PARABLES in the EYE of the STORM

PARABLES in the EYE of the STORM

Christ's Response in the Face of Conflict

Stanley A. Ellisen

Grand Rapids, MI 49501

Parables in the Eye of the Storm: Christ's Response in the Face of Conflict

Published by Kregel Publications, a division of Kregel, Inc., P.O. Box 2607, Grand Rapids, MI 49501. For more information about Kregel Publications, visit our web site: www.kregel.com.

Library of Congress Cataloging-in-Publication Data
Ellisen, Stanley A.
Parables in the eye of the storm: Christ's response in the face of conflict / Stanley A. Ellisen.
p. cm.
Includes bibliographical references.
1. Jesus Christ—Parables. I. Title.
BT375.3 .E45 2001 226.8'06—dc21 00-062944
CIP

ISBN 0-8254-2527-1

Printed in the United States of America

1 2 3 4 5 / 05 04 03 02 01

CONTENTS

FOREWORD

ALL OF US WHO WERE privileged to sit under Stan Ellisen's teaching have been waiting for this book to come out, since it was our beloved mentor who opened up to us the mind of our Lord, as revealed in the parables. Dr. "E's" love for the Gospels and the life of Christ contained therein has affected my life, and I am sure the lives of many of his students, for all eternity. Much of my love for the four Gospels and the parables of our Lord I owe to the excellence with which my mentor studied and the enthusiasm with which he taught.

Ellisen quotes Hillyer Straton, who once said, "If you define literature as the dramatization of life, Jesus stands supreme among the literary figures because of His parables; no one else remotely approaches Him." The importance of the parables is evident from both their number and their referent. They account for more than one-third of the sayings of Jesus, and the primary referent is the kingdom of God. Maybe nowhere in all of the Gospels do we find the mind and heart of Jesus like we find them in the parables.

Unfortunately, probably no other teachings of Jesus have been more maligned in their interpretation or have been used to advance more private agendas than the parables. The hermeneutics of the parables was the subject of the author's doctoral dissertation done at Dallas Theological Seminary some thirty years ago. His method employed here is to be distinguished from allegorization, moral generalizations, redaction criticism, and the destructive approaches of the Jesus Seminar. As it relates to other genres, the parable is differentiated from the figurative language of allegory, fable, and myth. Parable is a subsection of wisdom genre that contains a range from the shorter one-sentence sayings of Jesus to the more full-length parables.

The hermeneutical approach in this book appreciates the delicate balance between the literary, historical, and theological concerns. The gospel texts are taken as authentic material. This means that both the parables and their accompanying interpretations are believed to be the message of Jesus as He gave it. Ellisen was committed to the acceptance of the Bible on its own terms and treating the material as it stands in the finished text. The book is concise and to the point. His purpose was to briefly exposit each of the parables to discover its historical interpretation and contemporary applications. This book suggests five guidelines for interpreting a parable, which are then applied to the parables themselves: (1) discover the problem that made the parable necessary, (2) seek the central truth of the parable, (3) relate the details to the central truth, (4) clarify and authenticate the central truth, and (5) discover the intended appeal of the parable for proper application.

The author believed the parables should be understood within both the literary contexts of the Gospels as well as the historical contexts of the life of Christ. The purposes for the parables of Jesus are interlocked with the various audiences for which they were crafted. The parables were meant as teaching aids for the disciples, apologetic responses to Jesus' enemies, and convicting challenges designed to evoke appropriate decisions from the uncommitted. Jesus used the parables to reveal more truth about the kingdom program of God to the receptive, while for the rejecting hearts the parables were employed judicially to conceal these new kingdom truths.

If one is familiar with works on the parables, to state that much injustice has been done to the life and teachings of Jesus is a recognizable understatement. While many books on the parables treat a selected number, the reader will find here virtually every parable treated with equal attention to its setting, need, central truth, and wider application. Ellisen identifies four kinds of parables: similitudes, example stories, symbolic parables, and parabolic sayings. One of the writer's unique contributions was his understanding that each of the four styles was intentionally used by Jesus at a particular time in the chronology of His ministry, as warranted by the historical need.

The parabolic sayings were used as aphoristic barbs to describe the forecasting shadows of rejection as hinted by the responses of the leaders to Jesus' claims to be the Messiah. The referent of the similitudes is the mystery aspect of the kingdom of God that would extend from the time of the Messiah's rejection by Israel until the time of their reception at the end of the present age.

The example stories and full-length parables were used to describe the drama of life within the present age of the kingdom and the need to be ready for the future kingdom. The author chronicles the ministry of Jesus in parables in chapters highlighting the entrance into the kingdom, servanthood, human responsibility and divine concern, anticipating the coming kingdom, rewards in the kingdom, warnings to those who would reject the message of the kingdom, and the accountability required by Jesus at His return.

Dr. Ellisen was a word craftsman and a biblical artisan. His wit and love of puns comes through in the text of this book. The use of contemporary illustrations and creative writing also makes this informative book a pleasure to read. My mentor proved what he had always told me: "Since Jesus was never boring; neither should we be."

Key principles are stated in creative and picturesque stylings. In the parable of the Unforgiving Servant from Matthew 18, the statement is made, "Love does, indeed, turn vengeance inside out." Theological expressions are also well defined. From the parable of the Good Samaritan we learn, "One's neighborhood is as broad as his or her circle of influence or ability to reach, without regard to race, color, or social status." Another example can be offered from the account of the Rich Fool. The rich man "had factored God out of his world, forgetting that when there is no rain, there is no grain."

Contemporary illustrations are woven into the applications of the first-century stories to bridge the biblical world to ours. To help us identify with the community of praise in heaven over the recovery of the lost in Luke 15, the world's rejoicing over the recovery of little Jessica who fell into the well in Midland, Texas, is recalled. Enigmas like the seeming unearned praise for the Unjust Steward in Luke 16 is linked with a strange fascination in the northwestern United States over Dan B. Cooper, who parachuted from a plane over southern Washington with $200,000 of hijacked money. Though never heard from again, his evil act has likewise become legend and is even celebrated in some cities.

This book is informative as well as interesting as a basic text for the interpretation of parables. It hits its mark. The book is grounded in a belief of the inspiration and resultant inerrancy of Scripture. The message of Jesus is taken seriously. This work will be a helpful addition to the growing body of parabolic literature. I commend it to your profitable use.

—MARK L. BAILEY
January 2000

PREFACE

WITH LIBRARIES BULGING with books on the parables, one might ask why anything further needs to be said. Why add to the bulge? The uniqueness of this book lies in several areas. It is first of all strongly conservative in dealing with the biblical text. That is strangely missing in many current works on the parables, for human literary considerations often tend to compromise biblical inerrancy. Yet it is essential to recognize that, though the Gospels are the products of human authors, they were written under the superintendence of the Holy Spirit. That recognition alone obviates much of the circuitous research of historical critics who spend much time searching for what is already established, namely, the "authentic words of Jesus" (cf. John 14:26). That recognition also enables a more straightforward approach.

A second unique feature of this work is that it builds on the chronological order of the parables. Their historical contexts and movement are all important. They were not given as isolated sayings or bits of prudence to catalog as a group of proverbs. Rather, they tie together as essential links in a chain of events. Their sequence, in fact, reveals a grand panorama of the kingdom program as revealed in the ministry of Christ. They are kingdom-oriented. But it also reveals a diabolic movement that gradually builds from a group of local irritants to a final conspiracy of national repudiation. A nefarious plot is unfolded. Though ignored by many, this chronological approach serves an essential function in revealing the full impact of the parables.[1] That, of course, is impossible if chronology is not stressed.

Having done my doctoral dissertation on "The Hermeneutics of the Parables" some years ago, I've had a keen interest in both teaching them and observing the rise of modern methodologies. A whole new literature is in vogue today, quite different from the old standbys of R. C. Trench, Siegfried Goebel, William Taylor, G. C. Morgan, or even C. H. Dodd and A. M. Hunter. To indicate the direction of this work, let me briefly note two broad trends that have developed in the past half-century and claim prominence today in parable interpretation.

The most obvious is that of historical criticism, which generally denies the plenary accuracy of the four Gospels. From at least the time of Adolf Julicher (1886), these scholars have viewed the text as products of various creedal groups in the early church and see as their first task to "peel off the transitional layers" of oral and creedal accretions. From their pens has flowed a vast literature as they grope to find the "authentic words of Jesus" through various literary analyses.[2]

The fruit of that approach is glaringly evident in recent publications of the Jesus Seminar (*The Five Gospels,* and so on), whose editors blatantly applaud taking "scissor and paste to the gospels."[3] They give more credence to the "Gospel of Thomas" (37 passages) than to the gospel of John (only 9 words). One thoroughly schooled in that system as an author of one of their standard works in Germany, Dr. Eta Linnemann, has renounced the whole charade. Her lengthy appraisal of it is that historical-critical theology "does not deserve to be called science."[4]

This battle over the text is reminiscent of the native setting of the parables; they were born in the eye of an awesome storm. Truth's foundations were being lashed. In the modern struggle, critical scholars are not less intense, as divine superintendence is summarily dismissed in favor of humanistic analyses. While successfully renouncing the allegorism of medieval times, they have proliferated their methodologies to the point of defending a new kind of existential allegorism. The result is that there is little consensus among them as to what the parables either say or mean.[5] Specific or "correct interpretation" for some is even deprecated.[6]

Another broad trend that has quietly emerged is that of conservative scholars who subscribe to literary analysis, but with a general acceptance of textual inerrancy. Having richly gleaned from the literary critics, they yet stoutly defend the text and discern much of their touted scholarship as mere pedantry. "Not everything that claims to be a literary approach to the Bible actually is," writes Leland Ryken.[7] This conservative response is wholesome in that it seeks to rediscover the literary aesthetics of the parables while cautious of its humanistic tendencies.

The danger, of course, is to become so caught up with the concerns of literary form, structure, and critical evaluations that precision and convictions concerning the historical context are weakened. As Linnemann has warned, the basic premise of historical-critical theology is that "the Bible is to be viewed as a creation of the human mind and cannot be handled any differently than other products of human mental activity."[8] She further quotes Werner Kummel as saying, "Hence there is no other access to the understanding of the New Testament writings than the method of historical research which is valid for all writings of antiquity."[9] Linnemann's final caution is that "whoever gets involved in historical critical theology will end up in a similar situation. One can no more be a little historical-critical than a little pregnant."[10] While informed of the values of modern research, it is well to be forewarned also of its pitfalls.

With those broad trends in view, we seek in this work to highlight valid conservative principles for parable interpretation. Our emphasis is not on literary analyses and structures for specialists, but rather on practical guidelines and balanced expositions for practitioners. Written in popular parlance, its design is to help pastors, teachers, and students discern the basic message of each parable in order to pursue its broader applications. Jesus' stories were spoken to be understood by common people, not necessarily deciphered by literary experts. In this work, then, we have kept critical matters to a minimum to highlight the positive that caviling so often obscures. The positive, properly founded, usually carries its own punch and apologetic.

ACKNOWLEDGMENTS

THE PUBLISHER GRATEFULLY acknowledges the assistance of Dr. Dan Lioy (Th.D., D.Min., Trinity Theological Seminary/University of Liverpool; Th.M., Dallas Theological Seminary) in the completion and editing of this work. Dr. Ellisen was not able to complete chapter 14 prior to his death. Dr. Lioy contributed both chapter 14 and the Epilogue to this work, in keeping with the methodology and principles of interpretation that Dr. Ellisen set forth in the previous chapters.

Part 1

KEYS TO UNDERSTANDING THE PARABLES

Chapter 1

JESUS' UNIQUE TEACHING AIDS

EVERYBODY LOVES A STORY, and Jesus told some dandies. He was the superb storyteller. For this alone He might have become famous. His unique brand of tales He dubbed parables, and they are acknowledged as the most delightful literary gems of the race. As Hillyer Straton once said: "If you define literature as the dramatization of life, Jesus stands supreme among literary figures because of His parables; no one else remotely approaches Him."[1] The beauty and power of these portraits have long challenged both scholars and skeptics, commanding the attention of all. More than for Mark Twain or Will Rogers, when Jesus opened His mouth in parables (Matt. 13:35), people stopped to listen.

The importance of these gems of Jesus is illustrated by their prominence in His overall ministry. He communicated one-third of His sayings in story form. This suggests how impossible it is to get a true grasp of His message apart from the parables. Much of His teaching on the kingdom, in fact, was given in this way. And since His kingdom program underlies the New Testament, the full impact of the gospel is blunted without them. We, therefore, come to the heart of the Lord's ministry when we listen again to His captivating parables on the kingdom.

HISTORIC DIFFICULTIES IN PARABLE STUDIES

Despite their beauty and simplicity, these anecdotes of Jesus have often baffled interpreters. Sunday school stories, indeed, yet they challenge the keenest theological minds. A dark, elusive quality seems to stalk them. This has spawned a wide variety of phony doctrines, and the cults have a field day scrimmaging for their support. The parables' innocent simplicity seems fair game for anyone to exploit. Many expositors and students even today are queasy and uneasy in teaching the parables. They love them as colorful illustrations, but hardly as bona fide revelations of fresh truth. Like the much neglected "types" of the Old Testament, these delightful tales of Jesus easily succumb to benign neglect or fanciful manipulation.

Intrigued with their grandeur and seeming forthrightness, we might wonder how they could come to such a state of mystery and uncertainty. Several prominent reasons for this plasticity may be noted by way of introduction.

The Allegorizing Craze

The first is the mischievous tendency of history to allegorize the parables. This is the practice of extracting elaborate meanings from all parts of the story, developing doctrinal points that may or may not relate to the historical setting. It is an ancient homiletic device with admitted appeal for the application-hungry preacher, seducing his creative juices to freewheeling exposition. Its basic problem, however, is that it is largely subjective; it traffics in eisegesis rather than proper exegesis. It forces the Word of God to intone the rhapsodic diatribes of men. We rightly turn in disgust from such harangues as trumped-up pieties, far afield from the historic settings of Jesus' ministry.[2]

The Tendency to Generalize

A second reason for parable neglect is the opposite tendency to draw mere generalizations from the stories. This is the search for moral maxims of proverbial wisdom.[3] Such a quest is readily understandable as a reaction to anathematized allegorism and has enjoyed wide popularity in the wake of Julicher's work.[4] It is still a penchant of many parable interpreters today.

This approach admittedly sounds like a useful hedge against wild excesses. Yet its urge to purge is acknowledged to have gone too far; it almost denudes the details of revelatory truth. Being reactionary, it was unbalanced in its zeal to scuttle the errors of church history. To relegate most of the details to mere "drapery," as it does, tends to undercut many obvious lessons Jesus taught in context. His stories, then, become innocuous illustrations of commonly known truths. This practice of gleaning mere proverbial maxims trivializes the parables.

The Modern Fad of Redacting the Text

A third problem is one that has mesmerized the modern critical school. This is the fancied need to recover the true text.[5] Assuming that the early church edited ("redacted") the Gospels, they see many parables as having been misplaced and in need of correction and restoration to their original settings in Jesus' ministry. Therefore, the first business of an interpreter is to rediscover by critical analyses the true settings in which they were spoken to discern the original lessons Jesus taught. So prominent is this preoccupation by these researchers that it has been called their "keynote" in parable studies.[6] For the vast majority of them, it is naive and unscholarly to accept the text at face value without some literary reconstructions.

Though popular and intriguing, this approach inevitably limits the understanding of the parables to an elite group of analytic scholars. For those without such skills, the stories remain mere enigmas with teasing mysteries. Though its proponents are greatly impressed by their ingenious thumping of past errors, we can ill afford their trade-off concerning the text. Without a reliable text, the ground for exegesis is eroded and futile. It leaves us in a sea of subjectivism not unlike that of the allegorists from which modern studies claim to have rescued us.

This reminds us again that the interpreter's task is not to judge or rearrange the text, but rather to explain it as given by the Holy Spirit. What Siegfried Goebel said many years ago is still true today: "Until two members of the advanced 'Critical' school can be found to agree, the expositor may justly decline their guidance."[7] An inerrant text is the only ground for stable exegesis.

The "Kingdom" Question

Another area of difficulty in parable interpretation concerns the "kingdom." What is this kingdom about which they speak? Though the parables purport to explain the kingdom, there is great diversity of opinion as to what that kingdom is. Does Jesus here proclaim the coming of the Old Testament Davidic kingdom? The New Testament spiritual kingdom? The coming millennial kingdom? Or is it the "realized eschatological" kingdom made popular in recent times? That question has long perplexed expositors and still does today. To appreciate Jesus' explanations, it is essential that we recognize what aspect of the kingdom He is describing in these stories.

Redemptive Applications

Another problem to be noted is the relation of the parables to God's redemptive program. Did Jesus explain the plan of salvation by parables? So pervasive are the allegorical interpretations of the ancients that this is rarely even considered a problem. It is assumed as a given. In drawing truths and principles from the parables, however, it is important to remember that redemptive theology was rarely given in figurative language. The Lord gave the plan of salvation in plain-literal declarations so that all true seekers might respond to it.

In the history of interpretation, this practice of allegorizing or milking the details for redemptive nuggets has been all but universal. Truths foreign to the context (often marvelous to behold) have often been unearthed. This penchant is native to us all and perhaps laudable in its pretense to "preach the gospel." We easily justify it on this account and congratulate ourselves for "spiritual" thinking. Its perniciousness is that it often substitutes the pious platitudes of the preacher for the Lord's intended message. Clever and apt though such analogies may be in stressing redemption, they fail to fulfill their designed intention. They ignore or neglect the specific truths Jesus taught in each parable in favor of some imaginative one, thus sacrificing the Spirit's blessing and power.

This reminds us again that the first responsibility of a Bible expositor is to convey the primary lesson taught by the Lord. Only then should we move to principles and applications. The Spirit jealously guards His Author's prerogative, insisting that we first spell out His message before pursuing any well-intended applications. Though the theme of redemption is certainly central to the gospel, it may or may not be central to a particular parable. Forcing it to bend to our pious machinations easily confuses both the doctrine of salvation and that of the kingdom.

Summary. These devious tendencies are some of the pitfalls to sane Bible interpretation that often plague preacher and student alike. The wise interpreter will guard against the dangers they present. With the Spirit's guidance and sound, biblical principles of interpretation, however, we can be sure that the native meanings of these literary jewels of Jesus await our discovery with powerful applications. As the ancient proverb once said: "It is the glory of God to conceal a matter; to search out a matter is the glory of kings" (Prov. 25:2 NIV). The Lord delights to play "hide and seek" with His truths—allowing us the joy of discovery. Especially is this true of Jesus' instruction by parables.

HISTORIC SETTINGS OF THE PARABLES

Strangely, Jesus is the only storyteller of the New Testament. Though writers of the Old Testament and later rabbis used parables on occasion, none of the apostles presumed to teach this way. They evidently considered this method of Jesus too hallowed ground for them to tread. For whatever reason, Jesus' parables have been left as a unique monument to His teaching. They also served several purposes that are quite evident when we recall the different people to whom He spoke.

Jesus' Varied Audiences

Jesus' general audience, of course, was the Jewish community of Israel under the Law. The church had not yet been instituted, awaiting the coming of the Holy Spirit at Pentecost (Matt. 16:18; Acts 1:5–8). Also, the circumstances that brought on the parables were not what one might expect. They were not festive occasions calling for light-hearted entertainment by a friendly fireside. Rather, they often came as Jesus' response to opposition and unreceptivity. Animosity usually lurked in their backgrounds.[8] His use of full-blown parables, in fact, only began after Israel's leaders blasphemed His miracles, which in turn called forth His introduction of the new kingdom program for the church. In that scenario, Jesus spoke to three basic groups of people—His disciples, His enemies or rejecters, and a mixed multitude of potential friends or foes. Each group had special needs to which He ministered.

Instructing the Disciples. Jesus' primary target in these stories, of course, was His disciples, whom He sought to train. The Twelve, in fact, were chosen shortly after the leaders conspired to kill Him (Mark 3:6–14). It was then that He resorted to concentrated parabolic teaching as He began a series of special instruction for them (Matt. 13). Having anticipated an impending messianic kingdom with political power, the disciples needed Jesus' special counsel to ease the shock of this change of kingdom direction. They needed to know the significance of their new roles and responsibilities. To present these delicate truths, the Lord brought into full play His parabolic method. With simple stories He gently reassured the downcast band, teaching, from the logic of nature, important truths to prepare them for the difficult days ahead.

Responding to Foes. Besides His friends, Jesus also drew a motley group of adversaries who continually dogged His trail. Among them were the scribes, Pharisees, and leaders of Israel who had decided in caucus that He must be eliminated (Mark 3:6). Having heard His claims of messianic authority and witnessed His supernatural credentials, they yet closed their minds to His call for repentance. For that reason, they would now be denied further truths about the kingdom (Matt. 13:13). The Lord was not in the habit of flaunting His family secrets before scoffers. Though He did address them later in parables to prick their consciences, He would not "cast [His] pearls before swine" (7:6 NKJV); to have increased their knowledge about the kingdom would have only increased their judgment. Their rejection of His mercy called for special treatment, and Jesus' parables were His effective way of handling them. In the words of Joachim Jeremias, the parables were His "weapons of controversy."[9]

For these adversaries, then, the parables were but mystic nonsense, except when Jesus called their bluff in judgment. To this unique use of the parables as literary missiles we will return in a later discussion.

Challenging the Curious Multitude. The third group to which Jesus spoke was a mixed crowd of both friends and foes. An inquisitive bunch, they were largely uncommitted and riding the fence concerning His claims. Characteristically restless and curious, they easily acquiesced to bellicose leaders or roving pundits. Not greatly savvy on theological issues, their main interests were filling their stomachs, clamoring for political liberation from Rome, and doing their religious rituals. As the common "show me" variety, they looked for a holiday and a handout.

To this motley crowd Jesus spoke in the universal language of the workaday world. He spoke about sowing, reaping, fishing, journeying, shepherding, building, bread making, and the like. For these waverers, His stories were designed as an alert, forcing them to decide between Him and His muttering, creedalistic foes. The picturesque scenes He painted beautifully fit this purpose of appealing to all who heard Him, whatever their backgrounds. For the most part, however, these fence-sitters loitered on the fringes as the Lord instructed His believing band and parried with His conniving foes.

JESUS' PURPOSE IN USING PARABLES

Each of these groups, then, required the Lord's special attention and suggested His varied purposes in telling stories. Through them He sought to both reveal and conceal truth as He challenged the people to think and act. To the receptive He gave revelation; to His enemies He gave puzzles; to the mixed multitude He gave challenges, prodding for decisions. Let's notice the part each of these purposes played in His ministry.

Jesus' Revelational Purpose

In His role as Prophet, Jesus' main purpose was to give instruction. He came as a revealer of truth, being the Truth incarnate. This purpose pervaded also His teaching by parables. In this way, His stories were different from those of the rabbis and other teachers, who used various anecdotes as illustrations. Jesus' stories were not just illustrations. They were fresh revelations of divine truths.[10] As in all His teaching, Jesus often introduced significant doctrinal concepts in His parabolic discussions. To deny this revelation aspect (as many do) is to deny also the important truths He taught at this critical time of instruction. His truths in parable form were not mere proverbial wisdom or tired givens. They both revealed and illustrated the new truths He was teaching.

In asserting this doctrinal feature, however, a word of caution is always necessary. The history of interpretation loudly decries the practice of building doctrine on parables. Irenaeus very early declared that "the parables cannot in any case be the original or exclusive foundation of any doctrine."[11] Had he left out the word "original," his rule would have been more accurate, for originality was a distinctive feature of Jesus' message as He taught by parables. Many initial truths of the mystery form of the kingdom, for instance, were introduced in the parables of Matthew 13. To see them as mere illustrations of truths already known misses the crucial emphasis of the kingdom the Lord sought to teach in that chapter.

With this recognition, great care should be taken that these doctrinal truths of the parables be strongly confirmed. Such confirmations should be sought in their immediate contexts or later, direct revelation. An example of such revelation is the prophetic content in various parables. James Smart has reminded us of this principle: "A definition which included in its scope the prophetic use of the parables would have prevented interpretations from falling into this false channel" of mere platitudinous truths.[12] Many great exegetes have recognized this doctrinal content as part of the warp and woof of the parables, a fact we would only underscore at this point.

The question naturally arises as to why Jesus revealed doctrinal truths in the figurative garb of parables. Why not expound such truths in plain literal or direct statements? The answer is found in the purpose of figurative language. The colorful language of figures in the Bible was never meant for mere art or entertainment; it was designed for emphasis.[13] Figures were exclamations! Jesus told parables to highlight or underscore difficult points He wanted to make. His stories commanded attention to stress those truths, inviting further inquiry or response. This purpose of revealing unsavory or difficult truths to the responsive was, of course, one of His major intentions in teaching by parables.

Jesus' Judicial Purpose

As previously noted, the Lord came not only to reveal, but also to conceal truth. It was not His purpose that all who heard Him should fully understand. As with the *mashal* (proverb) of the Old Testament, His parables do have an enigmatic quality. This may come as a shock to some, but the Lord frankly declared this in Mark 4:10 –12, underscoring His blinding intention for scoffers. Though it may sound preposterous to us, it was of His wisdom in that setting. Lurking despisers stalked Jesus' trail, seeking to trap and condemn Him. Such conspirators had no claim on His truths, and the Savior spared them further judgment by withholding those secrets from them.

This blinding feature of the parables has always been a challenge to interpreters, and it is almost universally denied by higher critics of our time. The reaction of F. C. Grant is typical: "It is simply impossible to view Jesus' parables as designed to withhold His teaching from anybody."[14] How, then, do they handle this blunt statement by Jesus? Numerous approaches have been taken.[15] The crucial passages are Matthew 13:10–15; Mark 4:11–12; Luke 8:10 (cf. John 12:38–40), and the disputed terms are Matthew's use of "because" *(hoti)* in explaining Jesus' parables where Mark uses the conjunction "in order that" *(hina)*. One speaks of "result" and the other of "purpose." Each quotes Isaiah 6:9–10 to confirm the consequence of divine judgment.

> Therefore I speak to them in parables; because *[hoti]* while seeing they do not see, and while hearing they do not hear. (Matthew 13:13)

> To you has been given the mystery of the kingdom of God; but those who are outside get everything in parables, in order that *[hina]* while seeing they may see and not perceive. (Mark 4:11–12)

One seems to attribute the blinding effect to Israel's obstinacy and the other to the Lord's judgment. How do we reconcile these seemingly contradictory emphases on "free will" and "predestination"? Solutions have been sought in collateral passages, the Aramaic Targums (Aramaic was Jesus' original language), and in Hebrew idioms. The following considerations should be noted.

Arndt and Gingrich note that the conjunction *hina* often serves "as a substitute for the inf. of result ('ecbatic') or consecutive use of *[hina]*. . . . In many cases purpose and result cannot be clearly differentiated, and hence *[hina]* is used for the result which follows according to the purpose of the subj. or of God. As in Jewish thought, purpose and result are identical in declarations of the divine will." Arndt and Gingrich then note many New Testament references.[16]

The point of the passage, then, appears to be that Christ employed parables as a *result* of His antagonists' hardness, and for the *purpose* of withholding certain truths from those hardened. Matthew stresses one aspect, Mark the other. The leaders' blindness and hardness were willful and self-generated, resulting in incapacity.

It is also to be noted that the Greek particle rendered "lest" *(mepote)* in Mark 4:12 (as well as Matt. 13:15; and the Septuagint of Isa. 6:10) has reference to those hardened (the nearest subjective antecedent), rather than to the activities of Christ in the preceding verse. The fear suggested by the "lest" refers to the disposition of the rejecters. In other words, they hardened themselves, lest (or, for fear that) they should be "turned again" or converted.

To get the full force of this fear it should be noted that the Greek words rendered "and be forgiven" *(kai aphethe autois)* are better translated "it should be forgiven them." Wuest comments: "The singular number of the verb . . . ostensibly refers to a single sin, in this context, the willful rejection of the truth."[17] Floyd Filson expresses it this way: "Jesus says that they fear they may see and hear and understand, and turn back, that is, repent."[18]

We can better appreciate this pejorative use of the parables if we look more closely at its *intent* and its *extent.* Its *intent* was certainly not to deprive anyone of salvation, though many have assumed this predestinarian flavor from Mark 4:12 (Matt. 13:13ff.; Luke 8:10). The context, however, does not deal with salvation, but rather with the consequence of the leaders' blaspheming Jesus' messianic credentials and taking counsel to destroy Him (Matt. 12:14). That was evidently "the sin" they were reluctant to confess and seek forgiveness for (Mark 4:12).

It was "on that day" (Matt. 13:1) that Jesus gave these parables of the kingdom, confirming the leaders' rejection as a fulfillment of Isaiah 6:9–10. To assume these rejecting leaders might have been saved had they better understood Jesus' parables is entirely gratuitous. Jesus rarely gave the plan of salvation by parables, but always in plain, literal language for everyone to grasp. His intention of hiding certain truths of the parables was not to deny them salvation, but rather to spare them further judgment for rejecting further light.[19]

Second, the *extent* of this blinding purpose was evidently quite limited. The parables involved appear to be just the four spoken to the multitude by the sea (Matt. 13; Mark 4). All others addressed to adversaries were either explained or self-evident. The truths of these four concerned Jesus' new kingdom program, which would mainly concern the church, truths that would have only enraged and further condemned the Savior's opponents. They had already maligned His messianic credentials as the work of Satan (Matt. 12:24–26).

It is therefore puerile to minimize this judgment aspect of the parables, following as it does the leaders' outright contempt. To suppose the Lord would indiscriminately divulge kingdom secrets to calloused and indifferent scorners is to misconstrue both His grace and His judgment. The view that Christ forever excluded any hearers arbitrarily from salvation must certainly be guarded against, for the fault lay not with either the *seed* or the *sower,* but rather with the *soil,* as He had just emphasized. Paul explicitly declared that it is the "god of this world" (2 Cor. 4:4) that blinds the minds of those who believe not. Though the Lord never blinded anyone to the truths of salvation, He did withhold these family secrets from those who had rejected and blasphemed His messianic credentials.

Jesus' Decision Purpose

In all His ministry, Jesus constantly struck for decisions; likewise in His parables. Each one carried both an indictment and an appeal. The indictment was to the rejecting nation and the appeal to those yet pondering whom they should follow. Most of Jesus' stories, in fact, show this element of challenge in which the issues were clear-cut, the indictment unmistakable, and the appeal urgent. His colorful stories called for action.

This feature of pressing for decisions made Jesus' parables especially unique. They were three-pronged, blending *persuasion* and *challenge* with *description.* While they instructed the mind, they pricked the conscience to activate the will. Passivity was never an option with Jesus. He left no neutral ground. In His parable of the Talents Entrusted, for instance, the servant who hid his talent and refused involvement was called wicked and slothful (Matt. 25:14–30 KJV). Likewise, the priest and Levite in the Good Samaritan (Luke 10:30–37). Jesus' descriptions often brought His audiences to a crossroads, demanding personal decisions. In this way the parables became life-transforming.

Summary. Jesus spoke in parables to fulfill several purposes. The diverse backgrounds of His hearers called for extraordinary wisdom in communicating His message. Readapting the storytelling method of the rabbis, He transformed it into a triple teaching tool of His own to meet those needs. With it He challenged the minds, hearts, and wills of His hearers. As the master Teacher, He braided simple anecdotes into a tapestry of revelation for the faithful, puzzles for the scorners, and enticing challenges for those yet riding the fence. The parables became Jesus' stock-in-trade literary tools to deftly communicate new and often difficult truths about the kingdom.

These colorful stories, however, were always to the point, explaining some aspect of the kingdom. Since the subject of God's kingdom is often misunderstood, we need to recall its overall meaning to see how it applies to the parables. What specifically is this "kingdom" about which Jesus spoke in parables?

Chapter 2

THE KINGDOM OF THE PARABLES

THE BIBLE HAS MUCH TO say about kingdoms, especially the kingdom of God. What is meant by God's *kingdom?* Though the term is often used in the Old Testament, it is never defined. Coming to the New Testament, we are relieved to find that the parables of Jesus propose to explain the kingdom. Yet we discover that here also the term is used in a variety of ways, leaving us hard pressed to know precisely what it means. To understand the parables of the kingdom, we need to look broadly at the overall concept of the kingdom in the Bible.

What, then, is this "kingdom of God" about which the Bible speaks? Though tomes have been written on it expressing many views, it is generally agreed that the term speaks about three things: God's "authority," God's "realm," or His "exercise of authority" over that realm.[1] The kingdom may be defined broadly as "the rule of God over His creation."[2] The kingdom of God, then, is a realm over which He reigns, exercising sovereign authority in the outworking of His program. To get a feel for Jesus' use of the term, let's briefly trace its origin in the Old Testament.

THE OLD TESTAMENT KINGDOM OF GOD

In the operation of His universe, God rules by delegated authority. When Lucifer was created, he was given sweeping authority to rule for God (Isa. 14:12ff.). But he soon rebelled and usurped that authority for himself. Adam and Eve were also assigned authority over the earth by God, but they likewise rebelled (Gen. 1:28). In the following chapters of Genesis, we read the sorry saga of their children as one of continued rebellion—despite God's chastening judgments.

When the Lord later called Abram, promising children and a great nation, His intention was that the patriarch's descendants should rule the earth for Him as a theocratic people. Yet they also rebelled and suffered countless judgments for spurning God's laws. In the process of time, that chosen nation was struck down, dispersed, and denied kingdom rule for one basic reason: they failed in their franchise to rule for God. His fierce judgment for this rebellion of His chosen people underscores a central fact: the kingdoms of this world belong to the Lord. He alone sovereignly delegates its ruling authority.

Those failures by Israel, however, also pointed to the world's need for a righteous ruler. To fill this need, the Lord promised the coming of a Messiah who would rule the earth in righteousness; He would reign as God's sovereign King. That promise was given in many ways and certified in several covenants: He would come as the seed of the woman (Gen. 3:15), the seed of Abraham (Gen. 22:18; Gal. 3:16), the Son of David (2 Sam. 7:12; Mark 12:35), and as the Messiah, the anointed of God (Dan. 9:25).

Concerning these grand expectations the prophets of Israel literally buzz. Joel, Micah, Isaiah, Daniel, Ezekiel, and Zechariah unitedly speak about that One who would come to reign in righteousness and peace. As a mighty King, He would judge the nations, purify Israel, and establish justice. He would lead His people as a Shepherd and govern the earth with a rod of iron.

That is how Malachi, the final prophet, brought the Old Testament to a close. Though Israel was in despair and virtual eclipse among the nations, the prophet dispelled that gloom with a final reminder of the Messiah's eventual coming in a blaze of glory. In His time, the "Sun of Righteousness" would come to purge and heal the earth (Mal. 4:2). Under Him, a new day of righteousness would commence in which the rule of God would be established over all the earth. In that hopeful suspense, Malachi left the faithful of Israel waiting for the coming of that promised King and kingdom.

THE NEW TESTAMENT COMING OF THE KING

After four hundred years of prophetic silence and much affliction, Israel's Messiah finally did arrive. He came precisely as promised. To inaugurate His ministry, He was introduced by another Elijah who shook the nation with his thundering announcement: "Repent, for the kingdom of heaven is at hand" (Matt. 3:2). What was this "kingdom" about which John the Baptist spoke?

The Kingdom Ministry of John and Jesus

Viewed from the historic context, it is inescapable that John referred to that about which the former prophets had spoken. His focus, however, was the presence of the King Himself (Matt. 3:3). Though the Old Testament concept of the Davidic "kingdom" included also the political and social aspects, John saw those as subsidiary to the King's presence. John saw his own prophetic mission as preparing Israel for the Messiah's coming, ostensibly to inaugurate that prophesied kingdom.

It is therefore important that these physical aspects of the kingdom not be dismissed in John's introduction. The notion of a spiritual kingdom in human hearts without these outward dimensions was foreign to the thinking of the prophets, as well as to John.[3] For him to announce the coming of such an abstract kingdom would have been much too late, for such was present from the time of Adam.[4] Rather, John introduced the person of the Messiah in Old Testament terms of the reestablishing of David's empire. That was also the gist of Gabriel's message to the shepherds: "The Lord God shall give unto him the throne of his father David; and he shall reign over the house of Jacob for ever" (Luke 1:32–33 KJV). Like David, Jesus was anointed for kingly service long before receiving the throne.

The gospel of Matthew, in fact, introduced Christ to the New Testament by confirming His physical rights to the throne (Matt. 1:1–17). As Joseph's oldest son (legally), Jesus was heir to David's throne through Solomon, just as prophesied (2 Sam. 7:12–13). Jesus alone was so qualified. In John's later introduction of Jesus to Israel, the same longings for a King and kingdom were evident. Those physical aspects constituted the nuts and bolts of what the prophets foretold, and that was obviously what the disciples looked for in the early ministry of Jesus (Luke 1:70 –74).

The Messianic Kingdom Rejected

When the leaders of Israel came to reject Jesus as King, however, they also inadvertently forfeited His kingdom. Their attitude of scorn soon infected the people as well. Though the capricious masses loved Jesus' healing clinics and "magic manna," they soon fell into lockstep with the leaders. They were reluctant to abandon the system. To this the Lord responded with remarkable grace, allowing them to exercise their freedom of choice; He would not force Himself on a recalcitrant people. His call was to those of faith who would respond in penitence to His grace. Repentance, however, was hard to come by in Israel.

For us, that rejection presents a baffling theological enigma. How do we explain Israel disowning the very Messiah they long anticipated, failing to recognize Him? How could they miss His obvious credentials—mighty miracles confirming His messiahship (Isa. 35:5–6; Matt. 11:3–5)?

Two reasons stand out. First, the leaders ostensibly were turned off by Jesus' lowly background. He came from despised Nazareth. They were mortified that their "Teacher of Righteousness" would come from "Galilee of the Gentiles." To them He was an uncouth foreigner.

Second, Jesus' teaching personally piqued the leaders. He demeaned their religious practices as put-on pieties and stepped on their theological toes. When challenged, He wouldn't kowtow to them even to quote their favorite scholars. He disparaged their tidy rituals of cleansing from defilement, while He Himself boldly ate with publicans and sinners. To top it off, Jesus brusquely marched into the temple and overturned their money tables in preparation for Passover. Called "Annas' Bazaar," this was their most lucrative operation of the year, which Jesus saw as spiritual burlesque. To them He was an iconoclast, a bull in a china shop, bent on wrecking their whole pious enterprise. Thus, they regarded His elimination as necessary to save the nation, not to mention their professional clout with the people (John 11:50).

These excuses, however, were only cosmetic. The underlying cause lay much deeper. The Lord put His finger on the leaders' basic problem when He solemnly declared to the Pharisees in John 8:44: "You are of your father the devil." He saw the nation as obsessed by evil and the whole religious system under satanic control.

It's no wonder that John the Baptist, who began as a priest, refused the temple courts as his base of operation; rather, he fled to the deserts to issue his call. As he did, he also denounced the religious leaders as a "brood of vipers" (Matt. 3:7). Such a gang of cutthroats would obviously have little room for the Messiah; neither His Person nor His program appealed to them. Other considerations of differing theological views were really incidental to the central fact that Satan and his henchmen had taken over the nation. Like a band of religious pirates, they had commandeered the ship of Israel, and the last one they wanted on board was God's Messiah.

The leaders' rejection, however, was really a two-way street. Not only did they reject Jesus; He also rejected them. That was apparent as early as the Sermon on the Mount when He condemned the leaders' hypocrisy before the people. His so-called "irenic" sermon was really a "declaration of war," focused on the self-righteous Pharisees and their legalistic system. Even at that early stage, He roundly scored them on both their doctrines and practices. Having all the trappings of true religion, they had concocted a colossal system of counterfeit piety that trafficked in pride rather than penitence.

This was especially tragic in view of the courageous and godly character of the early Pharisees (Puritans) who had doggedly fought the inroads of heathen idolatry. In their meticulous concern for scruples, however, they somehow lost sight of their divine mission. Their legal system, which was designed to point to the Messiah, was twisted into a tool of the Devil to renounce Him at His coming. In Jesus' final confrontation with the leaders, the Lord denounced their hypocrisy with the most scathing anathemas of the Bible (Matt. 23:13–33). Having caricatured God's Law, they came also to spurn His grace and despise His personal presence when He came.

With this in mind, it was inevitable that this two-way rejection would eventually come. For God to fulfill the promises of the Messiah's glorious reign under such leadership was unthinkable. That aspect of His kingdom program had to be temporarily scrubbed. As the apostle John declared: "He came unto His own [things], and His own [people] received Him not" (John 1:11 KJV). In keeping with His covenant warnings (Deut. 28–29), God again gave the people their requests, but sent leanness and deprivation of the kingdom to that generation of Israel (as He had done to a previous one in the wilderness; Num. 14:27–34). In the meantime, the Lord had contingency plans ready to implement.

The Messianic Kingdom Sidetracked

What, then, were the consequences of this cosmic mutiny and rejection? Was this the leaders' unpardonable sin? It is important to note that the consequences were both immediate and long-range; but they were not final. The immediate upshot was that Jesus refused any further miraculous signs to the nation; He turned His ministry more to individual needs (Matt. 12). Muting His messianic proclamation (16:20), He focused His ministry on Gentiles and outcasts while preparing the apostles for a future ministry.

The long-range effect was that Israel would be sidetracked in God's kingdom program. The rejecters would indeed get their wish; Jesus would take His leave from the nation for an extended period of time. During His absence, the ancient promises to the fathers would be on the back burner, so to speak.

That change, however, did not nullify God's ancient covenants. The unbelief of rebels can never alter His faithfulness. Anticipating such unbelief in the Old Testament, the Lord often reaffirmed those covenants, adding His oaths for emphasis (Ps. 89:33–36). If unbelief could have invalidated God's vows to the fathers, the nation itself would never have survived to produce the Messiah. Their unbelief was almost endemic, like an addiction or way of life. Even Abraham himself showed this trait as he bargained with God for Ishmael, being impatient in waiting for unborn Isaac (Gen. 17:18). The Lord's purposes, however, were not subject to change.

This reliability of the Lord to keep His covenants was often underscored in the Old Testament; it rested on His faithfulness, not that of the Israelites. Nor could even the rejection of the Messiah alter those promises. The Lord simply put that program on hold while fulfilling other divine goals. In so doing He emphasized a significant lesson for all nations: God is obliged to no generation of sinners who spurn His grace, be they religious or pagan. Not even His chosen race was exempt from this principle.

Jesus, in His Mount Olivet Discourse (Matt. 24 –25), gave a final confirmation of Israel's future restoration. Though the nation would face scattering and near extinction, He vowed that He would eventually return to establish them as a kingdom of righteousness. They would be regathered and restored in the end times. Until then, however, Israel's kingdom program would be sidetracked; but it would not be forgotten.

THE MYSTERY ASPECT OF THE KINGDOM

The rejection of the Messiah by the leaders presented the disciples with a major crisis. Having looked for Jesus to quickly set up His kingdom rule, they were hard-pressed for logical answers to this unexpected turn of events. Could He really be the Messiah if the religious leaders opposed Him? How could the Old Testament covenants be fulfilled without them? And what would now happen to God's kingdom program? Was it to be scrapped, or what new form would it take? The small group of disciples were doubtless baffled by this debacle and desperately needed the Lord's special counsel.

At precisely this time Jesus began to reveal the "mysteries of the kingdom" (Matt. 13:11). A mystery in the Bible is not something mysterious; nor is it something difficult to grasp. It is rather the revelation of a truth not previously made known. The term was first used in Daniel 2:18, when God first announced the coming period of the "times of the Gentiles." Likewise in Matthew 13:11, Jesus spoke about a new kingdom program involving Gentiles, but different from that made known in the Old Testament.

Matthew explains these mysteries as truths about the kingdom, "hidden since the foundation of the world" (Matt. 13:11, 35). They unveil a new program of God, distinct from the covenant plan for Israel. The time of its duration is often called the "interadvent period," extending from Jesus' first advent to the time of His return. Some call this an "intercalary period," as inserted into a previous calendar of events. Though Jesus did not elaborate on its purpose at this point, the apostles later show it to be basically the time of Christ building the church (which Paul also called a mystery; Eph. 3:3–6). Jesus' purpose in Matthew 13 was simply to reassure the distraught disciples that God was not taken aback by this rejection; His kingdom purposes were neither thwarted nor aborted. They would simply take a different course for an extended period while the King attends to His broader purposes of world redemption.[5]

To introduce this new program, Jesus chose the literary device of parables. Though not a new technique, He honed it anew for His own unique purposes. As previously noted, He deftly used parables to accomplish two significant purposes: to enlighten some and enshroud others. The faithful were enlightened as to the new direction of God's program, while rejecters were treated to innocuous puzzles. A more appropriate vehicle to serve these purposes could scarcely have been chosen.

Summary. Though the parables speak about the kingdom, their sphere of revelation is not the whole of God's kingdom. They say very little about the Old Testament kingdom revealed by the prophets, for instance, or about the New Testament millennial kingdom. Rather, the parables outline a new direction for God's kingdom program during the interadvent period.

More specifically, the parables describe the operation of that kingdom from the time of Jesus' rejection to His future reception by the nation. Though that includes the time of Christ building His church (Matt. 16:18), that was not Jesus' point in the parables. He simply introduced His bewildered group to a divine change of kingdom emphasis for an extended period of time. The parables admirably fit this transitional purpose.

Chapter 3

THE UNIQUE NATURE OF JESUS' PARABLES

TO APPRECIATE THE PARABLES, we need to bother ourselves with some rather mundane questions. For instance: "What on earth is a parable, for heaven's sake?" The question is most apropos. Traditionally, it is known as "an earthly story with a heavenly meaning." Popular idiom would call it one of Jesus' "like" stories. Not bad for quickie definitions. But to better understand how Jesus used it and its more specific meanings, we should briefly recall its basic nature and various forms.

THE PARABLE AS A FIGURE OF SPEECH

From a literary standpoint, the parable is an extended figure of speech presented as a story. As such it is related to many other figures, but has a special quality and function of its own. What then is a figure?

A Briefing on Figures

The term "figure" (Lat. *figura;* Gr. *tropos,* a turning) may be defined as "a word, phrase, or narrative used in a different sense than normal." It signifies a turning from its ordinary or literal meaning to a "tropical" (or figurative) meaning.[1] To illustrate, "The Lord is my Shepherd" (Ps. 23:1) does not mean that God is a herder of four-footed, woolly animals. Rather, it simply emphasizes that God cares intensely for His people; He is like a shepherd in the sense of caring for His sheep.

The genius of a figure is its trait of familiarity. It portrays something familiar to build a bridge to the unfamiliar.[2] By describing the known, it gently reveals the unknown in comfortable, commonplace terms. It is user-friendly. In the process, it also locks the description into one's memory. This feature of familiarity, then, is essential to the nature of a figure; without it, it would be meaningless. Thus, a figure is not mysterious in the sense of being unintelligible; it is, in fact, a friendly escort between two realms of truth.

Its Primary Roots. We're all familiar with the two root figures of *simile* and *metaphor.* The simile makes a *stated comparison* using a linking word such as "like" or "as."[3] "All we like sheep have gone astray" (Isa. 53:6 KJV), is a classic example. The metaphor differs in being an unstated or *informal comparison* in straightforward terms: "We are . . . the sheep of His pasture" (Ps. 100:3). Notice the difference in emphases; whereas the simile gently states that one thing *resembles* another, the metaphor boldly and warmly declares that one thing is or *represents* another. A third basic figure is "hypocatastasis" (rarely even noted), a figure that makes its point by an even stronger implication: "Go and tell that fox" (Luke 13:32; i.e., everyone knows he's a fox).[4]

Relating the Parable and Allegory. It is from these root forms of simile and metaphor that the extended figures of parable and allegory are derived.[5] Like the simile, the parable is a stated or formal *resemblance,* as in the introductory phrase, "The kingdom of heaven is like . . ." (Matt. 13:31). It often makes this declared analogy. The classic allegory, however, is like the metaphor or hypocatastasis, using *representations* to portray or personify its likenesses.[6] Jesus used this in John 15:5, "I am the vine, you are the branches." It is bold in its declaration of one thing representing another and usually obvious in its meaning.

Since the parable and allegory are similar and easily confused, it is important that we know how they differ. In speaking about parables, we refer to its Semitic usage in the Gospels, rather than its broad literary class. Boucher has noted this distinction: "In the ancient sources the term [parable] and the literary compositions do not neatly and exactly coincide. . . . The word 'parable' . . . had a wide range of meanings in both the Bible and classical literature. Today, however, we do not employ the word in all of those ways."[7] As A. M. Hunter reminds us, the antecedents of Jesus' parables were not in Hellas but in Israel.[8]

The major problem in parable interpretation throughout church history has been their obvious allegorical features that seem to make them "allegories."[9] How are these details to be understood? Since Jesus Himself interpreted the details of several and okayed its propriety (Mark 4:13), interpreters have pursued every avenue in search of their meanings. The early church manipulated them to battle the Gnostics, who had already used them to confirm their heterodox views, only turning them to their own advantage. They learned to bend their meanings to suit their own purposes. Especially did they turn them into salvation messages, seemingly unconcerned whether they fit the context.

Though the sane interpretations of the Antiochene fathers fought this wild trend, the allegorisms of the Alexandrians prevailed to become the norm for over a thousand years. The writings of Augustine and the allegorists became almost canonical, and the last word was thought to have been spoken in exegesis. Not until the Renaissance and Reformation were they effectively challenged, especially by Calvin. He is said to have gone "arrow-straight" for the central point in the context. Yet the plague of allegorism persisted in the "historico-prophetical" works of Johannes Cocceius and Campegius Vitringa (c. 1660) and continued unabated in many quarters until the onset of literary criticism in the nineteenth century.

Adolf Julicher (1888) is often cited as the pathfinder for modern parable interpretation in that he sounded the death knell to this allegorizing craze. Yet he did it by compromising the veracity of the text; he practically dismissed Jesus' interpretations as additions by the early church. Others, however, have maintained the trustworthiness of the text through much of history, and with such restraints as those of Chrysostom, Calvin, and Siegfried Goebel, interpreted only those details that fit the context. Rationalism, in other words, wasn't needed to squelch the "monkey tricks" of medieval allegorism.

In the modern period, however, a new kind of allegorism is being defended. Both liberals and conservatives regard Julicher's one-point view as extreme and narrow, and see allegorical elements as endemic to parables. In some ways the parable and allegory are synonyms. Two- and three-point parables are often seen as norms with some advocating polyvalence. As B. B. Scott says, "A methodology that seizes on the one-point of likeness as a parable's meaning destroys the parable."[10] The difference that should be emphasized, says another, "is between a story which in itself is allegorical and the arbitrary allegorization of one which is not."[11]

Perhaps the balanced conservative view is that of David Wenham: "The interpreter must not force them into one mould, but must seek to identify the particular points of emphasis and to distinguish the points that are significant from the narrative details which simply add colour to the story."[12] That is not far from the views of early conservatives such as Chrysostom and Calvin who, while maintaining scriptural inerrancy, sought the central truth and related only those points that fit the context: "Interpret the elements in the parables that are urgent and essential. . . . do not waste time on all the details . . . and be not overbusy with the rest."[13]

Though the literary critics have blazed the trail of research through the vagaries of form criticism, redaction, structuralism, and the existentialism of the new hermeneutics and language-events, they still have more questions than answers. In their quest for the "historical Jesus," writes Blomberg, "their most reliable findings . . . actually support the defender of the parables' authenticity."[14] The plague of medieval allegorism has certainly been scotched and a balanced view of recognizing some allegorical parts in the stories is well authenticated. Jesus finely etched in these allegorical features as an artist, not as an artisan to fill a mold. Clues as to how He intended them must always come from the historical context.

Having recognized the overlaps of parable and allegory in using allegorical features, several distinctions, however, should also be recognized to refine one's work of parable interpretation.[15] Their differences help to point up the unique nature of Jesus' stories. Let's first define the parable and then note its distinctions.

The Parable Defined

The term "parable" is a transliteration of the Greek word *parabole* (*para,* along side, and *ballo,* to cast). It literally means "to cast along side of." In its Hebrew and Greek usages *(mashal* and *parabole),* it had a variety of meanings. As noted, however, most writers recognize a more restrictive or technical usage in the New Testament.[16] A working definition of this biblical usage will help us appreciate its significance. It is "a fictitious but true to life story, designed to teach some specific lesson in the spiritual realm, usually concerning the kingdom."[17]

This definition expresses several features unique to the parable: (1) Its story is fictitious; that is, it is devised rather than actual. Its interpretation is in the spiritual lesson, not in the fabricated story. (2) It is always true to life. Unlike the fable where animals might talk and trees walk, the parable is never a distortion of real life. It is never fantastic, but always in line with reality. This gives it its persuasive power; it can't be argued with. (3) The lesson it teaches is invariably specific, rather than general, and always in the realm of religion. Grand generalities may be drawn from it, but that is not its focus. It deals with specific historical problems that call for answers. (4) Its primary lesson is a "central truth" rather than a conglomerate (though it may involve several points). Unlike the so-called "allegory," which attaches meaning to most of its parts, the parable generally has but one or a few points of tangency. It does not "walk on all fours," as does the allegory.

These constitute the basic features that describe and identify the parables of Jesus. They make His stories unique, nicely fitted to portray His new truths about the kingdom.

The Parables Distinguished

As Richard Trench once observed, we can best appreciate the parable by distinguishing it from other figurative stories.[18] Noting these contrasts will help to identify its salient features. Other narratives that are similar but different are the fable, the myth, and the allegory.

The Fable. This figure is similar to the parable in that it is also concocted, but it lacks the spiritual character and realism of the parable.

Its departures to the bizarre and unreal are usually obvious. This sharply distinguishes it from the parable, where the story never strays from the realm of reality.

The Myth. This also has similarities to the parable, but differs in other ways. It distorts reality by seeking to interpret history with a blend of fiction. Purporting to explain the historical, it often adds imaginative or mythological figures and events. The parable, on the other hand, never presumes to confirm or interpret history, though it is always true to life. This preserves its quality of having but "one interpretation," and that primarily in the spiritual realm.

The Allegory. The figurative narrative most often confused with the parable, of course, is the allegory. Both figures belong to the broad literary family of "allegories" and, as such, both have corresponding "allegorical" meanings.[19] There is, however, a range of degrees of such allegorical explicitness in language, as Ryken points out. He defines a parable as "a brief narrative that explicitly embodies one or more themes," and an allegory as "a work of literature in which the details have a corresponding conceptual meaning or set of conceptual meanings."[20] Though the parable has affinities with the allegory in making such correspondences, it revolves around a central point and theme. The allegory may or may not be true to life, and each detail usually has a counterpart meaning.

To better understand this elusive figure, we should note two sharp distinctions in the allegory's character and two in its interpretation. In character the allegory can be recognized by its obvious use of fantasy and metaphorical language. In *Pilgrim's Progress*, for instance, the reader is led through fantasy-land and readily recognizes it as such. This does not affect its point or lesson, for it makes no pretense of being true to life; its descriptions do not pretend to be genuine. This allows for a rich use of metaphors, which is another of its distinctions. Paul illustrates its use in his allegory of spiritual warfare in Ephesians 6. The allegory abounds in individual analogies. As such, it is often called a "description in code." It never hides its figurative garb.

Interpreting an Allegory. Because it differs from the parable in character, the allegory also differs in interpretation. Here again, there are two distinctions that stand out. The first is that an allegory has significant meaning in most of its parts. Being a description in code, its details must be deciphered to catch its meaning. In contrast to the parable, the allegory does "walk on all fours."

Second, the allegory almost always contains its interpretation within itself.[21] For this reason, allegories themselves are not usually hard to understand. They explain themselves in one way or another as they proceed. Few would debate, for instance, the lessons of *Pilgrim's Progress*, for the drama constantly explains itself. In Jesus' allegory of "The Vine" in John 15, this interpretive feature is abundantly evident as the Lord progressively interprets each part.

Such is never true in Jesus' parables where suspense and surprise keep the story in tension to engage the hearers. Though they may include several metaphors, these are never explained within the story. The interpretation may directly follow (as in the Sower and the Tares in Matthew 13), but it is never blended in the story as in allegory.

Thus, the parable is quite distinct from the three figures of fable, myth, and allegory. Though similar to them, it has a character quite unique to itself. Recognizing these features and distinctions will help to reduce the problems one faces in interpreting the parables.

The Bible's Aversion to the Allegorical Method

In reviewing the allegory and its distinction from the parable, it is important to note how the "allegorical method" ("allegorizing") is foreign to both. Though often confused as being the same, they are entirely different. One is a story, the other a method of interpretation. Failure to observe their distinctions has resulted in great confusion in church history.[22] The Bible does use allegories, but it never uses or approves the allegorical method of interpretation.[23] Let's briefly distinguish the allegory from the allegorical method.

As already noted, the allegory is a group of descriptions or metaphors related by a central purpose, each having a specific meaning or truth. It is important to note that each has a specific, literal meaning, not a variety of meanings. The allegorical method, on the other hand, is a way of interpreting historical events or sayings with "several levels of meaning."[24] It does not presume to interpret allegories, but histories, giving them other meanings than the normal. As with Origen's ingenious allegorical interpretations, the least obvious (so-called "deepest") is considered the most spiritual; it is also the most far-fetched. This differs sharply from the allegory where each metaphor has a specific meaning.

We might ask how the allegorical method got started. Isn't it used in the Bible? The short answer is, Never! Historically, it originated in Greek philosophy and religion. It was used as an attempt to reconcile the mythologies of Homer and Hesiod (which were often grotesque and absurd) with the more rational philosophies of Plato and Socrates. For them the allegorical method was a compromising tool, assigning different meanings to the mythological parts. These etymological manipulations seemed to allow them the "best of both worlds," retaining the revered traditions of mythology along with the wisdom of the philosophers. It was, in essence, a "tongue-in-cheek" compromise of fable and philosophy.

The pity is that this method later crept into the early church as certain Hellenist Christians sought to reconcile the Old Testament with Greek philosophy.[25] In the same way that they harmonized Homer with the philosophers, they presumed also to harmonize Moses with them. That played havoc with Old Testament history, as it did likewise with Jesus' parables when applied to them. The heterodox were admittedly the first to resort to this game of chicanery, but the orthodox were not far behind.

Thankfully, the Reformers as well as modern critics have roundly anathematized that devious method, but it still dies a slow death in interpretation. Few approaches to Scripture have been so mischievous in turning the text into putty for any interpreter to remold. It has no place in interpreting Bible allegories, and is even more foreign when applied to the parables.

Advantageous Qualities of the Parable

For what reasons did Jesus use the storytelling method of teaching? Why not doctrinal outlines laced with documentations? Why not simple questions and straight answers? To fully appreciate Jesus' use of parables it is essential that we recognize several qualities in them that especially attract and engross the human mind.

The Universal Attraction of Stories. The first and most obvious is the universal attraction of stories. Everybody loves a story. It is far more appealing than a naked argument. Stories have the unique quality of entertaining while they instruct; they take you on a vacation. Rarely does an audience allow a good yarn to be interrupted. Its unraveling almost guarantees listening ears.

The Mind's Allurement to Analogies. A second attraction the Lord's parables exploited was the disposition of the human mind to enjoy analogies. Like fitting pieces of a puzzle together, we enjoy making comparisons and finding links. It gives our egos the joy of discovery, so essential to good learning. The mind thus engaged is tickled with its own ingenuity, hardly noticing fatigue. This mental fascination Jesus exploited on many occasions, challenging His audiences to think; He wanted them to make their own discoveries. This illustrates again the Lord's technique of playing "hide and seek" with the truth, rewarding those who earnestly seek (Prov. 25:2; Heb.11:6). Such intriguing analogies were the stuff of His parables.

The Desire for Simplicity. A third attraction to which Jesus appealed was the mind's desire for simplicity. Rather than appealing to the IQs of intellectual highbrows, His stories were usually quite simple. Simplicity, of course, is not superficiality. It is often a step beyond complexity, pursuing it to the point of unity. Though the truths Jesus taught were most profound, they were not mental gymnastics. Easy diction and familiar objects were His trademarks. Planting, plowing, fishing, bread-making, and even children playing games in the streets were His story plots. So simple were these sayings, they almost embarrassed the worldly wise—until Jesus nailed them with His punch line. Outflanking their intellectual pride, He spoke profound truths in simple terms to be understood by those with open minds.

Appealing to the Hearers' Objective Judgment. Fourth, Jesus' stories solicited the objective judgment of His hearers. His style was tact itself, even in addressing the unreceptive. Rather than brashly pronouncing judgment, He often created a story drama of scenes they were familiar with, inviting them to be the judge or jury. These seemingly innocuous stories about someone "out there" lured the audience into making an objective judgment of themselves. Too late they found themselves trapped by their own verdicts from which they couldn't escape. This ploy of objectivism is reminiscent of Nathan's parable to adulterous King David, who unwittingly condemned himself, as if judging another. Jesus, however, rarely had to say, "Thou art the man!" (2 Sam. 12:7 KJV).

In this sense, Jesus' parables became sharp swords that laid bare many an evil heart. As James Smart observed, "This use builds on the fact so plain in human life that we see and condemn faults quickly in others to which we are quite blind when they are present in ourselves."[26] Human nature has an uncanny ability to see its own faults in other people. Jesus appealed to this remarkable sensitivity to act as a mirror for self-judgment. His parables often reflected this as He pressed them home for application.

To these unique qualities of the human mind Jesus constantly appealed as He revealed His new kingdom program through parables. They were deftly designed to enlighten, convict, and challenge His audiences as He introduced these striking revelations.

JESUS' FOUR KINDS OF PARABLES

The Lord's character as Creator is reflected in His style of stories. Though His narrations were simple in content, they were anything but stilted. They were not spun out of a single mold. Some had similar plots, but the overall group was quite diverse.

In this variety of some fifty parables proper, we can trace several literary forms that Jesus used.[27] The different forms will often suggest clues as to the truths they convey. A vehicle, for instance, often tends to reveal its cargo: you don't expect the morning mail when a furniture van stops by. Likewise, the specific conveyers Jesus used often provide hints concerning what He taught in content.

Though various categories have been used, four literary groupings appear obvious: *similitudes, example-stories, symbolic parables,* and *parabolic sayings.* The first three are quite generally recognized, though different writers use different nomenclature.[28] The last, however, should also be noted as a group of short sayings that the Gospel writers also call parables. Let's briefly note the significance of each for interpretation, noting the last first.

Parabolic Sayings

Jesus was a master at one-liners, often called "parabolic sayings." Like proverbs, they crisply deliver a sermon in a sentence. Jesus gave these in various ways, as short statements, questions, or commands, each in essence compressing a narrative into a single sentence. For instance, the statement, "If a blind man guides a blind man, both will fall into a pit," is a potential drama in capsule form (Matt. 15:14–15). Called a parable, it is "narratory" in scope. Being pithy and pointed, these sayings were sharp communicators. The Lord especially peppered His early ministry with these short gems, as will be noted.

Similitudes

The Latin word "similitude," which means "likeness," identifies this second group of parables. Though the term is sometimes used of allegories, its more restrictive meaning is that of "a germ parable expanded into a moving picture and seen as a generalization" (though its lesson is not a generalization). As such, it portrays a normative action of what a person generally does, rather than a specific incident. Its appeal is to the logic of what one would normally do under similar circumstances. This can be seen in Luke 15:4 ("What man among you, if he has a hundred sheep"), which describes a common activity with a logic that is unassailable. It assumes their full agreement in the natural realm to enforce it in the spiritual.

The similitude is quite easily recognized by its series of actions in the present tense. Unlike parabolic sayings, the similitude describes a moving picture of drama. Jesus used the logic of the similitude in various parts of His ministry.

Example-Stories

The "example-story" is just that—an example of the truth being presented (sometimes called "illustrations"). It doesn't compare two realms of reality as the others, but rather gives a specific example of its truth in a single realm. This especially contrasts with the similitude. As Adolf Julicher wrote, "The story is itself an instance of the proposition being demonstrated."[29] Jesus used these stories to teach broader principles by specific instances. Only four such were actually given, all recorded by Luke: the Good Samaritan, the Rich Fool, the Rich Man and Lazarus, and the Pharisee and Publican Praying (Luke 10:30–37; 12:16–21; 16:19–31; 18:9–17).

It should be noted that allegorical elements are especially foreign to this type, inasmuch as it deals with but one realm of reality. It doesn't symbolize God, for instance, as a king, a father, or some other figure, but simply calls Him "God." In these stories we meet the priest, Levite, Pharisee, rich man, and the like, all specifically identified. The Lord was quite blunt in these parables, keeping metaphors to a minimum as He encouraged or leveled indictments on specific groups.

Symbolic Parables

The fourth classification, called "symbolic parables," makes up the largest group (sometimes called "allegories"). These are similar to the example-story in that they describe a specific event, but are different in that they involve two realms of reality. A scene in the physical is portrayed to teach specific truths in the spiritual realm. The Prodigal Son, for instance, describes a father and son in the earthly realm to impress truths about God and man in the spiritual (Luke 15:11–32).

Unlike the similitude, this type of parable may depart from the normal or generally expected. This unexpected turn in the story may, in fact, be its major point. In the story of the Tares, for instance, a natural process of sowing is portrayed, but this is followed by the unexpected act of an enemy sowing darnel by night (Matt. 13:24–30, 36–43). Such a twist would be contrary to the nature of a similitude, destroying its logic; but not for the symbolic story. It often specializes in surprises. This group, in fact, constitutes nearly two-thirds of Jesus' stories.

Summary. This variety in the makeup of Jesus' parables displays His creativity, but it also helps us to more sharply discern His lessons. He had many difficult secrets of the kingdom to reveal. To do that, the Lord used an assortment of literary vehicles. Recognizing these will greatly enhance our study as we develop basic guidelines for interpretation. They will also be apparent as we later study individual parables and the relation of each to Jesus' ministry.

Chapter 4

GUIDELINES FOR INTERPRETATION

THOUGH THE STORIES OF Jesus were rather simple, the lessons He taught are not always caught. Some have been notoriously missed. Few areas of Scripture, in fact, have been so misunderstood—and misapplied—even by the learned and pious. Piety is certainly essential, but it does not guarantee accuracy, for one can be sincerely wrong. How, then, can we properly understand the parables, and how can we be sure we have the lessons Jesus intended? Several keys to interpretation should be noted that are especially pertinent in treating these stories of Jesus. We may call them general guidelines.

GUIDELINE 1: DISCOVER THE PROBLEM

Jesus told parables to solve problems. He was neither an entertainer nor an anxious preacher cranking out moral applications. Rather, His primary focus was on the historic scene and its needs. Discovering the problem of answering to those needs, then, is the first key to interpretation. If we don't know what we're looking for, in other words, it is doubtful we will find it or even recognize it when we do. Solutions and problems must be tied together. How, then, do we discover this first clue to interpretation?

The problem sought is almost invariably found in the context, often at the heart of the preceding discussion. It may be in the prologue or the epilogue. At times the parable itself will help to identify it. Where several stories follow each other, it is probable that their problems will grow out of each other. Such is the case with the four parabolic sayings of Matthew 9:12–17, the kingdom parables of Matthew 13, and the three stories of the lost in Luke 15.

This initial step of seeking the problem is all-important, though often overlooked.[1] Attempting interpretation apart from the problem is an exercise in futility, for only the problem can properly point to the lesson. This principle reproves our tendency to allegorize by making a passage confirm some valid truth of the gospel that has little relation to the context. It also cautions against the practice of generalizing truths from pet phrases that may be catchy, but are hardly related to the problem. In recognizing this, one simply asks whether an interpretation is what Jesus had in mind or the product of an impulsive imagination.[2]

This search for the problem may appear laborious and an impediment for creative preaching; it may seem like mere busy work. It is, however, most rewarding and essential in exposition. Any titillating points one might dredge up unrelated to this native problem will soon fade into insignificance when the real problem is discerned. Pursue the search for the problem first; don't leave "home base" without it.

GUIDELINE 2: SEEK THE CENTRAL TRUTH

Having discovered the problem, the solution will usually stand out, since a specific problem demands a rather specific answer. Jesus was not coy or evasive about this. That answer in the parables is known as the "central truth." It is the primary lesson being taught, though related truths may also be involved. Everything revolves around it. Its discovery is not really difficult, for clues often appear throughout the context and in the story.

The prologue may suggest the central truth, as in the Good Shepherd of John 10, where the evil leaders are contrasted. At times the epilogue will point it out, as in the Evil Spirits Returning in Matthew 12:45. The central truth may come in a blunt question by Jesus following the story, as in Matthew 21:31: "Which of the two did the will of his father?" On several occasions, of course, Jesus Himself gave an extended interpretation. That central truth, however, is always related as an answer to the problem in context.

For the apprehensive in this search, a word of encouragement is in order. Don't panic. The central truth is never hidden or mystical, but nearly always prominent; it is usually evident, rather than far-fetched. Its discovery requires common sense, not mesmeric clairvoyance. As R. C. Trench once noted, "it will scarcely need to be defended and made plausible with great appliance of learning, to be propped up by remote allusions to Rabbinical or profane literature, by illustrations drawn from the recesses of antiquity."[3] If such is required, it is tolerable evidence that one has scored a miss and hates to admit it.

The central truth, then, comes as an answer to obvious questions of the common people in Jesus' audiences. The point or lesson He taught was not for the intellectual sleuths, to send them scurrying to their theological scrolls or crystal balls. Such were, in fact, the very skeptics from whom Jesus' truths were hidden. Rather, He taught the humble and believing, making His points quite evident for them to catch. We are not, therefore, to be embarrassed by the obviousness of a central truth in its context; it may turn out to be a bolt of lightning in the historic setting. Discerning this central truth is the heart of the process in uncovering the lessons in Jesus' parables.

GUIDELINE 3: RELATE THE DETAILS TO THE CENTRAL TRUTH

Interpreting details brings us to the crux of the fuss in parable interpretation. It is well to remember in considering the various details that, though all contribute to the central truth, not all relate in the same way. Some do have metaphors to be interpreted, for instance, though not all. Chrysostom long ago warned against being "overbusy with the details," sensing the need for balance in expounding them.[4]

Two extremes in church history have been noted in handling the details. Origen of Alexandria and Johannes Cocceius found hidden meanings in every detail, many of which were foreign to the context. Adolf Julicher, on the other hand, fought allegorism so vigorously that he denied significance in any of the details, limiting the central truths to broad generalities. Both of these extremes have erred in handling the text, as is generally acknowledged; one violates it by additions, the other by subtractions. What, then, is the balanced way of handling the details without either distorting or neglecting them?

As with all Scripture, it is important to first recognize that none of the details are superfluous in Jesus' stories. Each is given to serve one of two basic functions: it may contribute directly to the central truth, or it may contribute to the realism of the story. To appreciate these functions, let's review the significance of each.

Details Contributing to the Central Truth

Around the hub of the central truth Jesus occasionally interspersed metaphors, weaving them into a corresponding plot. These were given to press home the story. In the Wicked Vinegrowers (Matt. 21:33–39), for instance, the "vineyard" is a figure of Israel (as in Isaiah 5:7), the "vine growers" are the leaders, the "servants" represent the prophets, and the "son" depicts the Lord Himself, as Jeremias acknowledges.[5] These are so obvious that they hardly need explanation. Each detail strikingly underscores the central truth, as Jesus later explained: "The kingdom of God shall be taken from you, and given to a nation bringing forth the fruits thereof" (Matt. 21:43 KJV). In earlier parables the Lord specifically interpreted allegorical parts (The Sower and the Tares), leaving the disciples a significant paradigm to follow (Mark 4:13). In so doing, He summarily rebuked any squeamishness we might have to recognize occasional metaphors as allegorical parts. In His example-stories, in fact, Jesus specifically named some of the individuals or groups involved in the story plots.

Recognizing metaphorical parts for many today seems to suggest a throw-back to the errors of allegorism and its wild interpretations. The two, however, are worlds apart. Since the time of Joachim Jeremias' break with Julicher, most interpreters, in fact, do recognize the place of metaphorical relations in the details.[6] We have noted elsewhere that many modern expositors reject the authenticity of the interpretations given by Jesus, attributing them rather to the early church.[7] This notion builds on a form critical view that requires the reader to slash through the Gospels with structural analysis to rediscover Jesus' actual words.

This approach, as we have noted, violates the very text it presumes to interpret, taking a narrow, concocted view of what a parable can or cannot teach. The opinion of A. T. Cadoux is characteristic: "The speaker who needs to interpret his parables is not master of his method."[8] It might have been more circumspect for him to have said, "The interpreter who needs to remodel the text is not master of his interpretive method." We prefer to stay with Jesus' interpretations as He responded to the disciples.

This admitted use of metaphors by Jesus, however, does not give us freewheeling license, but limited latitude. Many of the parables Jesus explained had very few points of resemblance. As in the Unjust Steward (Luke 16:1–8), for instance, Jesus often used some pretty shady characters to represent God and believers. Their questionable ethics and character, however, did not affect the central truth, for He simply used man's natural logic in that parable to impress the lesson of preparing for the future. His point was simply the greater logic of "making friends for eternity." The steward's dishonest character was obviously not what the Lord commended.

This sparing use of metaphors cautions us against overpressing the meaning of metaphorical details. Like the Old Testament types, Jesus' symbols were used to impress one truth, not a vast complex of truths. Jonah, for instance, typified Christ in but one way, the prophet's experience in the place of death; it certainly was not in Jonah's character.

The same observation can be made of Jesus' symbols. To draw doctrines from the metaphors of the "leaven," the "elder brother," or the "poor man" Lazarus deserving paradise is vastly overdrawn. Enlarging on the "pearl of great price" as a symbol of the church may delight the fancy as it calls to remembrance exquisite truths of the gospel, but that was hardly Jesus' point. His emphasis to the disciples at that time was the extreme value of the kingdom, as the story makes abundantly clear. Drawing clever meanings from symbols may serve to mesmerize the mystics, but it also tends to minimize the central truths taught by Jesus. Don't overwork the symbols or metaphors.

Details Used for Realism in the Story

Though all the details are important, not all add to the central truth. Many serve as "drapery details," making the plot more realistic. These might be removed without affecting the essential meaning, but not without affecting its realism. Without these background details, the parable loses much of its persuasive power. Jesus constantly appealed to that which transpires in the natural realm to make His point clear and unarguable. That is doubtless one reason He used parables rather than allegories or fables, which often stray into fantasy and make-believe. His parables were always true to life, and many of the details were given primarily to enhance this realism. They lend color to the stories, making them more life-like and therefore more persuasive.

The question naturally arises: "How do you tell the difference?" Which details contribute to the central truth and which serve primarily for realism? The key is the "historic naturalness" of the analogies. Would Jesus' hearers have understood them as symbols or as mere incidentals in a realistic story? A. M. Hunter has suggested a good standard: "If then you meet something in a parable which almost cries out to be taken symbolically . . . ask yourself: would this detail carry this symbolical significance for the men to whom Jesus spoke?"[9]

Nicely stated. That is the essence of historical interpretation. If a symbolic meaning is questionable or foreign to the historic setting, it is wise to recognize it as a prop or drapery enhancement, woven in for realism. Forced symbolisms tend to cast the whole lesson in doubt; natural interpretations tend to confirm them.

GUIDELINE 4: CLARIFY AND AUTHENTICATE THE CENTRAL TRUTH

That the parables are revelatory should not be questioned. They were spoken specifically to reveal new truths about the kingdom program. Being figurative, however, they are in special need of double-checking to verify the truths they teach. To do this, one should first press for clarity and unity in the central truth. They were given to clarify, not to mystify, and their interpretations should reflect this crispness of meaning. This can be done by first stating the problem in the form of a question, and then briefly stating the central truth as an answer to that question.[10] Be satisfied only with clarity. If it can't be stated in rather simple terms, the probability is that either the problem or the central truth being taught has not been clearly discerned.

With a clear understanding of the central point, one should then check its validity with the rest of Scripture. This check is often called the "analogy of Scripture." It performs a safeguarding function against the inroads of error and is especially important with the parables. In evaluating the new truths being taught, however, one should not demur because a truth was not previously revealed. Revelation is progressive. The vital test is whether it is corroborated by its context and in harmony with later revelation. This test of overall Scripture is especially important in deriving doctrines from the parables.

In this connection it is well to remember that the doctrinal focus of the parables is not so much on the redemptive program as on the kingdom. Seeking the lost, for instance, is not related to the atonement in the parables, but rather to restoring God's kingdom. This is seen in the story of the Prodigal Son, where the sinning boy comes to his father, seemingly on his own; but that is not the point.

Finding the doctrines of propitiation, reconciliation, expiation, and redemption in these stories only pauperizes those doctrines. Such building of redemptive theology on the parables easily leads to error in neglecting the God-ward aspect of the atonement. Therefore, it is wise to remember that the Lord's primary focus in these parables is God-centered. They concern that which was lost to His kingdom and how He is reclaiming it. This does not minimize redemption, but rather highlights the divine side of the story of the kingdom.

GUIDELINE 5: DISCOVER THE INTENDED APPEAL

Most of the parables carry an appeal and are designed to evoke a decision. Jesus' presence called for action. He appealed to the mind and conscience to elicit a decision of the will. His stories were not given to entertain, but rather to instruct and involve. Proper interpretation should bring this out.

This appeal is sometimes explicit in the prologue or epilogue and sometimes implicit in the story or context. In the parable of the Sower it is found in the epilogue: "Therefore take care how you listen" (Luke 8:18). In the Ten Pounds Entrusted, it is implicit in the story with no need of comment before or after (19:11–27). At times Jesus' appeal was simply to be encouraged concerning the divine power and progress of the kingdom, as in the Seed Growing by Itself (Mark 4:26–32). The Lord's appeal was never hackneyed or stereotyped; rarely did He append an invitation. His style was full of surprises in arousing the human mind and spirit.

This challenge to the will was always paramount in Jesus' teaching. He constantly struck for decisions. To study the parables for mere curiosity without pressing for this divine appeal is to abort their purposes. Inherent in the central truth of each is a unique appeal for action.

Summary. The purpose of these interpretive guidelines is to ensure that the lesson drawn is what Jesus intended—one that comports with the historical and grammatical settings. The central truth will then answer the contextual problem giving rise to the parable and will be supported by its various details. All the details are significant, but not in the same way. Some add substance to the truth, while others simply give color for realism to strengthen its persuasive power. Its telling will often involve an indictment coupled with an appeal for action. Jesus' words were spoken to activate His people for service.

It should also be noted that these guidelines are not meant to insist on a mandatory order of interpretation. Rigid adherence to rules is not their design. Many parables can be understood without a step by step approach, and we will do that with some in the following chapters. Where difficulties and uncertainties arise, however, it is important to have a checking procedure to build confidence in the interpretation and to open up the full range of truths and possible applications. This is especially important for those new to the parables and uncertain how to approach them. Hopefully the following chapters of interpretation and application will bear this out.

Part 2

THE PARABLES RELATED TO JESUS' MINISTRY

Chapter 5

HINTS OF DISASTER IN JESUS' EARLY PARABOLIC SAYINGS

GREATNESS RARELY BEGINS with celebration. The birth of Jesus went almost unnoticed by the world. Even the year of His birth is uncertain. He was born in poverty and raised in obscurity, leaving little record of His early life. Though heir to the throne of David through Solomon, Jesus had anything but a royal welcome. Rather, He was born in a barn in Bethlehem and grew up in the despised village of Nazareth in "Galilee of the Gentiles" (Matt. 4:15).

Why was Jesus not born and raised in Jerusalem, the city of the King? The answer is obvious, if you put yourself in the shoes of Joseph, His legal father, who was well aware of His right to the throne in the Davidic line. Joseph also knew the murderous tactics of Herod the Great, who ruled the land. At his jealous caprice many heads had rolled whom he suspected of treason—even two of his own sons and favorite wife, Mariamne.

For this reason, Joseph and Mary raised Jesus in relative seclusion, carefully guarding the secret of their royal lineage. Even their neighbors in Nazareth were unaware of Jesus' true identity, hardly inclined to vote Him the "local boy most likely to succeed." Some even saw Jesus as illegitimate and a shame to respectable society. To most He was just the son of Joseph and Mary. They also saw Jesus as a young carpenter who never married, but who supported His widowed mother. When Jesus later came to speak in their local synagogue, they were amazed at His performance. He came to earth as the Son of God and the world's Savior, but He came with His Godhood veiled in human flesh.

JESUS' PRESENTATION TO ISRAEL

This veiling of Jesus' divine nature for over thirty years is admittedly hard to conceive, especially in light of the many Old Testament predictions about His coming. But that modesty and mystery were part of the divine plan. When Jesus presented Himself to Israel, He didn't flash before them a dossier of royal credentials demanding regal homage. Nor did He summon a special session of the Sanhedrin to announce and authenticate His presence. Jesus came, rather, as a commoner from the hills of Nazareth preaching a gospel of righteousness. To those who challenged Him, He never flaunted His unique credentials—never did He mention His virgin birth or royal genealogy. He simply identified Himself as the "Son of Man."

The purpose of this self-abnegation, however, was not to hide Jesus' identity, but rather to seek commitment on a higher level. He wasn't looking for shrewd entrepreneurs to build His kingdom; the worldly-wise need not apply. Rather, He called men and women of faith whose primary concern was for spiritual realities. Elderly Simeon and Anna in the temple were of this stripe and became His first disciples. In the divine plan, this mode of identification was strikingly effective. It turned the national dilemma about Jesus' messiahship from a hassle over credentials into an issue of trust in His Word. Out of this background of obscurity He was able to reap a spiritual harvest of the faithful without suing for national recognition. How it threw off the self-serving and superficial is one of the ironies and mysteries of history.

John the Baptist made Jesus' first presentation to Israel. Though of priestly descent, John came as a prophet out of nowhere with a message of unprecedented spiritual challenge. Nor did he politic with the moneyed bureaucrats or cavil over minutia. His pulpit was a stump in the wilderness from which he hailed the nation to the mourners' bench.

What was John's message? "Repent, for the kingdom of heaven is at hand" (Matt. 3:2). The rugged prophet spared no one but summoned all to repentance or judgment. His mission was to prepare the people spiritually for the Messiah's coming. In introducing Jesus, John harked back to Isaiah's grand redemptive song (Isa. 53:7): "Behold, the Lamb of God who takes away the sin of the world" (John 1:29). The messianic hero whom John presented was not a mighty man of war or Jewish Alexander who would conquer their enemies, but rather a Savior who would cover their sins. John called out the spiritual remnant, not the self-righteous hierarchy, to prepare for the Messiah's presence.

Jesus' Credentials as the Messiah

When Jesus did come on the scene for ministry, however, it was not with the thunder of John. Jesus' first year was one of comparative silence, while John continued to hound the nation for repentance. Jesus began slowly, almost reluctantly, awaiting their response. Quietly He moved through the hillsides, teaching in their temple, synagogues, and villages, gathering disciples. To confirm His messiahship, Jesus ministered to them with miracles of mercy. Rather than flaunting legal credentials, He displayed divine powers. These He did in great variety and abundance in His first two years of ministry. Jesus healed the sick, raised the dead, cast out demons, and relieved every kind of distress. Even nature itself bowed to His command. Surpassing by far the miracles of the Old Testament prophets, Jesus showed Himself to be the Creator and Giver of life.

What was Jesus' primary purpose in all this display of power? Was He really trying to meet the physical needs of people, or did He have some other agenda? He certainly was concerned for these crying needs, but He also saw their deeper need. Ministering merely to physical demands often produced greed rather than spiritual fruit. Jesus' primary purpose was to authenticate His Person and word as the Messiah (Matt. 11:5).

Confirming the Word was also the basic purpose of Bible miracles. As the prophet Isaiah declared, such powers were to be a unique feature of the Messiah's ministry; even John the Baptist had to be gently reminded of this when he doubted (Isa. 35:5f.). The Gospel writers often called those miracles "signs," for they pointed the nation to the Messiah's presence. They were His "calling cards," announcing His arrival.

The Nation's Response to Jesus' Miracles

Faced with such convincing proofs, how then did these children of Abraham respond? Not knowing the facts, we would imagine they gave Jesus a roaring welcome with shofars blowing throughout the land. Who wouldn't rejoice and bow before such awesome credentials of majesty? Such, of course, was not the case—how well we know. Rather, a rising tide of doubt slowly began to swell. The reasons behind that strange anomaly constitute the background of Jesus' early parables.

The Political Response. One of the first negative responses came from Herod Antipas, ruler of Galilee and Perea. During the winter of Jesus' first year of ministry, this profane monarch became irked at the judgment calls of John and slapped the prophet into prison. That effectively cut short his revival movement and became an ominous portent and cloud over the nation. It also provoked Jesus to move to Galilee. That move, however, was not for fear of Herod, for Galilee was also part of his turf. Rather, it was a subtle challenge to the impious ruler, laying down the gauntlet. For the next two years the Lord boldly ministered in this area, demonstrating His powers under the shadow of this scandalous son of Herod the Great.

The Religious Response. A polarization of religious opposition also set in toward the end of this first year, perhaps around mid-March. After cleansing a leper in Capernaum, Jesus sent him to the temple to fulfill the Mosaic ritual for cleansing (Lev. 14; Luke 5:14). That trip to the temple, however, had more than a ritual purpose. It was intended as a "testimony" to the priests (as noted by all three Synoptic Gospels; Matt. 8:4; Mark 1:44; Luke 5:14). A testimony of what? That the Messiah, the prophesied Healer, was on the scene.

This constituted a prophetic challenge to the whole Jewish Sanhedrin, notifying them of the Messiah's presence (Isa. 61:1; Matt.

11:5). That they got the point is evident by the next recorded event (Mark 2:1–12; Luke 5:17–25). The Pharisees and lawyers "from every village of Galilee and Judea and from Jerusalem" (Luke 5:17) soon converged on Capernaum. They came on a fact-finding mission to check out those rumored credentials, and Jesus didn't disappoint them. He gave them more than they asked for, in fact, in a public exhibition of healing.

But before healing a paralytic, Jesus treated these scholars to a short course in Christology 101—He forgave the man's sins. This was a rare procedure for the Lord, something He never did before or after. His purpose here was "that you may know that the Son of Man has authority on earth to forgive sins" (Luke 5:24). In a twofold demonstration Jesus showed that He was not only the Messiah but also God Himself with authority to pardon sins. For these men of the cloth, of course, this was sheer blasphemy. They saw it as the foulest kind of heresy and began to check and suspect everything He did.

The second occasion came soon after when Jesus called Matthew the Jewish tax collector to be one of His disciples. Since these "internal revenuers" worked for Rome, often lacing their pockets through extortion, the Jews saw them as apostates, traitors of the nation. In the same way, they saw Jesus' choice of Matthew as intolerable. Jesus had embraced the accursed thing, aligning Himself with the enemies of God. But, adding insult to injury, He then attended a banquet put on by Matthew where He lounged with a whole crowd of "tax-gatherers and sinners" (Luke 5:27–29). For the Pharisees this was open scandal and a repudiation of orthodoxy. The rift between them was growing into a chasm.

JESUS' FIRST PARABOLIC SAYINGS

Why rehearse this well-known history? Its importance here is that it constitutes the historic context out of which Jesus began to speak in parables. It lays bare the setting and problems involved as we review His early parabolic sayings.

The call of Matthew to join Jesus' cabinet occurred near the end of His first year. With the growing animosity of the leaders, Jesus seems to have changed His approach. He adopted this parabolic teaching method to portray by pithy proverbs the condition of Israel. Though they may appear rather innocuous, the Lord deftly used these figurative sayings as striking hints of an ominous turn of events. With a cluster of four such one-liners, He began at this point to indicate the essence of that change.

Parable of the Ministering Physician (Matt. 9:12–13; Mark 2:17; Luke 5:31–32)

The Problem and Brief Saying. Though that joyous feast with Matthew was something of a breakthrough for outcasts, it also became a catalyst for Jesus' new truths about the kingdom. In response to the grumbling scribes and Pharisees who resented His grace to "publicans and sinners," Jesus gave a caustic reply: "It is not those who are well who need a physician, but those who are sick" (Luke 5:31). To make sure they didn't miss it, the Lord embarrassed them with the obvious interpretation: "I have not come to call righteous men, but sinners to repentance" (v. 32).

The Central Truth. Jesus' reference to the leaders as "well" and "righteous" was obviously a tongue-in-cheek gesture of tact and graciousness. But beneath that parabolic garb was a subtle missile of judgment. In polite terms He called their bluff and alerted them to their own failures and negligence to duty. While He was tirelessly ministering to the outcasts and wounded, they were reveling in good "health" and scorning anyone gracious enough to care for the sick. Jesus could hardly have struck a more sensitive nerve, for they touted diligence to duty as their crowning virtue. To parade as children of God while ignoring the outcasts, Jesus implied, is to stand self-condemned before God.

Parable of the Wedding and Purloined Bridegroom (Matt. 9:14 – 15; Mark 2:18–20; Luke 5:33–35)

The Pharisees' charge that Jesus consorted with "sinners" called for another clarification. They had noted that while they were piously fasting, Jesus and His disciples were pompously feasting. Not only was He "slumming" with the outcasts; He was also sloughing on religion. They nailed Him with the question, "Why do you and your disciples laugh and feast on a fast day?" They saw Him as founding a cult of revelry.

The Problem in the Context. Jesus' answer came in the form of three parabolic sayings that portray a tragicomedy. The scene is that of a bridal party. Though the lesson is often missed, it is quite obvious when related to the question just posed. The first saying portrays a happy bridal party with a bridegroom who is suddenly snatched away; the last two describe the reasons for Jesus' startling announcement of departure. That is the basic problem He addresses here.

The Central Truth. Answering the question of fasting, Jesus explained: "The attendants of the bridegroom cannot mourn, as long as the bridegroom is with them, can they?" (Matt. 9:15). This picture struck a symbolism deep in Israel's tradition. Her covenant relation with the Lord was often likened to that of a bridegroom and bride (Isa. 50:1; Jer. 3:8; Ezek. 16:8; Hos. 1). The bridal drama of the Song of Solomon, for instance, recalled that relationship every Passover as the Israelites dutifully recited the book. Though Israel's harlotries had incurred a divorce, a future reunion was promised as joyous as that of her exodus from Egypt (Isa. 51:11; 54:1; Jer. 3:11; Ezek. 16:31ff.; Hos. 2:14–16). John the Baptist, in fact, introduced Jesus to Israel in the role of bridegroom (John 3:29).

This depiction of the Lord as a bridegroom was given to emphasize two points the Pharisees were missing. It first gave them a striking notification of Jesus' identity, and then dramatized the reason His disciples were feasting. He had come as the long-awaited covenant Lord, ready to fulfill His role as their heavenly Groom. Such an occasion called for joy, not mourning. His unspoken question to them might have been, "Why are you fasting when your long-awaited Bridegroom is here?"

That note of joy, however, was followed by a note of gloom: "The days will come when the bridegroom is taken away from them, and then they will fast" (Matt. 9:15). This spoke in a veiled way of Jesus' coming absence. It was one of His first hints of departing without fulfilling His kingdom mission for Israel, given shortly after the Pharisees had charged Him with blasphemy (Luke 5:21). He would, in fact, be "snatched away" (Greek, *aparthe*), suggesting a violent departure.

The New Patch and New Wineskins (Matt. 9:16–17; Mark 2:21–22; Luke 5:36–39)

As a follow-up to the Bridegroom saying, Jesus added two more pictures. They express some of the reasons He would be "taken away." The very idea of leaving, of course, was incomprehensible to His disciples, if He was indeed the Messiah. Wasn't the Messiah to remain forever (Ps. 110:4)?

The Problem and Central Truth. To answer this problem and explain the strange anomaly, the Lord gave two clues from familiar scenes, both relating to the spiritual condition of Israel. He first related her to an old garment, then to an old wineskin. Though patching old garments was common in that culture, everyone knew it was futile if the garment itself was rotten. The obvious reference was to degenerate Pharisaism, which was showing itself intransigent and beyond repair. The leaders' opposition to the reformation of John the Baptist made this evident. So rotten was the spiritual fabric of the nation that the attempted patch of John was pulling apart, leaving an even greater rift. John's disciples, in fact, were part of this audience (Matt. 9:14). With the prophet sealed up in prison, his grand patch job appeared to be coming apart at the seams.

The following saying of the New Wine served to further reinforce that point of Judaic corruption. Not only was her spiritual fabric corrupt, but also everything she touched became corrupt. In the figure of an old wineskin, Jesus illustrated this truth by recounting a familiar "practical joke"—pouring new wine into an old wineskin. Several methods were used to preserve new wine, the most common being that of using new skins or uncontaminated containers. Only a fool would use old skins over again for the simple reason they retained some of the old lees of fermentation, which would quickly ferment and explode the skins. Not only would the bottles break, but also the new wine would be lost. Jesus used this familiar act of stupidity to show the wisdom of His leaving.

Jesus' obvious point was the utter folly of any attempt to establish His kingdom with the present leadership of Israel. The whole Judaic system was honeycombed with old lees of corruption. This was evident in much of the priesthood, their oral traditions, and especially in their materialistic way of life. Hypocrisy was rampant. The original purist movement of the Pharisees had been taken over by false shepherds, who installed a revisionist system. So hardened and inflexible had it become that it was about to rot of its own fermentation. Yet those entrenched in the old system were oblivious to that corruption, insisting that "The old is good enough" (Luke 5:39). They had little appetite for the "new wine" of Jesus' message.

The Wider Significance. Don't miss the full impact of this parabolic cluster. Together they answer the question of why Jesus came and why He soon would leave. He came to bring joy to the nation as her heavenly Bridegroom, but would soon depart without fulfilling that marital union.

Why that unexpected departure? The three sayings in their settings suggest the answer. Two essentials of a glorious wedding were missing—the bride's garments of beauty (Ps. 45:13–14), and the pure beverage of fresh wine (John 2:10). Rather than garments of beauty, Jesus was met by tattered rags; instead of pure wine, Israel came with a jug of fermented traditions, ready to defile any new message from heaven. Being drunk and blinded by those dregs, she failed to even recognize the heavenly Groom when He came. Nor was He about to fulfill that union. He would simply forego the glories of that royal marriage until a future day.

This prophesied marriage of Israel to her covenant Lord should not be confused with His coming marriage to the church. Though similar, they are not the same. The Lord entered a marital union with Israel when the nation was formed (Ezek. 16:8, 32). He later gave her a bill of divorce because of her adulteries (Jer. 3:8), but promised a glorious restoration at her time of national repentance (Isa. 54:5–7; Hos. 2:14–16).

The name of that covenant Lord is "Yahweh," the Triune God. Jesus came to Israel as part of that Trinity, her promised Bridegroom.

Though the New Testament relation of Christ to the church is also portrayed in marital terms, it is a spiritual union to be consummated at the Father's house (2 Cor. 11:2; Eph. 5:27, 32; Rev. 19:7). It is an eternal marriage of God's Son to His heavenly bride. One is an earthly relation with His chosen nation, the other a spiritual union with His called-out church. The figure of marriage shows the intimacy of both relations.

Application. These first parabolic sayings impress an important principle that needs emphasis. Any religious system or instrument of God that puts traditional biases above God's Word and fails to purify itself, soon becomes blind even to God's presence. The Lord eventually discards such as dead wood. That was true of ancient Judaism and of many other kingdoms, and has often been demonstrated in apostate movements in church history. The Lord will not long tolerate any generation of sinners, be they religious or civic, who become too proud and egotistical to respond to correction.

PARABLES ON JESUS' NEW RELATION TO ISRAEL

During Jesus' second year of ministry, A.D. 30, several spates of parabolic teaching also took place. That year began on the second Passover after which the Sabbath controversy in the grain fields occurred (Luke 6:1). It ended the following Passover when He fed over five thousand (Luke 9:10–17; John 6:1–14). That year was action packed and a time of great public favor despite the leaders. During that period Jesus chose the twelve disciples, gave the Sermon on the Mount, performed numerous miracles, and ministered to great throngs in Galilee. But it was also a time of disappointments: clerical agitation continued to mount; John the Baptist was slain by Herod; Jesus declined an offer of the laity in Galilee to make Him King. He was becoming the center of great national controversy.

The Spread of Antagonism

Though Jesus' popularity with the people continued, His relations with the leaders steadily worsened. Shortly after that second Passover, He was twice charged with breaking the Sabbath (Mark 2:24; 3:2). This He acknowledged, but showed Himself Lord (or Maker) of the Sabbath, defending also the principle of doing good on the Sabbath. The leaders agreed to neither of these propositions, but were enraged at His brash temerity. Jesus had violated their Sabbath ritual, a sin akin to blasphemy. So miffed were the Pharisees that they joined forces with the Herodians in seeking ways to murder Jesus (Mark 3:6). This amalgam was epochal in itself, for they had traditionally fought each other tooth and nail.

It was following this unholy alliance that Jesus chose the Twelve to train for ministry. Part of their training was given in the Sermon on the Mount (Matt. 5–7). That famous address was doubtless spoken many times, primarily to clarify true righteousness. Its purpose, of course, was not to give a plan of salvation, but rather a true way of life. To underscore His principles, Jesus contrasted them with the ritual system of the Pharisees, thereby incurring again their pious outrage (5:20). He stressed that in both doctrine and practice a true believer seeks to please the Father, not to impress people. What startled the people and disturbed the leaders most was that Jesus spoke on His own authority, not that of the scribes (7:29). Six times He declared, "You have heard that it was said, . . . but I say," setting His authority over the "sacred" traditions of the elders.

For the religious leaders, this wasn't just heresy, it was treachery; it was an open declaration of war. They rightly discerned that Jesus' references to hypocrites in the synagogues, false prophets, ravenous wolves, and so on, were directed at them. He had painted them as sinister villains in vivid contrast with righteousness. Thus, in clarifying God's concern for justice and mercy, Jesus also threw down the gauntlet to their whole pseudo-religious system. Their intransigence was turning His mission of mercy into one of judgment.

Parable of the Spoiled Brats Playing Games (Matt. 11:16–19; Luke 7:31–35)

Jesus' parabolic language more and more reflected that change. During that summer John the Baptist sent messengers to Jesus, asking if He really was the Messiah. The doughty prophet was troubled as to why he should be locked up if Jesus was indeed that coming Emancipator. To this Jesus responded by pointing to His many miracles in fulfillment of Isaiah's prophecy (Luke 7:22; cf. Isa. 35:5–6). But He also paid tribute to John as the greatest of prophets, calling the nation to repentance. Yet these leaders continued to disdain both the prophet and his ministry.

The Problem and Central Truth. Noting this arrogance, Jesus unloaded one of His early judgment sayings. The leaders were showing themselves unresponsive to every work of God, like a bunch of snooty kids. Jesus saw them as spoiled brats playing games in the streets: "They are like children who sit in the market place and call to one another; and they say, 'We played the flute for you, and you did not dance; we sang a dirge, and you did not weep'" (Luke 7:32).

To make sure no one missed the point, the Lord carefully identified these players. The snobs were the leaders who showed their disdain for both John and Jesus. Like those haughty kids, they refused to "play ball" with any referee or messenger from God. To John's ascetic approach they responded with condescension, calling him demonic. To Jesus' social approach they feigned indignation, calling Him a drunkard. As their fathers did to the prophets, they also rejected God's correction in whatever tone of voice He spoke.

The Wider Significance. The abiding truth of this juvenile comedy should not be missed. As the Pharisees played a game of religion, arbitrarily changing the rules and calling the shots, so it is easy for any creedal system to succumb to self-delusion. Any leadership that becomes petty and impervious to God's correction is a candidate for judgment. To remain true and dynamic, every movement of God must maintain a responsive attitude to His leading and correction. Elite snobbery often follows non-response.

Parable of a Loan Officer and Two Debtors (Luke 7:36–50)

Jesus' Shabby Treatment as a Dinner Guest. Shortly after this slap at arrogance, Jesus was invited to dine with a Pharisee by the name of Simon. As Jesus arrived with other guests, however, He received a cool reception. Rather than being welcomed with the usual courtesies of a kiss, foot washing, and a touch of perfume, He was rudely ignored. In that culture such amenities were expected of a host as guests came in from dusty roads. Jesus then evidently made His way to the lowest seat as He waited for other guests to arrive and be welcomed by the host.

A Timely Intrusion from the Streets. That meal, however, was suddenly interrupted. A woman of the streets, known for her previous life of immorality, "crashed the party" and began washing Jesus' feet. Spontaneously, her tears flowed, wetting His feet (from behind), and she dried them with her hair while kissing and anointing them with costly perfume. Jesus graciously received this, but it left Simon and his party aghast. It could not have been a worse disaster for the proud host had a loose bull tromped through overturning the tables and delicacies. But he also saw this as proof that Jesus was naive and anything but a prophet. Reading his mind, Jesus commanded their attention with a brief parabolic missile. If the party needed an "after-dinner story" to pep it up, this one was wired for explosion.

Jesus then told the story of a loan officer who had two debtors who were unable to pay him. Though one owed ten times more than the other, the lender graciously forgave them both. With this brief portrayal, Jesus lured Simon into the plot with a simple question: "Which of them therefore will love him more?" (Luke 7:42). The logic was inescapable and Simon retorted, "I suppose the one whom he forgave more" (v. 43). That was all Jesus needed to make His point. Let's first note the problem and then the central truth.

The Problem Addressed. Jesus' response was not what Simon might have expected. Jesus ignored any superficial questions the Pharisee might have had such as, "Why did Jesus tolerate this sinful woman?" The deeper problem He addressed was Simon's misconception of himself. He imagined that he was not only far above this woman, but also quite superior to this visiting Rabbi from Nazareth. In playing host to Jesus, Simon's obvious intent was to humiliate Him before his invited guests, beginning with a shoddy welcome.

That was Simon's first mistake. Any other rabbi might have stomped out, but Jesus remained to press home a needed lesson. The brash intrusion and love of this woman of the streets provided the ideal setting. What the arrogant host had neglected, she graciously performed with finesse. Sensing the host's contrived humiliation, she boldly broke into the dignified dinner to lavishly honor the Savior. Her tears expressed not only her love for the Lord, but also her sympathy and deep shame for the Pharisee's shabby treatment of Him. In a lion's den of humiliation, this newly saved "Magdalene" boldly showered Jesus with her highest devotion.

From this tense scenario we can then express the problem Jesus addressed in this parable: "Who was the real sinner at the dinner?" He might have asked, "Will the real sinner please stand up?" Was it the brash woman, as Simon thought? Or might it be someone else? The haughty host soon supplied the answer himself as he clumsily stumbled into his own humiliation.

The Central Truth. Jesus' point was not that the woman's love earned her forgiveness, but rather that it showed she had already received forgiveness by faith (Luke 7:50). The Pharisee, on the other hand, revealed his lack of forgiveness by his rudeness and poverty of love. His cool welcome of "no water," "no kiss," and "no oil" for Jesus showed Simon had also received "no forgiveness." He betrayed the fact that the real sinner at his dinner was not the uninvited guest, but rather himself. Lack of love is always a dead giveaway in this game of "who's the biggest sinner?" In his pride and arrogance, Simon practically reared his own gallows, intending to hang Jesus.

The Lord, however, was not content with deflating this proud host. He sought rather to call the attention of the people to Himself as the Savior. Before leaving, He said to the woman: "Your sins have been forgiven" (Luke 7:48). This statement the guests rightly interpreted as His claim to being God, who alone can forgive sins. Besides claiming to be the Messiah, Jesus left them with something even more startling to think about—they had inadvertently dined with God, but had shamelessly treated Him with disdain.

The Wider Significance. The abiding truth of this beautiful story is almost unrivaled in its depth of meaning. Dignified ritual or arrogant pride does not display righteousness or true forgiveness. It is not aloof and condescending. Rather, it is God's gift to anyone who acknowledges his or her sins and accepts His mercy in Christ. Righteousness is shown by courageous and selfless love that stands up for the Savior.

This woman is sometimes called "Mary" because of the following passage, and could well have been Mary Magdalene, who was cleansed of seven demons (Luke 8:2). If so, she was then one of the women who stood by Jesus in His hour of ultimate humiliation on the cross (John 19:25). But she was also honored by the Savior on Easter morning as the first one to whom He revealed Himself in resurrection glory (20:16 –17). How appropriate!

PARABLES IN RESPONSE TO BLASPHEMY

As previously noted, Jesus' relations with the religious leaders began to deteriorate quickly after that second Passover. Several altercations took place between them during that summer, leading to an open break in the fall. Following the Sermon on the Mount in early summer, the question of Jesus' miracles increasingly became a national issue. Unlike John, Jesus peppered His ministry with unprecedented wonders. These confirmed His messiahship, as we have noted.

The Pharisees, however, concluded on other grounds that Jesus was an impostor. He didn't fit their carnal notions of a political Messiah and was an irritant to their bureaucratic system. Their problem, however, was that this "pretender" didn't just pretend; He backed His pretensions with mighty miracles. How do you answer the opening of blind eyes and raising the dead if Jesus is not the Messiah?

Parable of Satan's Divided Kingdom (Matt. 12:25)

The leaders' sultry rejection was equal to the challenge. Yes, Jesus does miraculous works, they said, but He does them in the power of Beelzebub, ruler of the demons (Matt. 12:24). This assessment was not just a snide remark, but rather had the official ring of Jerusalem's authority (Mark 3:22). Having reluctantly conceded His power to do miracles, they now attributed that power to Satan. Recognizing the firmness of this verdict by the officials, Jesus would desist no longer. They had gone beyond the point of mere doubt, and Jesus summoned them to a crucial confrontation (v. 23). Characteristically, He began His dress-down with a parable—one on the kingdom of Satan.

The Problem and Central Truth. The Lord began with a brief saying in the form of a proverb: "Any kingdom divided against itself is laid waste; and any city or house divided against itself shall not stand" (Matt. 12:25). Though crisp and almost a given, it was a little bit of dynamite. Its logic was irresistible, challenging the leaders' inane contention that Satan would oppose himself. Jesus' obvious point was that no intelligent being, kingdom, or home would intentionally destroy itself; and Satan is nobody's fool. Jesus thus rebuffed the leaders' own touted logic by showing it to be an obvious non sequitur.

But Jesus pursued the logic of that charge even further. He showed it to be a boomerang, returning on the leaders to incriminate their own children. "By whom do your sons cast them out? Consequently, they shall be your judges" (Matt. 12:27). Their foolish charge was an ever-tightening noose around their necks with their own sons doing the strangling. By a Freudian slip, they had convicted their own children of demonry.

Having defused the logic of this Pharisaic charge, Jesus then pointed to the only viable alternative. "If I cast out demons by the Spirit of God, then the kingdom of God has come upon you" (Matt. 12:28). His exorcising of demons simply demonstrated the presence of God's kingdom. Jesus had come to do battle with Satan and finally to bind him before seizing his kingdom. Therefore, to stand against Jesus was to align oneself with the Devil. To cap it off, Jesus warned that to impugn His work as satanic was to blaspheme the Holy Spirit, for Jesus worked in His power (Matt. 12:28, 31). That, Jesus further warned, was an "unpardonable" sin, eternally so (Matt. 12:31–32; Mark 3:28–29).

The Wider Significance. What then is this "unpardonable sin"? Jesus gave several clues, both negative and positive. First, it is not a sin that believers can commit, for it cannot be forgiven, even in the world to come. Nor is it the sin of finally rejecting Christ, for it is described as being against the Holy Spirit, not against Christ (though final rejection, of course, is unpardonable). Some would restrict the unpardonable sin to the special circumstance of the Pharisees blaspheming Jesus' works and, therefore, make it not applicable to our age. That would conveniently dispose of it as a continuing danger, but it would also change the language of the warning.

It should be noted that Jesus gave the warning in the form of a principle, of which the leaders' blasphemy was but an instance. That principle is stated in Genesis 6:3, "My Spirit shall not strive with man forever." Only the Holy Spirit can bring repentance, but His patience has a limit (2 Tim. 2:25). Anyone under conviction, of course, has not committed that sin, for conviction is evidence of His working. Though a harsh concept, it would be brash indeed to defuse Jesus' solemn warning about the Holy Spirit's sensitivity in this regard.

Parable of the Haunted House in Palestine (Matt. 12:43–45)

That blasphemous charge of the Pharisees constituted a watershed in Jesus' ministry. Two actions directly after strongly confirm this. The first was His refusal to give the leaders' any further messianic "signs," and the second was the stress on His new relationship to His people. Being told that His mother and brothers were seeking Him, Jesus delayed, pointing out that His spiritual family would now be related by faith, rather than mere physical ties (Matt. 12:46–49). Those who do "the will of My Father in heaven" are "My brother and sister and mother" (v. 50). This suggests a major disjunction in Jesus' ministry. From that point on He directed His mission more to outlying areas as He prepared His twelve disciples for their new and wider ministry.

The Problem Addressed. Before leaving the scribes and Pharisees, however, Jesus had one further ominous word for them and their generation (Matt. 12:41–45). Having heard a greater prophet than Jonah (who had received an immense response in Nineveh), and a greater wise man than Solomon (who had amazed the Queen of Sheba), the leaders' judgment would also be proportionately greater. To portray that judgment, Jesus related it to His recent exorcism of a demon-possessed man (v. 22). When a demon is cast out of a person, Jesus declared, it often returns to its old haunts looking for a place to flop. Finding it empty and refurbished, the demon eagerly declares squatter's rights and returns with a gang of seven others more wicked than himself. The final state of that man, Jesus said, is worse than the first.

What was Jesus' point in this strange story of the Haunted House? That He taught something more than the old aphorism of "the futility of mere self-reformation" is evident from His end-stress: "That is the way it will also be with this evil generation" (v. 45). He was not just parroting practical prudence or telling "Halloween stories." What then was His point?

The Central Truth. Jesus' obvious lesson concerned the spiritual state of the nation under its present leadership. That was the problem He noted in the prologue. They had experienced the greatest cleansing movement of history under John the Baptist, who came introducing the Messiah (Matt. 3:5–6). But John's brief reformation was being aborted by the leaders, who rejected not only him but also the One he came to proclaim (Luke 7:30). The final irony was that they were also shutting the door for themselves on the messianic age they sought.

This barring of the Messiah from their house, however, was not the whole story. An empty house needs occupants, or thieves and thugs will infest it. That was the condition of Israel. Their "haunted house" could not remain empty; it would soon become the habitat of the fiends of hell, as the parable suggests.

A more graphic description of Israel's condition in the wake of Jesus' crucifixion is hard to imagine. And as Paul explained in Romans 11:10 and 25, their hardness and demonic control continue even today in their blindness to Jesus. With all its broad-minded toleration for things religious, modern Judaism is as adamant as ever in denying the messiahship of Jesus. To receive Him as Savior is considered a sin against their culture and an "un-Jewish" act.

Though the scattered remnant has paid dearly for that rejection (driven almost to the regions of hell as wanderers in the world since A.D. 70), their national rejection of Jesus as the Messiah has not changed. That certainly does not justify the irresponsible and almost fiendish charge of the medieval church that the Jews were Christ-killers, for that only exacerbated their alienation. Yet, the Messiah is still locked out of the house as Israel plies a hazardous course with the "seven demons" still at the spiritual helm. Though that will not continue forever, there is no apparent exorcism in sight.

The Wider Significance. This parable of the Haunted House was not just for ancient Israel, but also was given as a spiritual lesson for all. God continually seeks to cleanse that He might occupy. Spiritual housecleaning, however, is useless without positive commitment. Negative religion by itself is futile and can be dangerous; the demons stand ready to move into any spiritual vacuum. Too easily we pride ourselves on repudiating evil without replacing it with good. Jesus here reminds us that God's work in any life is only half done when Satan or evil has been evicted. Christ must also be enthroned as Lord.

Summary. These initial parabolic sayings introduce us to a crucial turnaround in Jesus' ministry. They graphically portray His fallout with the religious leaders and the reasons for it. The first four of these brief sayings defended His ministry as Israel's Physician, suggesting also His coming absence because of her intransigence in responding to God. Their grand hopes of an early wedding celebration with the Messiah were dashed for what Jesus called their having become an "evil generation" (Matt. 12:45).

The next group of sayings further alluded to this growing antagonism in Jesus' stories of the Spoiled Brats and the Two Debtors. The leaders' arrogance was unbearable. Those exchanges then set the stage for His crucial confrontation with the scribes and Pharisees. Since they had accused Him of working with Satan, He showed them in these two final sayings who it was that was working with Satan—He or them. In the story of the Divided Kingdom, the Lord let them pronounce their own judgment by the logic of their own exorcisms. They argued themselves into self-condemnation. Then the story of the Haunted House gave an eerie description of Israel's spiritual condition following the Messiah's departure. Not only would their rejection abort John's reformation, but it would also open the door to a demonic horde that would infiltrate and harass the nation for an indefinite period of time.

These parabolic sayings dramatize the monumental changes that were taking place in Israel as the tide began to turn and the leadership coalesced against this Prophet from Nazareth. The brief sayings serve as a hinge, highlighting the events that turned Jesus' ministry to the broader world at large. In the wake of these Herculean changes, many questions needed answers. What about that long-prophesied kingdom they all looked for, the disciples wondered, and where do we go from here? Are the increasing rumbles of coming disaster really worth the cost and the hazards it might involve?

It is to that significant area of the Lord's instruction we turn in the next chapter as we listen to Jesus unveil the "mysteries of the kingdom."

Chapter 6

"MYSTERIES OF THE KINGDOM" UNFOLDED

Part 1: Its Planting and Growth

RECALL THAT THE FIRST major crisis of Jesus' ministry took place in the fall of His second year. He had ministered in Galilee for about eight months and was met by a groundswell of public acclaim. The people loved His gospel of goodies and magic works. After the Sabbath controversy with the Pharisees (Passover, A.D. 30), however, antagonism began to build. Spirited disputes with the leaders made it a hot summer both north and south. The result was a polarization of the people, bringing strained relations between Jesus and the Pharisaic lawyers. The dissension soon turned to sharp conflict that came to a head that fall.

The day of that spiritual eruption was one of the busiest of Jesus' ministry. During the morning, He mingled with a vast multitude, healing and teaching (Mark 3:20). One of those healed was a blind and dumb demoniac, leading to a discussion on demonism. In the exchange, the Jerusalem delegation rebuked Jesus' claim to forgive sins and charged Him with working in the power of Satan. It was then that He called their bluff, set them straight as to who was working with demons, and warned them of blasphemy. From that point on He refused them any further confirming signs. The polarization process was virtually complete.

THE DISCIPLES' DILEMMA CONCERNING THE KINGDOM

Following this break with the leaders, the Lord began to update the disciples on the changed status of the kingdom and what lay ahead. The nasty split with the Pharisees had left them stunned and confused. They had left all to follow Him, thinking He would fulfill their messianic dreams. As with the rest of the nation, they envisioned a glorious ascendance of the Messiah to destroy their enemies and establish Israel as a world power. He would, in fact, rule all nations. Jesus' coming and ministry had rekindled those dreams into a lively hope, which now seemed to be shot down by the very leaders who supposedly looked for Him.

This presented them with a colossal dilemma. How could the disciples be true to their Judaic faith if they spurned Israel's leaders to follow this "unauthorized" prophet from Galilee? Excommunication was inevitable. And what would become of the promised kingdom now that the King was being rejected? These were some of the perplexities the disciples faced as they left the scene of Jesus' break with the leaders. They were cowed by the religious system and confused by the whole turn of events.

But Jesus also faced a problem as Shepherd of this mystified flock. How could He divulge to them that the kingdom they looked for would now be put on hold?[1] How could He wean them from their expectations of immediate glory to the prospects of suffering? And in making this shift, how could He keep from shattering their faith in the grand Old Testament promises of the Messiah's coming?

The disciples' instruction at this point called for supernatural pedagogy. No more delicate lessons ever had to be taught. The Savior, of course, was the Master Teacher and set about the task with special teaching aids. Those aids to learning were the parables by which He unveiled the "mysteries of the kingdom" (Matt. 13:11). His use of these longer narratives was not a new teaching method; but He used them with such consummate skill as to make them not only incomparable, but eternal stories.

The Setting and Survey of Matthew 13 and Mark 4

Jesus gave this seminar at Galilee's shore. With a large crowd gathered, He spoke from a small fishing dinghy, addressing the people just off the beach. The rural setting of farming scenes in the surrounding hillsides was ideal for His subject and their hearing. This series of parables was the largest group He gave at any one time, and His audience here may also have been the largest.

"Mysteries of the Kingdom" Defined

These parables deal specifically with "mysteries of the kingdom of heaven" [or of God] (Matt. 13:11; Mark 4:11; Luke 8:10). Though Mark and Luke use the term "kingdom of God," Matthew phrases it "kingdom of heaven" in deference to his Jewish audience, who guarded the divine name from common usage. The terms are basically the same, both deriving from Daniel 2:44, "*The God of heaven* will set up a kingdom which shall never be destroyed" (emphasis added). In referring to it in kingdom terms, rather than redemptive, Jesus emphasized God's sovereignty in orchestrating this new program. Though redemption is certainly implied, Jesus' emphasis in the Synoptic Gospels is that of bringing individuals willingly under God's rule during the interadvent age. The actual designation of "church" was given some time later (Matt. 16:18).

The term *mysteries* sets these parables off as especially unique. A mystery in the Bible is not something mysterious, but rather a new truth revealed for the first time. As the Master Teacher, Jesus was not giving His class a rehash of old truths, but a preview or revelation of something new. He made this clear as the disciples first questioned Him on His use of parables (Matt. 13:11). His purpose was not to further describe the messianic kingdom, foretold in the Old Testament, but to reveal a new phase of God's kingdom previously unrevealed. To further underscore this point, Matthew quoted Psalm 78:2: "I will open my mouth in parables; I will utter things hidden since the foundation of the world" (Matt. 13:35).

Though Jesus came to Israel offering the Old Testament kingdom announced by John (and by Gabriel; Luke 1:32–33), that is no longer His appeal. The nation's rejection of His Person jettisoned also His kingdom offer to the people. For an indefinite period, the ancient promises to Israel will continue unfulfilled while the Lord enacts a new program of grace to all nations. This will stretch from His rejection by Israel to their reception of Him at His second coming. It is often called the interadvent period. In these parables the Lord portrays how that new program will commence and how it will progress throughout the age. It is basically the church age, though it extends a bit before and after the precise period of the church.

These parables, then, are called kingdom parables, each designed to describe an aspect of this program. There are nine in all, eight recorded by Matthew, three by Mark, and two by Luke. Following Matthew's order, we find that five were spoken to the crowd by the shore and four to the disciples as they met later in a house. To the crowd by the Sea of Galilee, Jesus gave no interpretations; but to the disciples He explained each one later in the house (Mark 4:34). Only the first two of these interpretations, however, are recorded.

These stories and pictures were from scenes familiar to the disciples, the first group focusing on farming and the home, and the last group on marketing or industry. An outline of these two groups of parables will help display the broad movement of Jesus' plan for the church as He introduced it in this new kingdom program.

PARABLES OF THE KINGDOM IN OUTLINE (MATT. 13; MARK 4)

I. Parables by the Sea—With a farming motif.
  A. Planting of the kingdom.
    1. The Sower—Why the small harvest and how will it end?
    2. The Tares—How does one explain the counterfeits?
  B. Growth of the kingdom.
    1. The Mustard Seed—Will it really grow?
    2. The Leavening Process—How will it grow?
    3. The Seed Growing by Itself—Why will it grow?

II. Parables in the House—With a marketing motif.
   A. Values of the kingdom.
      1. The Hidden Treasure—Is it worth pursuing?
      2. The Priceless Pearl—Is it worth the sacrifice?
   B. Responsibilities in the kingdom.
      1. The Fishing Net—Responsibility to reach and gather.
      2. The Household Steward—Responsibility to teach.

PARABLES ON PLANTING THE KINGDOM

Parable of the Sower (Matt. 13:3–23)

The activity of sowing is Jesus' subject in the first two parables of this series, first that of good seed, then that of the counterfeit. Farming, of course, was familiar to all in that culture, perhaps even in view as Jesus spoke. The season was late fall, the time when the people planted winter wheat before the latter rains.

Jesus' story involved a farmer who sowed his field randomly, as many farmers did, allowing the seed to fall where it would on the soil. Some fell on hard, wayside ground and were quickly snatched up by birds; others fell on rocky ground with shallow soil; some on thorn-infested soil; and a few on good ground. The obvious result was that only the good ground produced fruit. That harvest, however, proved to be an abundant one, up to a hundredfold. Despite everything, the farmer reaped a bumper crop.

The Problem Addressed. The evident purpose of this parable was to shed divine light on the puzzle of how Israel's leaders could reject the long-awaited Messiah and His kingdom. Their continued obstinacy was incomprehensible to this believing band, leaving the disciples numb with shock. As dark shadows began to fall, they needed the Lord's special counsel on that enigma to keep their faith anchored and their hopes alive. What, they pondered, was its cause, and what would the Lord now do about His kingdom?

The Central Truth. Though this parable alludes to Jesus as the Sower and the word of God as the seed, its central focus is on the soil of Israel. The fruitlessness of Jesus' message in that soil was producing also the scuttle of His kingdom offer. Before encouraging the disciples with the prospect of a fruitful spin-off, He first identified the cause of that apparent failure. It was neither the Sower nor the seed, but rather the barren soil of Israel. That was Jesus' central point. Having failed to prepare itself for the Messiah's coming (as exhorted by John), the nation had preconditioned itself for failure. Jesus pictured it as hardened in superficial ritual, shallow in spiritual life, and entangled with the thorny growths of political and personal ambitions.

The story, however, has a happy ending. In a small plot of "good ground" the word of the kingdom would take root and flourish—so profusely, in fact, that it would more than recoup the initial failure by the unresponsive. The Lord would not be the loser in terms of reaping a harvest, though that evil generation of Israel would suffer loss. Though the chosen nation would be set aside temporarily as God's instrument, the Lord's spiritual purpose of establishing His authority in the hearts of people would not be thwarted. The story has many applications, to be sure, but this central truth is foremost.

The Details Interpreted. Jesus Himself interpreted this parable in some detail, being recorded three times to make sure we get the point (Matt. 13:18 –23; Mark 4:13 –20; Luke 8:11–15). The *seed,* He said, is the "word of the kingdom" that He had sown. The four soils represent the various hearers of the word. These hearers refer to the people of Israel at that time, as evident from Jesus quoting Isaiah 6:9–10. Jesus did not identify the various soils, but made them quite apparent.

1. The Wayside Soil. The first soil symbolized hardened hearts, too callused to receive the word of Christ. Because of this, they were quickly deprived of it by the evil one. The scribes and Pharisees, who had just demeaned Jesus' work as satanic, admirably fit this description. Though their spiritual soil was originally good, it had become hardened by unbelief and lack of response. Their "Traditions of the Elders" had saturated the soil with a hardening and dogmatizing effect. In this soil Jesus' words found no root and the Devil quickly devoured them. The "harrumphing" religious leaders were a classic case of hardened soil.

2. The Rocky Soil. This represented soil that had little depth. As with much of the rocky ground of Palestine, it was incapable of supporting healthy growth. Its soil was a shallow layer of dirt over flat rocks that soon warmed in the sunshine, and with a little moisture quickly germinated shoots. But, unable to root, these growths would easily become scorched and soon wither.

This ground describes many of Jesus' early disciples who followed Him in the sunshine of His early popularity, but backed off when rejection set in and the going got rough. They were the superficial, party-going fans who loved His "signs" and "magic manna," but quickly deserted Him when the party was over and the ominous storm clouds began to rumble (John 6:66). Their number had no doubt peaked at this time.

3. The Thorny Soil. Jesus' words also fell among thorns, which symbolized those who gave their priorities to other things in life. It speaks of soil that is loamy and capable of good production, but infested with other growths. The weeds of worry, riches, pleasure, and personal ambitions were sapping its energy and choking out its life. The problem with such soil is not its hardness or emotional shallowness (as with the previous), but rather with the hungry weeds of personal priorities. These smother and starve the struggling shoots of the Word so that they die aborning.

The rich young ruler of Luke 18 is a case in point. As that virtuous and potentially great young man sadly turned away, the Lord emphasized the point of this figure: "How hard it is for those who are wealthy to enter the kingdom of God" (v. 24). Riches and pleasures so easily become thorns that usurp the rich nutrients of the soil and deprive the Word of its necessary cultivation and oxygen for growth. Though lush and seemingly innocent in their early stages, these sprouts become increasingly vicious and deceitful as they mature. They tend to choke out spiritual life. Purportedly seeking the best of both worlds, they usually end up submitting to other priorities. Many such showed up in Jesus' ministry, calling forth numerous warnings from the Savior.

4. The Good Soil. Jesus' words also found a portion of noble soil in Israel. The parable showed this ground to justify the whole farming operation, yielding a rich harvest. This Jesus identified as those "who have heard the word in an honest and good heart, and hold it fast" (Luke 8:15). They listen attentively to the words of Christ, evaluate them honestly, and respond with spiritual understanding and commitment.

These individuals differ from the previous soils basically in their disposition toward truth; they are honest and responsive. Though not necessarily religious in background as the hard-soil hearers, they respond to truth; though not necessarily as emotional or impulsive as the shallow, rocky-soil hearers, they are decisive and dependable; though not always as energetic and gifted as the thorny soil, they are resolved and committed in their spiritual priorities. In turning to Christ they make Him Lord of their lives. From these the Lord reaps a rich harvest that more than compensates His loss in the barren soil.

These details interpreted by Jesus are admittedly allegorical metaphors, but they are not interpreted allegorically. Rather, they revolve around and support the central truth, relating solidly to the historic setting with one level of meaning. Jesus deftly used this portrayal of Israel to describe the many factors that brought about His impending change of ministry.

The Application for Today. Though the interpretation relates to the historic setting of Jesus' ministry, it is also rich in applications for Christian living today.

Lesson 1: Preparation of the Soil. Its first lesson is the need to properly prepare the soil if the word of the gospel is to be effective. Though the sower's work of planting is essential, the work of preparing the soil is not less so. Good seeds do not normally germinate in unprepared soil, regardless who sows them. Even the Savior Himself could not produce in barren soil, as the story makes clear.

This is not to excuse non-production, but simply to recognize that great, persuasive preaching or witnessing do not always bring a harvest. Such proclamation of the Word will certainly fulfill its divine purpose, but there may not be an immediate response (Isa. 55:11). Many of the prophets, for instance, ministered without immediate results, and even the Lord's ministry ended in seeming defeat and despair. But those thankless ministries served to prepare the soil for a later, bountiful harvest.

Lesson 2: Widespread Planting. A second point Jesus made in this parable is the need to sow the good seed with careless abandon on all kinds of soil. The sower is not to be selective, for the good soil is not always apparent. We easily mistake the good for the bad and vice versa. In Jesus' ministry, for instance, the disciples considered the Samaritan woman to be "poor soil," or a futile prospect on which to "waste" the seed of the Word (John 4:27). She was immoral, foreign, unspiritual, and uninterested— hardly a candidate for evangelism. Yet Jesus' careful planting of the seed brought from her a ready response, with the result that she went home and won her whole town.

Lesson 3: The Problem of Failure. This story also suggests that a sower of the Word must be prepared for a good deal of seeming failure. The ratio of failure to success portrayed in the story is three to one. Anyone planting the Word must not be deflected by the lack of immediate success. If the experience of Jesus and the apostles is any indication, failure may, in fact, characterize much of one's ministry. Which of the prophets experienced immediate and overwhelming success (except for Jonah who couldn't handle success)? In God's kingdom work, the Devil often comes up the winner in terms of immediate results. That was also the apparent outcome of Jesus' ministry, but He was not deterred by it. He looked rather to the final bumper crop.

Lesson 4: The Optimism of the Gospel. This parable also reminds us there is a splendid optimism to the gospel that should override any fear of failure. The divine Sower did not plant His seed to fail, but rather to succeed. Not only is He a good Carpenter; He is also an eminently successful Farmer. His Word will not return void, but will inevitably accomplish His purposes (Isa. 55:11); He is Lord of the harvest. As the Savior was not crushed or discouraged by failure, even at the Cross, so we as His workmen need that same "splendid optimism" as we continue to plant the seed for an abundant harvest. It's our business to plant; it's His business to reap. That is both a comfort and a challenge in the work of ministry.

Parable of the Tares Among the Wheat (Matt. 13:24–30, 36–43)

The business of planting, however, has other problems; it often encounters vicious competition. This parable follows that of the Sower as its corollary; they are given as two aspects of planting in the kingdom. The first concerns planting the good seed; the second, planting the bad or counterfeits. Having provided the disciples with the basis for "splendid optimism" despite seeming failures, Jesus now alerts them to the darker side. Sinister forces of Satan would also be at work usurping the soil and trying to destroy even that sown on good ground.

It might also be noted that in this parable Jesus moves from the abstract to the concrete, as Henry Swete has observed.[2] The *seed* of the previous parable was the "word"; now it is seen as "sons of the kingdom" (Matt. 13:38). This symbolizes the presence of worldly counterfeits growing alongside true believers as tares among the wheat.

Matthew alone records this parable, perhaps as a special reminder to his Jewish audience. As the parable of the Sower explains the human causes for the Messiah's rejection (the barren soil), the parable of the Tares Among the Wheat reveals some of the supernatural reasons behind it (an evil sower). It highlights the role of Satan in the process.

To make sure its lessons wouldn't be missed, Matthew included both the parable and Jesus' detailed interpretation. Though most modern scholars deny this came from Jesus, assigning it rather to later redactors, we accept it as the Spirit has preserved it in the authentic Greek text (though the Gnostic text of St. Thomas omits it). It not only supplies a significant historic explanation, but also underscores a very important theological point made by Jesus.

The Problem Addressed. Its problem relates solidly to what Jesus had just revealed in the previous story. The good seed was planted by Jesus, but failed to take root in much of the soil of Israel, especially the leaders. As Jesus withdrew His offer and appeal to that generation of leaders, He gave another reason for that withdrawal. That is the problem He here addresses: How could mere men divert the Messiah from setting up His messianic kingdom? If that coming kingdom was indeed an invincible work of God, what other forces could oppose it? That "who-dun-it" motif pervades the story as the problem Jesus deals with.

After identifying the culprit, Jesus deals with the further question of what should be done about questionable pretenders in the future. Should the disciples organize a religious posse or inquisition to stamp out hypocrites? Are the Lord's servants responsible to carry out culling operations?

This problem may then be stated as it relates to recognizing counterfeits: Are all who profess membership in God's kingdom true children of the kingdom? Are all those who pretend saintliness true believers? Can we tell the difference?

The Story of a Nocturnal Villain. The parable begins with another familiar scene of sowing, but adds something sinister—the work of a spoiler by night. While the farmer slept, an enemy perniciously sowed tares or darnel among the wheat. The Greek noun rendered *tares* (*zizania,* used only here in the New Testament) signifies wild or degenerate wheat, not just weeds or obnoxious thorns. These went undetected by the servants until the wheat began to bear grain and the tares turned up barren. But, rather than ordering the servants to cull them out, the farmer gave strict instruction to leave them until harvest so as not to disturb the wheat. At harvest time the reapers would handily weed them out for use as firewood.

The Central Truth. As noted, this parable was also interpreted by Jesus, but only to the disciples later in private. For the uncommitted crowd the story was just an entertaining "wild western" about the "good guys" and the scheming desperadoes who finally get it in the end. Many others have this limited view today, rejecting Jesus' specific interpretation. In His explanation, however, the Lord identified many metaphors or points of tangency that unveil a backstage conspiracy against the kingdom.

These metaphorical details have led some to view the story as an allegory. However, it does not have interpretive elements within itself as is true of allegories; if it did, it wouldn't need an interpretation. Nor does Jesus give meaning to all the details as in allegory; nor are several meanings given to them, as in allegorical interpretation. Rather, He simply used the metaphors as symbols to support the central truth by identifying the main characters. This He did also in many other parables (e.g., Matt. 13:19ff.; 21:28–45).

The central truth of the story is that the Devil will continue to plant a counterfeit kingdom of his own, using clones who masquerade as children of God. They are, in fact, almost indistinguishable from the true. Because of this similarity, the Lord denied His servants the work of weeding them out, lest they mistake the true. At the time of harvest the angelic reapers will take care of the culling, not the least fooled by the good looks or pious talk of counterfeits. They will then commit them to the same fiery fury as the blatantly wicked (Matt. 13:41–42).

The Appeal and Application The message of this parable looks both backward and forward. It looks backward as an explanation and forward as an alert for God's people.

Lesson 1: The Enemy Identified. In looking backward, it answers the contextual problem of why the religious leaders would reject the Messiah, the very One they had looked for to fulfill their kingdom dreams. Jesus placed the responsibility for that debacle squarely on the Devil and his children. The evil one had slyly planted his camouflaged agents in places of power to mislead and brainwash the nation. As the wizard of ooze and demagoguery, he had orchestrated their rejection of the Messiah.

Lesson 2: An All-Points Alert. The purview of this parable also looks to the future. Jesus put His disciples on special alert at this point concerning Satan's evil agenda in coming centuries. As he had taken over the leadership of Israel, he would seek to do likewise with this new instrument Jesus was forming. The Devil had already begun that ploy, in fact, by slipping Judas the betrayer into the midst of Jesus' band (John 6:70).

This notification of Satan's covert operation is really Bible-wide, certainly not unique to the New Testament. His phenomenal success with Israel was well documented, and Jesus only warned the disciples here about his continuing duplicity. The sly enemy would not be caught napping or flatfooted as God replaced the instrument of Israel temporarily for another. Counterfeiting God's work is the Devil's specialty and has been ever since he went into business for himself. At his fall he didn't say, "I will be a vicious green monster with a venomous tail"; rather, he said, "I will be like the Most High" God (Isa. 14:14 KJV).

Satan's main business, then, is counterfeiting or cloning the works of God. The Devil doesn't specialize in thorns and thistles, for they're too obvious; instead, he plants tares. Contrary to popular opinion, his grand desire is not the destruction of people, but rather their social preening apart from God; this makes them independent of God. Satan finds solace not in making his children to be drunkards, hobos, or criminals, but rather cultured humanists; he himself parades as "an angel of light" (2 Cor. 11:14). He knows that the virus of sin will ultimately destroy its victims, especially if he can just deprive them of the sense of their need for God. As the "cosmic copycat," the Devil deceives the unwary by crudely mimicking the works of God.

The pity is that this lesson of the Devil's deceptive handiwork has been forgotten so often in church history. As his henchmen took over Israel at the time of Christ, so Satan seeks to do likewise with the church. At this crucial time in kingdom history, Jesus here reminded His people that wherever the good seed of the kingdom is planted, the Devil's clones will also soon appear.

Lesson 3: Patience in an Evil World. Another lesson taught by this parable is the need for patience with the presence of evil. "Allow both to grow together until the harvest," Jesus said (Matt. 13:30). Culling and sniffing out counterfeits was not part of the Great Commission. Such patience, however, has never been in large supply. The church, like the heresy-hunting Donatists of the fourth century and the Catholic Inquisition of the thirteenth, has often busied itself in witch-hunts, to its own harm and distraction. As Richard Trench observed, "Every young Christian, in the time of his first zeal is tempted to be somewhat of a Donatist in spirit."[3]

Such culling operations, however, have only tended to exchange outward evil for inward pride and another brand of hypocrisy. The result has often been the sacrifice of many noble Cervantes on the altar of carnal zeal. The problem of mistaken identity so easily plagues us when we try to play Sherlock Holmes in spiritual things. Jesus twice warned against this practice in these kingdom parables, and Paul also echoed it in his caution not to judge one another (Rom. 14:4). The Lord's counsel here needs to be re-read by every generation: "Allow both to grow together until the harvest" (Matt. 13:30).

This prohibition, however, should not be pressed into wrong service. It should not be used to deny discipline in the church, which Christ also commanded in no uncertain terms (Matt. 18:15–18; cf. Acts 5:1–11). Nor does it mean condoning sin in one's home, community, or society where one has an influence. Compromise in either doctrine or practice widely misses the point of this passage.

Jesus here simply denies individuals the role of judging other believers by their own pet biases. As H. B. Swete once wrote, the "saying must be held to apply not so much to the public action of the Church as a body, as to the conduct of individual Christians towards one another."[4] It does not ban the discipline of outward or gross sins, but rather the judging of pretenders who fail to produce the kind of spiritual fruit you might expect. Our work, like that of Jesus, is the work of planting, not weeding.

PARABLES OF KINGDOM GROWTH

While the first two parables concerned planting the kingdom, the second pair concerns its growth. The evident problem in the context was the great opposition facing Jesus and His little band as they broke away from the Pharisaic system. Having incurred the enmity of both political and religious leaders, the question of survival would soon be of great concern. Jesus' small corps of followers were not people of prominence or influence in either politics or religion. They were mostly unschooled fishermen and common serfs with little political or social clout. Most came from despised Galilee.

How, then, could this ragtag crew defy the powerful juggernauts of Pharisaic Judaism and the Roman Empire, who were aligning against them? Was it realistic to believe this new kingdom program would survive or even get off the ground? Even the stoutest of hearts needed a word of encouragement at this point.

Those were the basic problems Jesus dealt with in the following two parables, first concerning the extent of kingdom growth, and then the process or power of its growth.

Parable of the Mustard Seed (Matt. 13:31–32; Mark 4:30–32; Luke 13:18–19)

Like the seed being described, this parable is small compared to the first two. Also, the writers do not include Jesus' interpretation, perhaps assuming we have grasped the broad lines of interpretation already given.

In this analogy the Lord answers another question about the kingdom by reference to a garden. He likens the kingdom to a mustard seed that begins small, but then grows to almost the stature of a tree. Most family gardens in Palestine included a mustard bush (black mustard) at one end of the field that produced food, condiments, and medicines. Normally it grew to a height of about ten to twelve feet.

The Problem and Central Truth. Though many analogies might be drawn from this pastoral scene, the context determines the narrow parameters of its meaning. The contextual concern was that of the growth of the kingdom in its beginning and end. The problem Jesus addressed was whether the new kingdom program He was instituting would really survive. Like Moses' doubts and fears when sent to deliver Israel from Pharaoh, Jesus' disciples had grave questions as to their survival in such a hostile world. Wouldn't they be snuffed out under the massive opposition forming?

Jesus' answer was that the new kingdom would grow to dimensions all out of proportion to its meager beginning. Though its starting nucleus consisted of mere fishermen, despised tax collectors, and redeemed harlots and outcasts, it would experience unbelievable growth. Jesus' logic was the common "garden variety" of the growth of the quaint mustard seed. Never mind the oddity of its insignificant size; its great growth was unarguable. The added detail of the birds nesting in its branches only demonstrates that greatness, for birds don't normally nest in bushes, but in trees. Like the mustard bush, the growth of Christ's new kingdom would also become a surpassing marvel, contradicting all odds against it.

Significance of the Details. One should be wary of drawing too much from the details of this parable, as church history has shown. The attempt of Clement of Alexandria to draw lessons from the fact that mustard "represses bile, that is, anger, and checks inflammation, that is, pride," is hardly in line with the problem in context.[5] The one feature noted by the Lord concerned its growth, which most of the details simply support with added realism.

A popular interpretation has been to relate the "birds of the air" (Matt. 13:32) to Daniel 4:20–22, making them a symbol of evil in the kingdom. Others have made the birds out to be the "great ones of the earth" who take shelter in the shadow of the divine kingdom. These views, however, assume that the *kingdom* described refers to all Christendom as the "kingdom of heaven" (but not the "kingdom of God"). They see this as the organized church where false doctrines and pretenders infiltrate to corrupt the kingdom.

Though the concept may be true (especially from other Bible references), it is not the point of this passage. Mark 4:30 speaks of it as the "kingdom of God," rather than "kingdom of heaven." That makes this interpretation virtually untenable, for nothing false is allowed in the kingdom of God (John 3:3, 5). Recognizing this detail of "birds making nests" in the branches is better seen as a note of realism to emphasize the great growth of the kingdom.

Other commentators have been bothered by Jesus saying that the mustard seed is "smaller than all other seeds" (Matt. 13:32), suggesting He made a scientific blunder. They point out that there are smaller seeds in that region. This supposed error is generally refuted by noting that the black mustard seed was the smallest of several varieties of mustard seeds in Palestine, or by recognizing the saying as a Hebrew idiom of something extremely small (17:20).

Either option might be an adequate explanation. However, it should also be noted that the Greek word rendered "smallest" *(mikroteron)* or "smaller than all" (Matt. 13:32) is a comparative form that sometimes serves as a superlative. Had Jesus meant the absolute superlative, "smallest," He could have used the absolute superlative form *mikrotatos.* Rather than charging Jesus with naiveté in science, it is well to acknowledge that the term could mean either "smaller" or "smallest," depending on its context. In other words, Jesus was not just accommodating Himself to the misconceptions of His time, but rather was accurate in all His statements.

The Wider Significance. This parable is unique in portraying the growth of a single seed, not a multitude as in the previous stories. That is, the parable describes the growth of the kingdom as a whole during the interadvent period. That growth, Jesus stressed, would be phenomenal and irresistible, despite demonic powers arrayed against it. Like the small acorn of an oak tree that grows through a crack in concrete to break it and tower over it, Christ's kingdom would irresistibly grow through the toughest of world environs. Though assailed by both religious Israel and political Rome, it would spread worldwide, while Israel and Rome would soon crumble in ashes. Not even the gates of hell (demonic forces) can prevail against it (Matt. 16:18).

This parable also highlights one of God's strange methods of building. He likes to start small to build large. He often uses a rejected Joseph or Moses to restore His people and build a nation; a despised youngster like David to slay the giant and lead the kingdom; a gory cross to build a golden crown; or a group of unlettered, fumbling disciples to teach the nations. In God's program the foolish, the weak, the base, and the despised are often the artisans of His trade, ensuring that all boasting is in God alone (1 Cor. 1:27–29). This parable of the tiny mustard seed is a mighty paradigm of that principle.

Parable of the Leavening Process (Matt. 13:33; Luke 13:20–21)

Jesus' second parable on kingdom growth relates to the domestic scene. It was also the last given to the multitude by the sea. Though its lesson is similar to that of the Mustard Seed, it pursues the theme of growth in another dimension. As the first parable dealt with the extent of kingdom growth, this one deals with the power and process of that growth.

The Story and the Problem Addressed. This rare saying takes us from the farm to the kitchen, portraying a woman at her daily chores (as if giving equal time to the distaff side). Women were often prominent in Jesus' audiences and the center of His attention on many occasions (in contrast to rabbis who taught only men).

This story depicts the common scene of a woman grinding wheat to make meal, and then inserting leaven in the meal to permeate and expand it. It was a familiar process enacted almost daily in Jewish homes, and Jesus had doubtless watched His mother and sisters many times at the task. No doubt His audience of listening women were delighted to hear Him take notice of their work. His recipe of meal (50 lbs.) appears large, but Jesus was never parsimonious in His gifts or pictures, especially in providing food (recall His provisions of wine, fish, bread, and so on). Perhaps His largeness of portion here related to the greatness of the kingdom about which He spoke.

The evident problem addressed in this parable flowed from the lesson just taught in the Mustard Seed. If this new kingdom was to attain such immense proportions against gigantic odds, how will this growth take place? Will the Lord recruit large armies to defeat their enemies as did David? Or will He organize a great temple system in Jerusalem and negotiate world peace as did Solomon? Perhaps Jesus might resurrect Moses and Elijah to defeat His Herodian and Pharisaic adversaries with fire, thunder, and drought. How helpful Moses' rod and Elijah's fire would have been earlier that day when the leaders blasphemed Jesus' miracles! The small band doubtless pondered these questions about how this "mustard seed" kingdom could possibly survive to become anything great.

The Central Truth. Though it is one of the shortest parables of the group, it is also one of the most controversial. Since its lesson has been so hotly disputed in church history, we should survey the main options before settling on a conclusion. Three basic views about the leaven have predominated.

The "Optimistic" View. This is the view that the gospel will work as leaven to eventually "convert the whole world," as Chrysostom expressed it.[6] As such, it will interpenetrate all society, affecting its "business life, social customs, the morals, the political life, the art, music and poetry of this world."[7] This was also the view of Augustine, who saw the "three measures of meal" as the "whole human race," represented by the three sons of Noah. In a similar way, Richard Trench saw leaven as the "word of the kingdom," which is Christ.[8] This optimistic view of the gospel permeating society was strongly defended by H. B. Swete, and has been enunciated by Simon Kistemacher in his fine work on the parables.[9]

The "Pessimistic" View. The second prominent view is often called "pessimistic" because it interprets *leaven* as evil that will spread through the whole of Christendom before Christ returns. J. N. Darby strongly articulated this position in 1845, and many others have adopted it, especially since World War I fairly punctured the optimistic dreams of a developing utopia. The social changes of moral degeneracy in today's world seem to favor this pejorative view of "leaven."

The biblical base used to defend this view is the Old Testament restriction on leaven for the spring Feast of Passover and Unleavened Bread. During that seven-day period the Israelites' houses were cleansed of leaven (though it was a required element in the two loaves at Pentecost; Exod. 13:3; Lev. 2:11; 23:17). Leaven then appears to symbolize evil or corruption. Both Jesus and Paul used it in this sense, warning against hypocrisy, malice, and wickedness (Luke 12:1; 1 Cor. 5:7). For these reasons many interpret *leaven* in this parable to be a symbol of evil invading Christendom.

The problem with this view, however, is that it makes the "kingdom of heaven" in Matthew 13:33 to be Christendom, distinguishing it from the "kingdom of God." It then makes the "woman," the "hiding," and the "leaven" to be symbols of evil in the organized church. Yet the gospel of Luke gives the same parable using the term "kingdom of God" (Luke 13:20). Since that kingdom is only entered by the new birth (John 3:5; cf. Luke 18:25), this view also faces an insoluble dilemma.

The warning against creeping apostasy is indeed an important biblical caution, but that doctrine should not be pauperized by such a shaky foundation. It has solid support in Luke 17; 1 Timothy 4; 2 Timothy 3, and so on, but was hardly a part of the context of Matthew 13. To its credit, this view rejects the unbiblical notion that the gospel will convert society by evolution. Yet it appears reactionary and insecure in trying to defend the doctrine of apostasy by this text. In the process it also misses the contextual lesson.

The "Contextual" View. The third view draws its lesson strictly from the immediate context and therefore is called the "contextual" view. In a sense it is both optimistic and pessimistic. By this view Jesus used the leavening process to portray the growth of the kingdom during the church age, showing its growth to come by a spiritual dynamic from within, not from without. Its likeness is not so much to "leaven," as it is to "leaven, which . . . ," emphasizing the activity of leaven or the growth process.

Jesus then was not using leaven as an Old Testament symbol for the scribal experts to decipher; rarely did He use theological symbols in His parables. Rather, He used it in the domestic sense of bread-making, which all understood. The scribes and Pharisees, in fact, were the very ones from whom Jesus' truths were being hidden (Matt. 13:14). Though leaven was purged from Jewish homes one week a year for Passover, everyone properly used it the rest of the year. Jesus' later explanation of the term as "evil" in Matthew 16:11–12 suggests the disciples had previously understood it in this domestic sense. As Dwight Pentecost has written, "the emphasis is not on the nature of yeast that could represent evil, but rather on the way that yeast works when it is once introduced into the mixture."[10]

This view appears to have the best contextual support, answering the problem of how Jesus' small "mustard seed" kingdom would grow in a hostile world of religious and political opposition. The leavening process laid stress on its inner source of power and growth. It pictures neither the ultimate triumph of the gospel in the world, nor the ultimate apostasy of Christendom, but rather the inner, spiritual power of this new kingdom as energized by the Holy Spirit (John 14:16–17).

The Wider Significance. In this parable Jesus stressed the true dynamic of His new kingdom program by portraying its nature to be that of a spiritual organism. As God's kingdom is entered by spiritual birth, so it will also grow by a spiritual process. Unlike the kingdoms of this world or even that of ancient Israel, it will not grow by the machinations of military might or ecclesiastical hierarchies, but rather by an inner spiritual power. This is the principle Zechariah urged upon the Israelites when they returned to build the temple against impossible odds: " 'Not by might nor by power, but by My Spirit, says the LORD of Hosts' " (Zech. 4:6).

The pity is that this spiritual key to growth has so often eluded the leaders of church history. That history is replete with ecclesiastical monstrosities that have arisen to supplant the Spirit's internal power, often with shrewd manipulations. It is admittedly more exciting and ego-building to organize ingenious techniques than to pray and patiently allow the Spirit to move from within. "Like a mighty army, moves the church of God," may be scintillating lyrics; but the thrust of Jesus (and Paul in Ephesians 6) is this: Like a quiet, spiritual, inner force, moves the church of God. Such growth and movement comes through the internal working of the Holy Spirit. By this He both generates life and spreads its growth to all parts of Christ's body.

The "Hiding" or Kneading Process. Jesus' picture of the woman "hiding" leaven in dough is, of course, part of the bread-making process. The Greek term rendered *hiding (enekrupsin)* does not mean "stealth" or "something evil," for these notions would be foreign to the idea of bread making. What woman surreptitiously sneaks the yeast into the dough? She "hides" or encloses it within the dough to enable its penetration and permeation.

That hiding, however, includes also the woman's periodic kneading of the dough to force the leaven into all parts. Without kneading, the leaven would cause a bloat in the clump of sourdough, while the rest would be unleavened and both parts inedible. I well recall as a boy watching my mother make bread dough, insert the yeast, and place it over the oven to rise. What amazed me was that she kept coming back to press it down by kneading it again and again. That kneading seemed unnecessary to me, but her wisdom prevailed as the dough grew larger and larger. Rather than pulling or stretching it, she brutally pressed it down, forcing the leaven to spread. The resulting growth was both amazing and delicious.

That analogy to church growth is hard to miss in the context. Though opposition from many sources is admittedly painful, it is often necessary for spiritual growth. Without it the church becomes sour or puffy (in the analogy of leaven). The book of Acts, in fact, many times illustrates this principle, as do the first three centuries of church history. Its periods of persecutions often served as outward kneading that the Spirit used to enable His power to flow throughout Christ's body.

In this way, the Spirit ironically puts the church's fierce enemies into divine service, using them as "kneaders" to promote its growth. It was when that kneading stopped at the time of Constantine in the early fourth century that a vast ecclesiastical organization took over. That, in turn, left the church in spiritual anemia during much of the Dark Ages. In light of this, we can further appreciate the counsel of James: "Count it all joy, my brethren, when you encounter various trials" (James 1:2). Admittedly this a strange notion by human reckoning; yet it is an important principle the Lord uses for the growth of His church.

Parable of the Seed Growing by Itself (Mark 4:26–29)

Mark alone has recorded this fifth parable by the sea, though omitting most of the others. It is also the fourth scene with a farming motif, and the third dealing with the growth of the kingdom. As the Mustard Seed stressed the *greatness* of its growth, and the Leavening Process the *power* of its growth, so this one shows the *inevitability of that growth* as sown with the Word. An interesting progression is unfolded. Though Mark places this parable before the Mustard Seed, it logically follows Matthew's thematic presentation of the planting and growth of the kingdom. As R. C. Trench noted, it seems to occupy the place of the Leavening Process in Matthew that Mark leaves out.[11]

The Story and Its Problem. This saying is a similitude-parable portraying another familiar aspect of farming. The process is so common that it is usually taken for granted. The Lord here unveils no great secrets of biology, but rather notes the obvious truism that a seed grows "automatically" (Greek *automate;* the term appears in a place of emphasis in Mark 4:28). As Kistemacher describes it, there is "the sowing, the growing, and the mowing";[12] but the farmer has nothing to do with the growing.

Growth, then, is not ultimately dependent on the farmer, but rather on the life within the seed and its inherent ability to draw nutrients from the soil and atmosphere. This does not disparage the work of plowing, fertilizing, cultivating, and weeding, but rather emphasizes that all those efforts are futile without the dynamic life within the seed. Nor does the parable mention the contributions of rain, sunshine, pollination, wind, and so forth, which nature provides. It simply notes that it is from this life-giving seed, through its various stages of growth, that the soil produces a harvest.

The contextual problem this parable addresses concerns another aspect of kingdom growth. Mark presents it as the third in a sequence of four, following the Sower and the Lamp. As the Sower dealt with the productivity of *good soil,* this one builds on the power and potency of the *good seed.* Like the previous two parables discussed in Matthew (namely, the Mustard Seed and the Leaven), this one also deals with growth, but highlights its automatic growth apart from human activity. With this in mind, we can easily discern the problem being dealt with: What must the sower do to guarantee that the Word sown will continue to grow and produce a harvest? Since Jesus is seen as the initial Sower in these parables, the problem concerns first His sowing of the Word, and then the fruitfulness of others who will also sow that Word.

The Central Truth. The primary point of the parable is that Jesus' Word of the kingdom will inevitably grow and come to fruition, regardless of whether it is tended. He had just spoken some powerful words about His rejecters and the new program of faith, noting also His coming absence and a time of mourning. Though the disciples didn't immediately grasp all this, Jesus anticipated their coming apprehension and here stressed the invincibility of His Word. That Word has within itself the inherent life and energy to stand against all foes and produce a crop. Its harvest is as certain as His planting. Though Jesus would be absent, the growth process would not flag for lack of tending, for its growth would depend on its own mysterious life and power through the Holy Spirit.

Some commentators have questioned this application to Jesus' ministry because of the statement, the "seed sprouts up and grows—how, he himself does not know" (Mark 4:27). They object to the idea that Jesus would "not know." It is important to remember, however, that a parable is not designed to "walk on all fours," as an allegory, but primarily to highlight a central truth. Some details are given simply for realism, not as meaning-loaded metaphors. The farmer's ignorance of how a seed grows is part of that realism. Since Jesus' ministry is definitely related here, His point is that His work of sowing the seed would unfailingly be brought to fruition by the tending work of the Holy Spirit.

The Practical Application. This parable is both an encouragement and a caution for those who spread the Word. It reminds us that God is Lord of the harvest, and we are only workers together with Him (2 Cor. 6:1). Having sown the Word, we are to commit its growth to Him, resting in His uncanny ability to bring forth a bountiful harvest. The principle is certainly not new, but rather runs through the Bible. Isaiah 55:11 expressed it at a time of Israel's degeneracy: "So shall My word be which goes forth from My mouth; it shall not return to Me empty, without accomplishing what I desire." Too easily we sell short the mysterious power of the engrafted Word to produce fruit.

In practice this principle has many applications. It reminds us of the need for patience with new converts, recognizing that the implanted Word will inevitably bring forth fruit. Our tendency is to fret and worry when growth seems slow in coming and then to prod and cajole slow-growers to "fall in line." This often results in "Christmas tree" fruit that is glittery and frothy, but not genuine. Jesus' counsel is to keep on sowing and leave the growth to God. As H. B. Swete put it, "The laws of spiritual growth will work themselves out silently and unseen, just as the laws of natural growth do."[13] Paul also gave this assurance in Philippians 1:6: "He who began a good work in you will perfect it until the day of Christ Jesus." God has His own schedule and climate for the growth and maturation of each.

This counsel, however, appears to run counter to much current emphasis on spiritual growth through calculated steps and techniques. The whole New Testament, in fact, seems to emphasize the need and obligation of all believers to promote spiritual growth. Jesus, in John 15, stressed the importance of growth in fruit-bearing. Paul, in 1 Corinthians 3, needled the carnal believers of Corinth to grow out of their baby stage of carnality. They were still on milk and couldn't handle meat. Hebrews 5–6 bemoans the same problem with the Hebrew believers who were just treading water and in need of being re-taught the elementary precepts of the gospel. How then can we reconcile this urgent concern for spiritual growth with the counsel of Jesus in this parable?

That paradox helps us to better understand Jesus' point in this brief saying of the Seed Growing by Itself. Those passages urging concern for growth also stress the fact that the Father is the One in charge of growth. He is the Farmer in charge of fruit production (John 15:1–2); He is the One who causes growth in the body (1 Cor. 3:6); and He is the One who has sworn to bless His people through His Word (Heb. 6:10, 17). The point of those passages is that growth comes from God, and we are workers together with Him in that process (1 Cor. 3:9). As the parable assumed that the farmer would fertilize, cultivate, irrigate, and so on, Paul also saw the apostles' work to be under the Father's direct supervision. Paul had planted, Apollos watered, and others cultivated; but God gave the increase (v. 6). Likewise, the issue of this parable is: Who is ultimately in charge of the harvest?

That issue was most important in Jesus' mind as He launched this new program for the coming age. The Father will produce His own kind of fruit in His own time. The apostles, teachers, preachers, or other believers do not necessarily determine the kind of fruit one should produce. True spiritual fruit comes in infinite varieties, not as something cranked out of a single mold.

The first "blades" may not be glamorous as they begin to grow. Nor do all believers come out of banana peels or corn husks. The Father alone knows the trees and shrubs of His garden and the fruit He expects from each. Our business is to sow the Word and encourage growth, but always to "sleep and rise night and day" with the assurance that the Father is the ultimate and only producer of genuine fruit. His role is not ours to usurp. Jesus sowed with that kind of calm and patience, and He exhorts His followers to do the same.

Summary. These three parables on the growth of the kingdom have a designed progression of thought. First, the Mustard Seed analogy emphasizes the coming greatness of the kingdom despite its small beginning. It will ultimately surpass all kingdoms in greatness. Second, the Leavening Process identifies the power by which the kingdom will grow as being internal rather than external. It will not conquer by military might or ecclesiastical edicts, but rather by the inner dynamics of the Spirit. Though pressured by external foes, that opposition will, in fact, serve to enhance its growth and stimulate a wider involvement by all.

Finally, the parable of the Seed Growing by Itself portrays the invincibility of its growth apart from human agencies. Not only will it grow despite outward opposition, it will also unfailingly grow by virtue of its own inner life as the Word of God. No human or demonic force can effectively stand against it. The kingdom belongs to God, and He will sovereignly see to its planting and productive growth.

Chapter 7

"MYSTERIES OF THE KINGDOM" UNFOLDED

Part 2: Its Values and Responsibilities

QUESTIONS ABOUT VALUES and responsibilities confront every entrepreneur going into business. Will it be worth the effort? What personal responsibilities are involved? Should I make the commitment? Those are, in fact, some of the basic questions we all face in life, largely determining our success.

At this point in Jesus' ministry, those questions also faced His loyal band of followers. Though His popularity with the people had been immense, the leaders were unimpressed. They, in fact, formed a dissenting coalition that began to harden into a counter-movement, putting in question His entire messianic mission. Having left all to follow Him, the little group was in a state of shock as they witnessed this crossfire. Their fond hopes of messianic glory appeared in jeopardy, giving them second thoughts as the roiled religious system bared its teeth.

To this personal trauma for His little band the Lord was not oblivious, but wisely called them out for a conference. They needed to see His long-range goals and have their vision steadied. Having just outlined His broad program for general consumption, He then turned to the more personal issues of the faithful with four additional pictures. The first two spoke of their sense of values and priorities.

PARABLES ON THE VALUE OF THE KINGDOM

Leaving the crowd by the sea, Jesus led His disciples into a nearby house for this after-meeting (Matt. 13:36). Perhaps it was their time for lunch, which they frequently ate together, and an excellent time for "rapping" and fielding questions. Jesus began this private session by first explaining His previous stories, which had left them a bit baffled, then zeroed in on their more personal anxieties. To the outside crowd He spoke only in parables, giving no explanations; but to this inner circle He was more intimate, discussing their part in the kingdom. For the first lessons, Jesus painted two scenes of marketing or exchange that would stick in their memories, applying them in two different ways.

Parables of the Hidden Treasure and Priceless Pearl (Matt. 13:44–46)

The first scenes had the aura of "get-rich-quick" fantasies, sure to fire up anyone's interest. In each a man stumbles on a fortune and uses his quick wits to make it his own. Who hasn't daydreamed about such a windfall with its tantalizing delights? In the first of these sketches, Jesus describes a man wandering through a field, accidentally discovering a treasure, perhaps left hidden by someone long dead. His response was to quickly pawn all his earthly goods to buy the field and acquire the treasure. As with any sudden windfall of fortune, the man was ecstatic and could hardly believe it was real.

The second portrays another dream come true of a pearl merchant who spies a priceless gem while searching for fine pearls. He also sells all he has to purchase this pearl of great price. Who couldn't identify with these earthly thrillers? The disciples were probably bug-eyed with interest.

We should note that only Matthew the gospel writer, who emphasized kingdom instruction, records these brief sayings. He gives more details on the kingdom than the others, showing the progression of Jesus' ministry in unfolding this new program. Since the emphasis of these two stories is so similar, it will be well to first review them together, then notice their differences. Both concern the marketplace of buying and selling to turn a profit. Let's first discover the problem, then the central truth and its applications.

The Problem Addressed. Recall that this had been a busy day for Jesus. In the morning He healed a deaf and dumb demoniac, was blasphemed by the Jerusalem lawyers for that healing, and then pronounced their house desolate and about to be taken over by demons. Their blasphemy was tantamount to rejection. For the disciples, however, it was also personal, gravely affecting their kingdom hopes. At this crucial point Jesus began to stress His new relationship of faith with His people that transcends racial ties. His family henceforth would be those who follow Him and do the Father's will.

How much of this the disciples immediately grasped is not certain, but they were probably overwhelmed. Their hopes of a soon coming Davidic kingdom with the glory of Solomon came crashing down. In terms of their own future, this was devastating since they had invested everything in Jesus establishing the kingdom. That "blue chip" investment seemed to be turning sour.

Besides material loss, the disciples were being estranged from their synagogue roots. Excommunication from the system appeared certain, for to follow this Nazarene was tantamount to renouncing their allegiance to Abraham. They would be pegged as traitors. It was one thing to follow Jesus in His quest for repentance and reformation; but to be part of a revolt against their cherished leaders was another matter. It meant forfeiting synagogue worship and all the temple rites with their beautiful pageantries of promise.

With this in mind, the problem Jesus addressed might be stated as a question: Is Jesus' new program, so despised by the religious leaders, really worth pursuing, especially in light of its immense cost for both them and their families? Are its many sacrifices really worth it?

The Central Truth of the Hidden Treasure. It is often noted that this story about sudden wealth involves some rather shady actions by the vagabond who finds it, hardly in keeping with Jesus' ethics. The vagabond's actions begin with a cover-up, and he seems to pursue some questionable means to a selfish end. The Lord, however, neither justifies nor condemns those actions, but rather relates them as the natural reactions of anyone who would stumble on such an unclaimed treasure. He simply presents it in terms of the wisdom of this generation (Luke 16:8), not questioning the normal custom of "finders keepers, losers weepers." People's savings were often kept hidden in a field, rather than in the house, and when a man failed to return from war, it might be lost for generations.

The point of the story is that this man was shrewd enough to recognize the value of a treasure that was up for grabs, and bent every effort to make it his own. He just used the smarts God gave him. The central truth concerning the kingdom, then, is that its value is so great that no sacrifice or effort should be considered too great to obtain it. Its worth far outweighs any cost or inconvenience it might involve. Vast treasures lay hidden in its coffers.

The Central Truth of the Costly Pearl. The point of this second picture is quite similar, perhaps added to further stimulate the despondent disciples. They needed a double dose of Jesus' optimism. Both parables portray shrewdness by the alert finder, and both emphasize extreme sacrifices in order to obtain their prize. Though the impulse of joy is only noted in the first, it is assumed in both. Neither begrudged the sacrifices required, and both were delighted and thrilled with their find. Thus, the central truth for both is the optimistic note that all is not lost, for Jesus' new kingdom program would more than compensate for any loss it might incur. Any personal sacrifices would turn a profit of immense joy in the long run.

The Different Emphases. The two stories, however, do have some significant differences. One describes a man of the field, while the other a pearl merchant. One acquires riches, but the other a gem of beauty. Perhaps the most essential difference, however, is how each found his treasure. In the first scene, the man accidentally stumbles on it; in the other, the man was searching. One was found by accident, and the other by diligent search. What do these details suggest? Together they highlight the lesson that Jesus' kingdom blessings were open to all, both to seekers and non-seekers (religious and non-religious). Great joy awaits all who will respond.

In the historic context the two entrepreneurs in these stories might well describe Jesus' varied group of disciples. He offered mercy and fulfillment to both publicans and puritans, both Gentiles and Jews. Among the Twelve, there was Matthew the publican, hardly an ardent searcher in religion, who quickly left his lucrative profession to follow Jesus. Andrew, on the other hand, was a pious seeker and disciple of John who left the "goodly pearls" of John to follow Jesus. Whatever their backgrounds, each found Jesus' kingdom infinitely worth pursuing. The disciples needed this cool analysis of their fortunes at this crucial juncture, for they were at a point of renewed challenge. Days of great opposition and commitment lay ahead when they would greatly savor this double dose of Jesus' optimistic candor.

Other Interpretations. Because these sayings lend themselves so handily to other analogies, it is instructive to note two others that have enjoyed popularity. They both see the hidden treasure and costly pearl as symbols, but interpret them in opposite ways.

The first is the view of Origen and many church Fathers that the treasure and costly pearl represent Christ.[1] He is the Treasure or Pearl that one should sell all to buy. That is still a widely favored view, affording intriguing analogies for preaching the gospel. Its usual confirmation is Paul's statement of suffering the loss of all things for Christ (Phil. 3:8). Jesus Himself declared that "no one of you can be My disciple who does not give up all his own possessions" (Luke 14:33; cf. Matt. 19:21). Origen pursued these metaphors even further, making the pearls sold by the merchant ("all that he had") to be "the law and the prophets." That fits nicely (or grotesquely) with his anti-Jewish theology (and allegorical method), but it hardly takes seriously the Lord's unchangeable covenants with Israel.

Those analogies are obviously far overdrawn. Though making Christ to be the exquisite pearl is a beautiful thought, it is extremely doubtful in this context. The Lord was not exhorting disciples to buy Him, or even salvation, but to be ready to sacrifice for the new kingdom program He introduced. It is therefore better to see the treasure and pearl as figures of the kingdom, not necessarily the King. Recall that in the previous parables of the Mustard Seed and the Leavening Process, those figures did not represent Christ, but rather His kingdom—the kingdom of heaven.

Another popular view of recent times is one that reverses the roles.

Rather than Christ being the treasure or pearl, He becomes the finder or purchaser.[2] The treasure and pearl that He finds then represent the church. This view is partly a reaction to the previous one that seems to suggest a works salvation in which the hearers purchase Christ.[3] Entrance into God's kingdom, of course, is not by a trade or purchase, but by the new birth (John 3:5). The view, however, does afford some interesting analogies, making Christ's purchase on the cross to include both the remnant of Israel (as the treasure in the field) and believing Gentiles (as the pearl from the sea). For these He joyously made His sacrifice.[4]

Though these analogies make intriguing vehicles for preaching New Testament theology, they have a dubious relation to the context of these parables. They appear to be answering questions that are foreign to the hearers. The Lord did not make known either the cross or the church until nearly a year later (Matt. 16:18, 21). Besides this anachronism, it also implies some questionable manipulations by Christ in acquiring the church. In selling "all that he had," did Jesus sell or dispose of all His sworn covenants with Israel? Impossible! Becoming poor does not mean He relinquished other relations to make this purchase.

It is better not to read the redemptive program into this discussion, for Jesus rarely used parables to discuss redemption. He spelled out the atonement and plan of salvation in plain, literal language that no one could mistake. That is John's emphasis in his gospel where he records almost no parables. It is good to remember again that the redemptive program concerns God's purchase for entrance into the kingdom; the kingdom program concerns the character, growth, and activities of those entering the kingdom. Though related, they are not the same.

Rather than making Christ a metaphorical figure in these parables, as either pearl or purchaser, it is better to recognize the two stories as Jesus' double emphasis on kingdom values. As noted, the disciples were in real need of His counsel at this time as their dreams of immediate glory were being shattered. To put it in present day marketing terms, they needed Jesus' comparative analysis, His market evaluation of this new kingdom program: Are its stocks really "blue chips"? Will its values hold up?

In these "stewardship" analogies Jesus declared Himself "bullish" on the kingdom. His market advice: Sell all other holdings and buy big into the stock of this kingdom. Don't hesitate lest you lose out on a grand opportunity. Though universally underrated and maligned by world brokers, this kingdom will spread worldwide and eventually pay handsomely in eternal dividends.

The Wider Significance. Few truths are in greater need of emphasis than the message of these twin sayings today. Shortsightedness can be fatal in investments, especially spiritual ones. The world's value system is geared to this life, emphasizing happiness now. Though the concept of God's kingdom lies in the back of everyone's mind (God "set eternity in their heart," Eccl. 3:11), the "tyranny of the urgent" easily muffles the "call of the eternal." Many of Jesus' later parables and sayings will return to this theme as He warns of the ever-present struggle people have between God and mammon. The touted victor on nearly every front is mammon, most scorning any voice to the contrary. But its joys and crowns are for a moment. Jesus here stressed the point that His kingdom pays dividends forever.

PARABLES ON KINGDOM RESPONSIBILITIES

As the first five parables describe the overall progression of the kingdom, the last four focus on individual responsibilities. They deal more with believers' personal concerns. As noted, only Matthew recorded these last four sayings. To Jesus' shaken cadre of disciples He first impressed the wisdom of wholehearted commitment—only those who invest will realize its benefits. That point naturally led to the question about how to invest. How does one get involved, and what role will each play?

In addressing this question of personal involvement, Jesus took His analogies from the industrial world of fishing and the domestic arena of household management.

Parable of the Fisher's Dragnet (Matt. 13:47–50)

Jesus' analogy of the kingdom to a fisher's net was, of course, familiar ground for the Twelve. All were Galileans except Judas, who was from Kerioth of Judea, and most had fished around Capernaum. This was one of the choice fishing grounds of Palestine, even supplying markets in Jerusalem. Over twenty varieties of fish swam on these shoals, where the mouth of the Jordan fed nutrients into the northern part of the lake.[5] It was but nine months earlier that Jesus showed these seasoned fishermen a "thing or two" in making a good catch from these waters (Luke 5:4–6). They had learned to respect Him even as a fisherman and would pay close attention to another good fish story.

This parable sketches the fishing operation of a team of fishermen who used a dragnet from a boat to encircle a large area of shallow water along the shore. The net Jesus describes is not the small snare usually cast from boats (*diktuon;* Luke 5:4; John 21:6), but rather the large seine net *(sagene).* This large enclosure would be drawn from the shore, rowing the boat in a semi-circle back to shore as the net dragged bottom.[6] Such an encircling procedure gathers "fish of every kind" (Matt. 13:47), pulling them to the shore. It is then that the inedible or unkosher fish are thrown out and the edible or kosher are retained (Lev. 11:10). The operation was a most efficient one, embracing everything in its sweep.

Jesus used this familiar process to emphasize a specific lesson. Though He likened the whole operation of seine fishing to the kingdom, His special focus was on the culling process. No one culls fish while the net is being dragged in. That process takes place after the harvest. What, then, was His specific point? Let's first note the problem, then the central truth Jesus stressed in His own interpretation.

The Problem. In this final pair of parables the Lord brought His discourse full circle with the issue of personal responsibilities. Rarely did He conclude an address without striking for decisions, and this was no exception. It was, in fact, a special time of commitment. Having instructed the disciples on the immense value of the kingdom, Jesus then anticipated their further concern: How can a group of unlettered fishermen invest or get personally involved in this new venture? Should they head for Rome to study politics, or perhaps enroll in the University of Alexandria to polish up on classical Greek? Maybe a stint at the rabbinical school of the Sanhedrin might sharpen their prowess?

On the contrary, Jesus met the disciples where He found them when He called them as fishers of men (Matt. 4:18–22). That call was not aborted, but now magnified as He elaborated the new challenge that lay before them.

The problem, however, concerned more than just fishing; it also concerned what the disciples did with the fish they caught. How selective should they be in "catching fish" was the issue. According to Leviticus 11:9–10, the Jews could only eat fish with fins and scales. Are disciples to be selective and set standards, culling out of the kingdom those individuals that don't meet their criteria? What about Gentile "fish"—or those with questionable backgrounds? Should the disciples assume the responsibility of judging which are genuine and which are not? Are fishers called to be "fish inspectors"?

The Central Truth. The obvious lesson in Jesus' interpretation is that the work of culling is not the responsibility of disciples or servants. Their work is to gather believers into the kingdom, not to judge or expel them by their personal opinions. That is Jesus' primary point in His own interpretation as He stressed the angels' part in the final judgment (Matt. 13:49–50).

Strange to say, many commentators mistake this final judgment as the central truth of the parable. The Lord's emphasis, however, is primarily on the separation of the wicked, with little said about the righteous. The obvious reason for this one-sided judgment is to stress the divine place of culling. Excommunication is not the work of the church. That is a judgment the Lord has reserved for Himself at the final day when He will dispatch special angels to sort out the wicked from the righteous (v. 49).

It is significant that this is one of only three recorded interpretations given by Jesus in this series (besides the Sower and the Tares). Its lesson is also quite similar to that of the Tares (vv. 40–43). Why, then, does Jesus interpret this one, but not the other five sayings?

The probable reason is that this parable might easily be misapplied without this explanation. The work of weeding out the false could be seen as a responsibility of the disciples along with their work of fishing, for that was obviously a further work of seine fishermen. To guard against that misapplication, Jesus enlarged on this fishing analogy to show that in His kingdom, the disciples' business is to fish, not cull. That was the basic point of Jesus' contrast. The church's missionary work is to reach out and encircle all possible, regardless of color, race, or gender. Judging and evicting pretenders is a work for which it is neither qualified nor commissioned. The Lord strictly disallowed this work of excommunication from His people.

The Wider Significance. As noted in the parable of the Tares, this restraint is not meant to deny the responsibility of discipline in the local assembly or the correction of immoral conduct or heresy. Jesus later spelled that out in Matthew 18. The church is responsible to purify itself by dealing with obvious sin in its midst and to promote the spiritual growth of all.

In that sense, we are our brother's *keeper*. But we are not our brother's *judges*. This parable forbids anyone the vain practice of consigning others to perdition (Rom. 14:4). Members of God's kingdom are too diverse in background and maturity for any mortal to make that judgment, including the apostle Peter. Ours is to reach and enclose all possible with the gospel net, leaving the separation process to the Lord of the harvest in His time.

Parable of the Household Steward (Matt. 13:52)

This final likeness of the kingdom is strangely omitted by many interpreters (e.g., Trench, Swete, Kistemacher, et al.). Without it they see a providential series of seven (number of completion?), ending on a note of final judgment.[7] Many others, however, do treat it as a parable, making the series in Matthew a full octave of eight notes on the kingdom (e.g., Keach, Morgan, Pentecost, Thomas, and Gundry). Its inclusion by Matthew appears to present an interesting symmetry of four pairs on planting, growth, values, and responsibilities in the kingdom.

As a powerful conclusion to the whole group, this parable forms a pair with the preceding one on fishing to emphasize a second responsibility of servants. The two round them out with personal applications. In this one the Lord as the Master Teacher challenged the disciples whether they had caught what He taught. And as a group of eager students, their spontaneous answer was "Yes." To which He then responded: "Here's what you should do about it."

The Problem Addressed. This brief give-and-take was used by the Lord to arouse the disciples' careful attention to His further assignment. The final problem He addressed is a question they might have asked: "We understand your instruction on becoming 'fishers of men' (as Jeremiah 16:16 also said). Is this then our sole responsibility, or are there other ways in which we are to serve?"

The Central Truth. Jesus' answer was simple and quite direct: "Therefore every scribe who has become a disciple of the kingdom of heaven is like a head of a household, who brings forth out of his treasure things new and old" (Matt. 13:52). Notice Jesus' unique use of the term *scribe.* This title recalls Ezra, the revered Sopherim scribe and priest, who re-taught the Israelites the Law after their return from captivity. Now that the Pharisaic scribes had become Jesus' enemies, He commissions a new group of scribes for the kingdom. The title itself was provocative at this time of new beginnings.

The disciples' effectiveness in this new commission, however, was dependent on their understanding the principles Jesus outlined. His question, "Have you understood all these things?" (v. 51), was a challenge to put those principles to work. Obviously not aware of all its implications, they answered in the positive. Perhaps He smiled at their naiveté, but then assigned them the work of a "ready scribe."

Jesus portrays this scribe as a "householder" (*oikodespote*—house despot), who brings from his treasure *(thesaurou)* adequate supplies for his family. As the Lord's stewards, disciples were to dispense from their store spiritual riches for the household of faith. A discerning steward, He stressed, should be knowledgeable of all his supply of treasures for the welfare of his household. The question is, what were these treasures of "things new and old" (v. 52) that the disciples were to dispense?

Many allegorical suggestions have been made, but the context is the key. Having just introduced His new kingdom program in the aftermath of the leaders' rejection, Jesus' obvious reference was to this. He focused on this new kingdom program, inasmuch as the leaders had rejected the old. As His newly appointed stewards, the disciples were to recognize this change of direction and instruct all the household concerning this fresh revelation concerning the kingdom.

Jesus' Final Appeal. This concluding parable then stressed the need to both understand and give instruction about the movement of God's program. Though the disciples looked for the messianic kingdom to soon appear, they were to recognize a change in that plan. Because the King had been rejected, that program would now remain on the back burner for an extended period of time (John 1:11). The disciples' business as stewards during this interadvent period is not to fret about "Paradise lost," or try to establish a new hierarchy of Israel to take its place. They are rather to serve the rejected Messiah in His new household of faith until He returns. As *fishers of men,* they are to gather in the lost; as *stewards,* they are to care for and instruct those in the household.

Summary. This had been a long day for Jesus and His troop with many healings, disputes, clashes, and discourses. He had grappled with demons and denounced His opponents in open combat. Then Jesus met with the curious crowd by the sea and later with His faithful band in a private house. The crucial issue of the day was the subject of the kingdom, and the disciples were given a crash course on its change of direction. Though they obviously didn't grasp all its implications, they were given its basic outline and introduced to their personal responsibilities.

The calamitous events of that day had no doubt stunned the disciples, and Jesus' new teaching method left them a bit bewildered. But during the weeks and months ahead He would further develop those instructions. He would unveil His plan to build the church and other aspects of His redemptive program. For the present, however, He simply allayed their fears concerning the leaders' opposition and this new direction of the kingdom. Calling them "mysteries of the kingdom" (Matt. 13:11), He had now introduced His family secrets as a foundation for further instruction.

Aftermath of the Seminar

It is striking to note the immediate consequence of this discourse. Quite often Jesus' great discourses were followed by a series of events that seemed to challenge His plans. Recall the aftermath of His baptism when Satan tempted Jesus to gratify Himself rather than please the Father. A monumental confrontation took place. Following the Sermon on the Mount a series of mighty miracles took place, demonstrating Jesus' divine authority over the leaders' traditions, capping it with a second insurrection. Such phenomena were especially highlighted when Jesus confronted the entrenched forces of darkness.

Supernatural Conflicts. In the aftermath of these kingdom parables, that demonic challenge was again evident in several open demonstrations. Mark 4:35 records that "on that day when evening had come," the disciples boarded a small boat to sail across the Sea of Galilee to the country of the Gerasenes (modern Khersa). On the way a fierce storm arose while Jesus slept, almost sinking the boat. The Lord's response to this tornado of wind and waves was, "Hush! Be muzzled" (*siopa, pephimoso;* v. 39, author's translation), using a term similar to His muzzling demons (Mark 1:25; Luke 4:35). The next day as the disciples arrived at the other side, they were met by two fierce demoniacs, namely, individuals possessed by a legion of demons (3,000 to 6,000; Matt. 8:28). When confronted by Jesus, the two bowed as the demons pled Him for mercy to stay their final judgment. Why these unprecedented acts of demonic power at this time?

The context reminds us that these events occurred shortly after Jesus had exorcised demons at Capernaum and gave a telling parable about the Devil's strategies. That brought out the greatest concentration of demons recorded in Jesus' ministry to challenge Him. As Geldenhuys has noted, "demon-possession is a phenomenon which occurred almost exclusively, . . . on an amazing scale, during Jesus' appearance on earth."[8] Though modern critics might deny its authenticity,[9] the context relates this directly after the demonic response to His open attack on them the previous day. Jesus accepted the challenge by giving a mighty demonstration of His personal power—first over nature, then over the demon world—to bolster the flickering faith of His disciples following the seeming debacle of the day before. Jesus had little time for demon excursions.

That massive assault and destruction by demons should not be misunderstood. The scoundrels seem to have won a victory by associating this loss of two thousand swine with the Messiah's presence in Gentile country. As someone said, the demons made "deviled ham" out of the pigs by drowning them. Why, then, did Jesus allow this? Was He outflanked by the demons?

We should first clarify that this was not a judgment on the people for raising pigs, an unkosher food, for Jesus declared that all meats were then ceremonially clean (Mark 7:19). His mission was not to judge their lack of ritual. Rather, the point is that Jesus allowed this association of loss with His presence to emphasize a changed approach in ministry. Jesus here challenged the people to believe in Him, despite material loss, simply because of His demonstrated Godhood. One who could command the vast spirit world could also provide for the material needs of people.

The Wider Significance. This constituted a radical change in Jesus' evangelistic approach. To the Jews across the sea at Capernaum, He had performed many miracles, pampering them with goodies. The result? A glut of superficial "freeloaders" and a blasphemous charge by the leaders that Jesus was in cahoots with Satan. Meeting their material needs strangely produced little more than greed and blasphemy. Jesus then declared that their generation would see no more of His messianic signs (Matt. 12:39). In line with His own counsel, He would no longer "cast His pearls before swine."

This new approach reflects what Jesus had just taught in parables. His kingdom program would flourish and grow, but not by the lure of material and physical gratifications. Rather, it would encircle the globe by the gracious attraction of His Person as preached by those who, like the Gaderene demoniac, have been liberated from the shackles of sin.

Chapter 8

PARABLES ON ENTERING THE KINGDOM

THOUGH THE SYNOPTIC PARABLES emphasize God's kingdom program, they do not present the plan of salvation, as such. It is the gospel of John that especially spells that out—in nearly every chapter. The Synoptic parables do, however, discuss various problems concerning entering the kingdom. Salvation, of course, is the overall theme of the Bible and most prominent in Jesus' ministry. But, as Daniel in the Old Testament deals with the kingdom, and Isaiah with redemption, so the Synoptic parables explain the kingdom, and the gospel of John stresses redemption.

As previously noted, it is perilous to force redemptive theology from the parables. The reason is that they give partial pictures and mainly discuss the rule of God in His kingdom. To draw redemptive theology from the Prodigal Son, for instance, easily leads to a kind of "do-it-yourself" redemption. The prodigal practically saves himself, picking himself up by his bootstraps to go to the father's house. That is not the point of the parable, as we shall see. Though the two programs are related, they stress two different purposes of God, one the reclaiming of His kingdom, and the other the redemption of people.

Since the redemptive program is part of the kingdom program, however, the parables do have many references to salvation. They often discuss the question of "entering the kingdom," such as who are invited and their attitudes. Several such parables were given as

Jesus turned His ministry focus to the outcasts. Let's pick up His trail to catch the historical background as He moved from the introduction of the kingdom in Matthew 13 to His further instruction the following year.

JESUS' MINISTRY TO OUTCASTS

Following His busy day of calling the leaders' bluff and blasphemy and instructing the disciples, Jesus' ministry took a definite turn. He began concentrating more on outlying areas; He also dealt more with individuals than with the nation, as such. Though He performed many miracles and healings, these were not given as "signs" to the nation. Many, in fact, were done in private, instructing those healed to keep it quiet. The mighty miracles of stilling the storm and commanding the demon world, for instance, were not displayed for the unbelieving nation, but rather for disciples and outcasts. Jesus exemplifies this new focus on individuals in Matthew 11:25–30. It occurred after He denounced the unheeding "wise and intelligent" of Israel: "Come to Me [out of the corrupt system], all who are weary and heavy-laden, and I will give you rest" (v. 27).

Assuming the date of this watershed event to have been in the late fall of A.D. 30, we can trace a period of nearly a year in which no parables were given or recorded. Nevertheless, it was an action-packed year in many ways. A brief review of some of the significant events of that year will provide the background for another group of parables.

Rejection at Nazareth

Shortly after the debacle at Capernaum and His trip to Gadara, Jesus traveled to His hometown of Nazareth. There He was rejected for the second time (Mark 6:1–6). So deep-seated was the rejection this time that it had spread also to "his own relatives *[suggeneusin]* and in his own household" (v. 4). Jesus was "without honor" even among His brothers and sisters. That situation evidently continued throughout the rest of His ministry until after His resurrection (John 7:5).

During the late winter and early spring of A.D. 31, Jesus sent the disciples on their first preaching mission. This was directed to all Israel. Despite the leaders' opposition, Jesus insisted that everyone hear His messianic solicitation (Matt. 9:35–10:42). This message the disciples carried quite wide, even to Herod's court. It was during this mission, however, that Herod, after imprisoning John the Baptist for over a year, had him beheaded. For Jesus and His band, this violent death of the forerunner was another ugly portent, indicating the mounting unbelief and rejection of the nation.

Rejection at Capernaum after Feeding Five Thousand

The martyrdom of John, however, led to another busy weekend for Jesus and His disciples, ending in another general rout. All four Gospels record this event, which took place at Passover in A.D. 31 (John 6:4). While mourning John's death, Jesus and the Twelve sought seclusion across the sea, but they were trailed by the crowd, who were hungry for more miracles. After feeding the five thousand (about 20,000 altogether), Jesus refused their pretentious offer of kingship (v. 15). Why did He turn down this grassroots initiative by the people, especially after the disciples had just returned from their mission of miracles in which they offered the kingdom (Matt. 10:6–7)?

The obvious reason was soon apparent; the crowd's whimsical vote was a sham. It was the response of their stomachs, not their hearts. This they demonstrated the next day after Jesus refused to give them more "magic manna"; they deserted Him en masse. The king they wanted was a bread king, a "Burger King," one who would fill their mouths and pander their passions. Refusing to be their "candy man," Jesus was then abandoned by nearly the whole crowd. Even the Twelve were a bit edgy in the aftermath (John 6:66 – 67).

The historic significance of this event was that it confirmed Jesus as the Prophet proclaimed by Moses, whom the people also acknowledged (Deut. 18:15; John 6:31). Yet they rejected Jesus as the Messiah. Besides being rebuffed by the elite leaders from Jerusalem (Mark 3:22), He was now being deserted by the common people of Galilee. Not only was He rejected by His hometown of Nazareth, He was now repudiated by His adopted city of Capernaum. This then signaled His further withdrawal to outlying areas, first going north to the Gentile region of Tyre and Sidon. Far from forcing Himself on a recalcitrant people, Jesus left them to begin a traveling ministry with the Twelve to other needy areas.

Traveling to Gentile Regions. Jesus' third year of ministry apparently extended from the feeding of the five thousand to the Transfiguration.[1] It was a year of diverse ministry. We can trace His journeys to Tyre and Sidon that summer and back through Galilee to the ten Gentile cities of Decapolis that fall (Mark 7:24, 31). During this time, Jesus' sparring with the leaders was only sporadic, which may account for the fact that His parabolic sayings were also quite limited. Much of this time was spent instructing the Twelve as they traveled through these northern regions.

Attending Two Feasts in Jerusalem. In the fall and winter of A.D. 31, Jesus attended two Jewish feasts in Jerusalem. One was Tabernacles (October 15–22), and the other was Dedication (Hanukkah, or Feast of Lights, December 25). Though He had not attended Passover (John 6:3–4) or Pentecost that year because of the growing animosity, Jesus did venture to Tabernacles, arriving secretly and late (7:10). The general topic of conversation there was the decision of the Sanhedrin and Pharisees to seize Jesus and have Him slain (vv. 25, 32). Yet He boldly taught in the temple, emphasizing His role as the Light of the World (8:12).

Two months later Jesus was at the Feast of Dedication, where the subject of "light" came up again (being the "Feast of Lights"; John 9:1ff.). His healing a blind man in Jerusalem on the Sabbath precipitated this discourse. That breach of sabbatical law was a challenge to the Pharisaic system and hung everyone on the horns of a dilemma. How could Jesus "break the Sabbath" and yet perform a miracle of healing even greater than that of the prophets?

The Pharisees had a ready answer—deny the miracle. They worked from the premise that breaking the Sabbath was a cardinal sin and, therefore, the healing had to be rigged—and the Healer a phony. The healed blind man argued in reverse. Knowing from his own experience that neither were phony, he lectured the learned leaders on the need to respond to the obvious: Jesus was from God (John

9:33). Levison has called this exchange "some of the finest flashes of wit and humor in the Bible."[2] Flushing and squirming for a credible answer, the Pharisees excommunicated the man from the synagogue on the spot.

That brings us to Jesus' parable of the Good Shepherd and His Sheep in John 10, the first spoken since the kingdom parables of Matthew 13. It was given approximately one year later.

Parable of the Good Shepherd and His Sheep (John 10:1–18)

Since this parable is not treated in most modern commentaries on the parables, it might be asked why we should include it. Even Warren Kissinger's definitive bibliography (listing 123 parables) has no bibliographic listings on this one. Earlier, more conservative works such as Benjamin Keach, Henniges, and Levison did include it, as well as the more recent study by Pentecost. For what reasons, then, do most commentaries today omit it and others include it?

Two basic reasons are given for leaving it out. The first is that it is not given by the Synoptics; the second, that it is usually classified as an allegory.

Concerning the first reason, it is important to recall the different purposes of the Gospels. While John emphasizes the redemptive program of the "Lamb" for individuals, Matthew highlights the kingdom program of the "Lion" for the nation. In nearly every chapter, John speaks about the way of salvation in plain, non-figurative language for all to understand. In this parable of John 10, however, the redemptive emphasis is joined with the kingdom emphasis to show how the old "fold" of Israel was being set aside temporarily for the new "flock" of the church. One fold was an "enclosure" (*aule,* not all sheep); the other a "flock" *(poimne)* of sheep. Jesus' use of a parable here admirably fitted this occasion as He again confronted His rejecters.

The second reason for this omission is that the story is not called a parable, but rather a proverb (*paroimia,* 10:6) or an allegory. Some commentators, therefore, regard it as being similar to the allegory of the True Vine in John 15. The two, however, are quite distinct. John 15 describes a vineyard scene with a string of metaphors, all of which are interpreted within the story. That feature identifies it as an allegory.[3] In John 10, however, we are given a story in one realm (sheep raising, vv. 1–5), followed by Jesus' interpretation in the spiritual realm. Though the story contains allegorical parts (as many parables do), it still retains the basic features of a true parable.

It is therefore essential that this story of the Good Shepherd be included in a well-rounded treatment of the parables. It is also crucial in the movement of Jesus' ministry as He struggled with the Pharisaic system and withdrew from it to begin building the church.

The Story and Its Problem. This parable portrays a most familiar scene, that of a shepherd and his sheep. The story form is a twofold similitude, describing first the entrance of false shepherds to the fold by illicit means, and then the coming of a true shepherd through the door of the sheepfold. Whereas the false shepherds climb through the back fence, the true one comes through the entrance and is admitted by the porter. The sheep, however, do not respond to strangers, but only recognize and follow the voice of the true shepherd, who leads them out to pasture. Following this parable, Jesus gave a rather detailed explanation, inasmuch as the disciples did not understand it (John 10:6–18).

The problem Jesus addressed is quite evident, with the Lord almost spelling it out. The religious leaders had just called Him a sinner for healing on the Sabbath, and they had thrown the restored blind man out of the synagogue. The questions the Jews must have pondered were: "Whom should we follow as the shepherd of Israel? Should we stay with the Pharisees or follow Jesus, who has opened blind eyes?" Incidentally, this Feast of Dedication commemorated the miracle of Hanukkah when supposedly the light burned eight days as the Maccabeans retook Jerusalem from the Syrians in 164 B.C.[4] It made an ideal time to ponder the nation's rededication to truth and light. Who, then, should the people follow?

The Central Truth. The story begins by Jesus identifying two kinds of shepherds, the false and the true. They are distinguished in two ways: first, by the way they enter; second, by the response of the sheep. In His interpretation (John 10:6–18), Jesus elaborates on these distinctions, showing the result of following each. Pursuing the false shepherds brings death and destruction, while following the true Shepherd brings life and abundance. Jesus then identified Himself as "the door" of the sheep, and later as "the Good Shepherd." This gave the parable a kingdom and redemptive emphasis.

The story's central truth is self-evident. Jesus came to Israel as her true Shepherd, entering through the door (namely, the virgin birth and other prophetic fulfillments). But, He found the nation taken over by thieves who masqueraded as shepherds with little concern for the sheep. Though the false shepherds had a large following, the true Shepherd was recognized only by the true sheep who followed Him. This dramatized what Jesus had just said to the Jews: "For judgment I came into this world, that those who do not see may see; and that those who see may become blind" (John 9:39). The true sheep, like the man just healed, were receiving sight, while the Pharisees who rejected Jesus were becoming more and more blind.

"I Am the Door." In Jesus' explanation, He introduced two more of the seven "I Am" statements for which the gospel of John is noted: "I am the Door" and "I am the Good Shepherd." These "I Am" statements served to confirm Jesus' identity as Jehovah (YHWH), the covenant God of Israel (Exod. 3:14).

Jesus' metaphor of the "door" sounds a bit confusing until we recall its significance in shepherding. The sheepfold was usually a fenced enclosure made from rocks in the field to keep out marauding animals. It had but one entrance for the sheep, which the shepherd guarded at night. G. Campbell Morgan quotes a shepherd who responded to George Adam Smith's question about why the entrance had no door: "I am the door," the shepherd replied. "The sheep go inside, and I come there and lie down across the threshold, and no sheep can get out except over my body, and no wolf can get in except over me."[5] This is an eloquent rehearsal of the point Jesus made here, though the local shepherd was unaware of it!

Jesus used this metaphor to stress that He was the only way of salvation, not one among many. He called Himself *the* door as the only way to life and abundance (*perisson,* John 10:10). After the healed blind man was cast out the door of the Pharisaic system in 9:34–35,

Jesus showed Himself to be the door to true life. Then, when the leaders rejected both Jesus and the blind man, Jesus portrayed those leaders as aliens to the true flock of God. The metaphor of the "door" fittingly portrayed Him as both the entrance and protector of life.

"I Am the Good Shepherd." Besides being the Door, Jesus is also the Guide and Guardian of the sheep. This caring function is stressed as He declares four times that He "lays down His life for the sheep" (John 10:11, 15, 17, 18). The sheep know His voice and follow Him. Though cattle may be driven, sheep only scatter when driven and must be led. Likewise, Jesus didn't say, "I am the good cowboy," but rather "the Good Shepherd." He leads rather than drives, and His disciples are called "followers."

The figure of "shepherd" was of special importance to Israel. In the Psalms the Lord (YHWH) is portrayed as the "Shepherd of Israel" who cares for and preserves His people from evil (Pss. 23:1; 80:1). The Prophets also warned against false shepherds. Ezekiel 34 gives a classic caution concerning the false leaders:

> Woe, shepherds of Israel who have been feeding themselves! . . . the diseased you have not healed, the broken you have not bound up, . . . nor have you sought for the lost. . . . therefore, you shepherds, hear the word of the Lord. . . . I shall demand My sheep from them and make them cease from feeding sheep, . . . but I shall deliver My flock from their mouth. . . . Then I will set over them one shepherd, My servant David. (vv. 2, 4, 9, 10, 23)

That key passage was doubtless on Jesus' mind as He gave this parable, and it probably struck fire in the thinking of the Pharisees. In it He reminded them of Ezekiel's familiar warning, portraying them as the ultimate villains in the Prophets' vision. Zechariah, in fact, carried this shepherd analogy even further. He noted that, due to the greed and insensitivity of false shepherds, the flock of Israel would be doomed to slaughter (Zech. 11:4–10). As a shepherd might break and discard his staffs, the Lord would break His staffs of *grace* and *unity*. In effect, He would no longer show the people favor and keep the nation united. Furthermore, the sword would "strike the Shepherd that the sheep may be scattered" (13:7).

Though the people hardly discerned the full significance of this, the Lord gave them a provocative Bible study in saying, "I am the Good Shepherd" (John 10:11). It was first a vivid declaration of His true identity. It revealed to all gathered in Jerusalem that He was the divine "I Am," the true "Shepherd of Israel" about whom David wrote. But having come to care for His flock, Jesus was being plotted against by false shepherds. Only their deep blindness and hardness of hearts can explain their obstinacy, which showed itself again in their attempt to stone Him (v. 31).

The Wider Significance. Jesus carried this shepherd analogy even further to portray His wider shepherding role for the church. Besides casting out His own sheep from the fold of Israel, He would also gather other sheep, which are not of this fold. Together these would become "one flock" (John 10:16). Whereas the term "fold" *(aule)* means an enclosure that may or may not have sheep, the word "flock" *(poimne)* signifies a sheepfold (sheep only). Israel's fold at that time not only contained sheep, but also wolves, serpents, vipers, and so on, as Jesus noted in Matthew 23. The new flock would have only sheep, gathered from both Israel and the world. For these Jesus would "lay down My life that I may take it again" (John 10:17). Following the resurrection, He would be their one Shepherd (Heb. 13:20).

Jesus' reference to this new flock as the church does not imply another ecclesiastical organization. Rather, it speaks of a spiritual "organism" of all believers of this age. As Israel was an organization with many physical members, but few true believers, so the organization of the church may also include a motley group of fellow travelers who are only pretenders. The true church, however, is a spiritual organism of only true believers.

The caution is that if the Devil was shrewd enough to take over the divinely appointed instrument of Israel, he will not fail to attempt the same thing with the church. His sinister ploy is to join churches and assume leadership, a plan he has used through much of church history. Though many such "folds" have succumbed to false shepherds and have had to be discarded, the Good Shepherd continues to guard and pasture His true flock.

A CHRONOLOGICAL NOTE—JESUS' FOUR-YEAR MINISTRY

From this point on a question is often debated by harmonists as to the dating of the events of Jesus' ministry, which also involves the parables. That question is the length of His ministry. Though debated by scholars throughout church history, it is generally agreed today that it covered a period of at least three years. This is based on John's mention of three Passovers (John 2:13; 6:4; 11:55) and the probability of another between chapters 2 and 6 (5:1 being Tabernacles). Though the Synoptic Gospels mention only the last Passover (Passion Week), they obviously relate to the events of John's chronology, which requires additional Passovers.

Most harmonies therefore accept the traditional view that Jesus' ministry spanned a little over three years, as propounded by Karl Wiesler in the mid-nineteenth century (Harold Hoehner, George Ogg, A. T. Robertson, Stevens and Burton, Thomas and Gundry, and so on). This view then places the remaining parables of Matthew 18–20 and Luke 9:51–19:27 between the Feasts of Tabernacles (or Dedication) in John 7–10 and the raising of Lazarus in John 11 (October A.D. 32 to late February A.D. 33).

Though this view is popular, it is generally recognized to have serious problems. The most difficult is relating Jesus' last journey from Galilee to Jerusalem as recorded in John 7:10 with His journey as recorded in Luke 9:51.[6] The crux of the problem is that the two journeys appear to have nothing in common. John 7 records Jesus' secret trip to Jerusalem in a matter of days. Luke 9–19 portrays His long travelogue through Galilee, Samaria, and beyond Jordan involving numerous stops. The two departures from Galilee simply do not relate.

Though it is possible to squeeze the many activities of Luke's travelogue somewhere into that winter before the raising of Lazarus in late February, such a compression is hardly plausible. The events and places are too numerous to fit. To propose such a furious pace for Jesus' final ministry a few months before the cross is hardly in keeping with His usual style of evangelistic travel and ministry.

There is, however, a viable alternative. Since the Synoptics record several events that suggest another Passover between the feeding of the five thousand and Passion Week, the idea of a four-year ministry has much in its favor. Limiting it to a three-year chronology is not required by the texts, for John's mention of three Passovers was incidental rather than meant to be exhaustive. If an unmentioned Passover is quite universally accepted between John 2 and 6, another unmentioned one between 6 and 12 is certainly possible. Nothing in the text militates against it, though tradition has adopted the three-year view.

For these abbreviated reasons, this presentation of the parables observes the four-year time structure of Jesus' ministry. In this view His ministry began in late winter of A.D. 29 (John's in the summer of A.D. 28, the fifteenth year of Tiberius; Luke 3:1), and concluded at the crucifixion in A.D. 33.[7] The five inclusive Passovers then occurred as follows: (1) At Jesus' first cleansing of the temple (John 2:13); (2) the first Sabbath controversy (Mark 2:23; Luke 6:1); (3) the feeding of the five thousand (John 6:4); (4) the Transfiguration (the time of the temple tax, which was during the Passover; Matt. 17:2, 24); and (5) the Passion week (Matt. 26:2). This time schedule is not given with even a mild form of dogmatism, but rather to provide a likely time frame to harmonize the various events and parables recorded.

Assuming this time structure, the kingdom parables of Matthew 13 were evidently given in late fall or early winter of A.D. 30, and the parable of the Good Shepherd about one year later, in A.D. 31 (at the Feast of Dedication on December 25). Both emphasized Jesus' changed kingdom program, the first after the leaders' blasphemy in Galilee, and the second after noting their blindness in Jerusalem. Each also commenced a new ministry of Jesus to different outlying areas.

Parable of the Unforgiving Debtor (Matt. 18:23–35)

We've all heard it: "To err is human, to forgive, divine." Does God always forgive? Does He have limits on His forgiveness? Does He ever withdraw His forgiveness? Careful, now. Why or why not? Why is it so important for believers to be forgiving? Is there a limit to what or how much we should forgive?

These are some of the first questions Jesus discussed with the disciples after He announced His plan to build the church. Like us today, they had some deep traditional hang-ups to surrender concerning the matter of forgiveness. For His "Sunday-punch" on this crucial issue, Jesus unleashed another parable to rivet His teaching on their minds and hearts.

The Historic Setting. In the spring of A.D. 32, Jesus led His disciples on a second northern journey, this time northeast to the district of Caesarea-Philippi. In this predominately Gentile territory, He revealed to the Twelve His plan to build the church and the immense cost of doing so. Jesus would be killed and raised again on the third day (Matt. 16:18ff.). This was His first announcement of the church, as such, and the first specific announcement of His coming death.

After Peter reacted with outrage to this suggestion of seeming defeat, Jesus then spoke about the cross each of the disciples would bear in following Him. For them this was heavy teaching and hard to swallow. But He also spoke about His coming again in great glory to recompense His enemies (v. 27). That was more to their liking.

As if to further bolster the disciples' faith, Jesus then took Peter, James, and John several days later to high Mount Hermon for a leaders' conference. Here they saw a vision of His glory as He conversed with Moses and Elijah. Besides getting a taste of His coming triumph, they also heard the Father emphasize the awesome preeminence of the Person of Jesus as His Son. His brilliance far outshone the towering figures of the Old Testament Law and Prophets (17:1–8).

Overwhelmed, the disciples came down from the mountain to receive further confirmations of Jesus' greatness and further instruction for the church. Being the time of Passover when the temple tax of a half-shekel was collected, the authorities sought to dun Jesus for His payment. To show both His compliance with the law and His vast preeminence over it, Jesus had Peter pay the tax by means of the disciple's favorite sport—fishing (v. 27).

When told to open the mouth of the first fish, Peter found the shekel waiting for him to collect. This was an immense miracle of omniscience and omnipotence for such a paltry sum! To those demanding it from Jesus, He paid a pittance, while also commanding the sea and the immense powers of nature! The disciples were left with one of the most unusual displays of His greatness and coming kingdom.

It was in the flush of this grandeur that Jesus began teaching the disciples the mundane principles of church relations. Though mundane, they were also foundational. When the disciples wanted to know more about Jesus' secrets of becoming great (how to be another Elijah, perhaps?), He spoke about humility. He showed that the way up is down. The way to win is often by losing, for any loss is better than causing a little one to stumble. The main business of life is to win the strays. Sometimes success comes by seeming defeat.

This led to the subject of how to treat a brother who sins. Does humility and meekness mean insensitivity to sin when a brother "sins against you" (Matt. 18:15; Byzantine text)? Are we to graciously overlook such offenses? Jesus' counsel was that the individual offended should first confront the offender and then consult the church. All of this, when bathed in prayer, is designed to win back the offender to repentance and fellowship. However, should the sinning brother still fail to respond, he is to be left outside the church to the judgment of God (v. 17). This was strong medicine for the disciples, especially after Jesus exhorted them to humility and meekness; nevertheless, it was essential to maintain purity and God's blessing.

Jesus' Grand Principle of Forgiveness. That teaching prompted Peter to raise the question of forgiveness (Matt. 18:21). Granted that the church should forgive and restore a brother who sins and repents, isn't there a limit to such forgiveness? Surely not ad infinitum?

In a spirit of generosity, Peter ventured the unheard of number of forgiving seven such offenses. The rabbis had set a limit of three, from Amos 1:3ff., and Peter outdid them by four.[8] (He may already have felt greater than Elijah.) Jesus' response to this expansive generosity was to smile and say, "try seventy times seven," or 490 (Matt. 18:22). His point was not that the disciples could blow their stack at 491, but rather to express the believer's obligation of unlimited grace in forgiveness. Yes, Peter, ad infinitum!

It was St. Jerome's observation that this was a striking contrast to the vengeance demanded by Lamech in Genesis 4:24. As that child of Cain demanded "seventy-sevenfold" vengeance from God for anyone avenging his murder for self-defense, Jesus called for "seventy times seven" forgiveness. Love does, indeed, turn vengeance inside out. Recognizing the unusualness of this concept, Jesus told a parable to illustrate the principle (Matt. 18:23–35).

The Problem Addressed. This is one of the few parables in which the Pharisees are not in the foreground or background. The disciples are here alone with Jesus as He discussed some in-house questions and obligations of the church. The problem addressed is quite apparent as expressed in Peter's question: "Lord, how often shall my brother sin against me and I forgive him?" (Matt. 18:21). Or, on what basis should a believer keep granting forgiveness to a brother who repeatedly offends him?

The Dramatic Story. This parable is simply a striking illustration of the principle just stated by Jesus, giving the reasons for it. His principle of unlimited forgiveness probably sounded too idealistic and "goody-two-shoes," if not dangerous, for even the most saintly. It would, in fact, hardly fly in most of our churches today. Perceiving the disciples' flinch, Jesus told a story with two dramatic surprises.

An oriental king decided to settle and balance his financial accounts, and, in the process, found one of his stewards hopelessly in debt to him. The steward owed him over ten million dollars (if 10,000 talents of silver; if gold, it was an even more prodigious amount). As Swete comments, the steward "must have embezzled the taxes of the whole country."[9] In accord with oriental justice, the king commanded that the steward and his family be sold into slavery, to which the steward responded with a plea for mercy, promising full repayment. Displaying immense compassion for his plight, the king then released him and completely forgave his great debt.

Then comes the jolt. This forgiven bum went out and found one of his buddies who owed him a paltry sum of less than twenty dollars. The greedy steward grabbed the man by the throat and demanded immediate repayment. To his plea for mercy and time to repay, the steward turned a deaf ear and heartlessly threw him in prison. When the king heard about this, he summoned the merciless steward, withdrew his forgiveness, and sent him to the tormentor, demanding full repayment of his debt.

This story has two surprise twists that would startle anyone. The first is the king's unheard of compassion in responding so graciously to the pleading of his debtor. The fabulous amount he squandered must have come from massive embezzlements of the king's revenues. But the tough monarch was so moved by the steward's plight and apparent deep supplication that the king wiped his slate clean, allowing him to make a new start. What a magnanimous display of generosity!

The second surprise comes in the lack of mercy this pardoned steward showed to a fellow servant who was indebted to him. Though this debt was a mere pittance compared to what the steward had been forgiven, he refused to show mercy. Rather, he demanded the "last pound of flesh" immediately. The story is one of monstrous ingratitude and insensitivity to a hurting neighbor! Had David heard it, he would have said, the steward "deserves to die" (2 Sam. 12:5).

The Central Truth. Jesus' point in this parable is crystal clear and for good reason. He wanted the lesson to be burned into our minds. As Pentecost has noted, it is imbedded in the response of the king to the wicked servant (Matt. 18:32–34).[10] In view of the immense forgiveness God grants us in Christ, no offense or number of offenses should be considered too great to forgive one who earnestly seeks it. The contrast of the two debts emphasizes this. If the huge debt makes the story seem unrealistic (far exceeding anything noted in the Old Testament), it does so for a purpose. It expresses the greatness of each of our transgressions for which no one is able to pay.

Peter's question, then, about how often he should forgive is answered in this contrast. To forgive seventy times seven comes nowhere near the immensity of what God has forgiven us in Christ. The ratio of the two debts has been calculated as 1,250,000 to 1, as Trench has noted.[11] When we recall Jesus' value of a soul as being of more worth than "the whole world" (Mark 8:36), the question itself becomes academic. Acceptance of God's pardon, not to mention also

His gift of righteousness, makes obligatory our surrender of every claim to take offense—or to refuse forgiveness to any offender who requests it.

It has been noted that the analogy of God with this king appears to put God in a bad light. Does God withdraw forgiveness once it is granted? Is His forgiveness contingent on our forgiving others? The real question is whether the person coming to God for pardon is really seeking pardon, or just release from debt. The schemer in Jesus' parable, in seeking the king's mercy, wanted to be released from his debt; but his failure to pass on that mercy showed he had not really received it. The steward merely snatched at the gift of freedom so that he could resume his merciless ways. The point is that God offers pardon to those who earnestly seek it as a gift of His mercy for positive good. Those who merely "use God" for personal gain eventually exhibit the fact that they never really received that mercy in the first place.

By now you have likely discerned an example of this merciless servant among the disciples. Judas Iscariot was a living portrait of the scoundrel. After having received the great gift of apostleship, he later exhibited unbelievable ingratitude. Not only did he grab the throat of another servant, but also he leveled his venom at the King Himself. Judas became a classic example of presumptuous mercy.

But lest we smugly pass this judgment off on Jesus' betrayers, notice how in His conclusion He pressed His caution to all of us: "So shall My heavenly Father also do to you, if each of you does not forgive his brother from your heart" (Matt. 18:35). Jesus' overall emphasis in this chapter was to guard against the sins of offense, first that of offending "little ones" who so easily stumble; then the offense of ingratitude in failing to forgive those who sin against us and desire restoration. God's mercy is such that it becomes conspicuous by its absence in those who are mere pretenders.

The Wider Significance. Jesus put this lesson in prayer form when He taught His disciples to pray: "And forgive us our debts, as we also have forgiven our debtors. . . . But if you do not forgive men, then your Father will not forgive your transgressions" (Matt. 6:12, 15). This was not given as a prayer of unbelievers for salvation, but rather as a prayer of believers for blessing. An unforgiving heart is no candidate for God's blessing and is really a stranger to God's Spirit. In God's forgiveness, His mercy triumphs over judgment (James 2:13). That attitude, Jesus said, should also characterize believers.

As forgiveness was one of the first lessons Jesus taught this group after announcing the cross, it was also one of the first lessons He demonstrated on the cross (Luke 23:34). There He called on the Father to forgive the Roman soldiers who crucified Him, for they did not know what they were doing. In the early church Steven also reflected that attitude with the result that one of his slayers, Saul of Tarsus, became the greatest missionary statesman of the early church (Acts 7:58–60).

That attitude of forgiveness is one of the most effective tools of the church against its enemies. The pity is that the later church failed to apply it to the Jewish people, whom they labeled "Christ killers"; the result was that they grievously alienated the Jewish people for nearly the whole history of the church. This points up our need to resurrect the lesson of this parable for the church today and for each of us individually. It is an art that needs polishing, especially in a day of growing offense.

To err is, indeed, human; but to forgive is not only divine, but also divinely commanded. The parable portrays this grace as a divine investment in us that we are to reinvest in others. God wants His investment to be reproductive in all His children.

Chapter 9

LUKE'S TRAVELOGUE

Parables on Servanthood

IN THE EARLY SUMMER OF A.D. 32, Jesus "set His face to go to Jerusalem" (Luke 9:51). This became a long, zigzag journey through Galilee, Samaria, Perea, and Judea that continued to the time of the Triumphal Entry. Luke is the gospel that describes this extended journey in what is known as "Luke's Travelogue" (9:51–19:27).[1] Having finished His ministry around Capernaum, the Lord began a final canvass of many other villages on His way south, often restating and applying earlier sayings in Galilee for these later audiences.

Jesus began this journey by sending disciples ahead of Him to prepare for His coming. Though the Twelve were previously restricted from going to Samaria (Matt. 10:5–6), these were sent first to that area (Luke 9:52). The Samaritans, however, met this initial probe with rebuff. The disciples' ministry, of course, was not so much a call to the nation as a call for individuals.

When the seventy were later sent out, they were elated on their return at their powers to heal and cast out demons (Luke 10:17). Yet Jesus did not share this elation over healings and exorcisms. Rather, He seemed to rebuke them in His following prayer, calling them "babes" (v. 21). His concern was for spiritual results: "rejoice that your names are recorded in heaven" (v. 20). By this Jesus gently reminded the disciples that their greatest gift was not to perform miracles, but rather to know the Father (v. 22). That clarification set the stage for Jesus' ministry in the coming months as He and His disciples traveled south. Using miracles only rarely, He taught by actions and parables many significant lessons on servanthood.

PARABLE OF THE GOOD SAMARITAN (LUKE 10:30–37)

This story is by all accounts the most popular of Jesus' parables. The very name has become a synonym for mercy and been adopted as the name of countless institutions and people-helpers. As often noted, the story has inspired the building of more hospitals than all the grand philosophies of people put together.

Though the Jews of Jesus' day had no time for the "half-breed" people of Samaria, Jesus never spoke disparagingly about them. He led the Samaritan woman of John 4 to believe, with the result that she won much of her city to Jesus. Later He healed a Samaritan leper who alone returned to thank Him. Though outcasts, their contacts with Jesus made them "Good Samaritans." The Lord was not averse to mingling with these foreigners (v. 9), a practice scorned by the Jews. This parable of the Good Samaritan subtly adverts to that ancient animosity, impressing a most important lesson on the Jewish leaders, as well as on the disciples.

The Probing Question about Eternal Life. The question precipitating this discussion arose as Jesus spoke about the disciples' gift of knowing the Father and salvation. This, Jesus said, was hidden from the "wise and intelligent" (Luke 10:21). Responding to this seeming taunt, a Jewish lawyer took offense and challenged Him on the subject (v. 25). The lawyer's first question was: "Teacher, what shall I do to inherit eternal life?" Sensing the man's adversarial tone, Jesus simply responded with the rabbinic method of posing another question: "What is written in the Law?" (v. 26). In reply the lawyer recited part of the Shema (Lev. 19:18b; Deut. 6:4–5), in which the Law commands people to love God and neighbor (Luke 10:27). As Levison has said, "It is believed among the Jews that any one who makes that confession before his death is sure of eternal life."[2] This Pharisee evidently felt smug confidence in his brief recital.

We might ask why Jesus didn't immediately explain the plan of salvation with such a verse as John 5:24, "He who hears My word, and believes Him who sent Me, has eternal life." Wasn't this a golden opportunity to preach the gospel? Why refer the man to the Law? The apparent answer is that Jesus used the Law to convict him, inasmuch as he didn't recognize that he was lost (1 Tim. 1:8–9). The man's question was quite defensive and hostile, not that of a seeker.[3] The Lord simply met him on his own turf, forcing him to personal introspection.

Notice, then, how Jesus finished by turning the question from debatable theory into practical theology by saying, "Do this, and you will live" (Luke 10:28). In essence He shifted the spotlight of examination from Himself to the critic. Finding that obvious reminder a bit demeaning, the law expert struck back with another much-debated question: "Who is my neighbor?" (v. 29).

The Problem Addressed. In both of Jesus' answers, He seems to have sidestepped the lawyer's questions, loaded as they were with rabbinic debate. Rather, He focused on the heart, dealing with the concept of "neighbor" to help resolve both questions. In Jesus' view, the man was not ready for the appeal of grace. This was shown by his belligerent, self-righteous attitude toward Jesus and all outside his own small circle of scribes and Pharisees. Their legal system had concocted a narrow view of "neighbor," excluding such people as Samaritans and Romans, or even Jews living in a Gentile or Galilean country.

With this recognition we can discern the basic problem being addressed: What does the command to love one's neighbor really mean? or, How far should we carry this business of love to fulfill God's Law? That, however, was only the surface problem. Since the story identifies key people who relate to Jesus' controversy with the leaders, the Lord evidently addressed a more personal question, one that also concerned many in the crowd: Who is really fulfilling God's Law, the religious leaders with their intricate ritual system, or Jesus, whom they accused of being a Law-breaker? The following chapter will explode that issue in a personal confrontation.

Jesus' Story About Crime on the Highway

Jesus' story to the lawyer simply portrayed a familiar scene on the perilous road from Jerusalem to Jericho. On this unpatrolled, mountainous descent to Jericho, some 1,200 feet below sea level, bandits and malcontents often roamed to strip any traveler brave enough to go unattended. It was known from ancient times as the "Bloody Road."[4]

One such lonely traveler, Jesus said, took that journey and was viciously attacked, robbed, and left half-dead. By and by two religious leaders came along in pursuit of temple duties, first a priest and then a Levite. Undoubtedly these clerics were well versed in the Law's command to show mercy (Mic. 6:8) and might have put their theology into good practice. But unfortunately, both apparently had a demanding schedule that day, inclining each to circle around the wounded man. It would not do to defile themselves for temple service. Perhaps they mumbled about what a shame it was that the "trash" of society should "get into fights like that."

Shortly after, however, a traveling Samaritan came along, saw the man's emaciation, and ministered to him with what he had. Seeing the man's need for continued care, the kindly stranger made his donkey into an ambulance, took the man to a nearby inn, and arranged for his continued nursing and rehabilitation. The Samaritan came as an angel of mercy to the dying man.

With that portrayal of stark contrasts, Jesus then invited this law expert to choose the "winner". "Which of these three do you think proved to be a neighbor?" (Luke 10:36). Not allowing himself to breathe the name "Samaritan," the lawyer admitted the true hero was "the one who showed mercy toward him." Then, with characteristic aplomb, Jesus dismissed the proud legalist with a crisp, "Go and do the same" (v. 37). Never pushy, Jesus simply gave him food for thought on the practical application of God's Law.

The Central Truth. The obvious point of the story is the clarification of what God meant by loving one's neighbor. A neighbor is anyone in need to whom we are able to minister. Such a person may not be lovely or a pretty sight—or even able to request aid—but a neighbor nonetheless. One's neighborhood is as broad as his or her circle of influence or ability to reach, without regard to race, color, or social status. A true neighbor ministers to such a person without regard for compensation.

It has often been noted that this story reflects three distinct attitudes: (1) That of the thieves—"What's yours is mine, and I'm going to get it." (2) The priest and Levite—"What's mine is mine, and I'm going to keep it." (3) The Samaritan—"What's mine is yours, and I'm going to share it."

The personal challenge for each of us is, "Where do I fit?" Ironically, Jesus' great conflict was not with the criminals of 1, but rather with the religionists of 2. The "I earned mine" attitude has, in fact, not lost its prominence in our day of modern America or, arguably, religious America. Jesus' admonition came loud and clear through the attitude of the gracious Samaritan: He ain't heavy; he's my neighbor.

Though the noble character of the Good Samaritan gets the spotlight in this parable, he really shared it with another in the historical setting. That was the one with the red face when Jesus finished administering the parable. We refer, of course, to the lawyer who asked for this dressing down.

The real villains of the story were not the thieves, but rather the priest and Levite. Why didn't Jesus choose a Roman or an Egyptian to fill these culprit roles? The reason is obvious. He wanted to portray the priest and Levite, both of whom were a part of the system the lawyer represented. Their ongoing struggle with Jesus was "daily news," for He was by now fair game for capture by the leaders (John 7:32; 8:59; 10:31, 39). In light of this, it would be naive to suppose that Jesus spoke this parable simply to inspire sweetness and kindness toward one's neighbor. As Bernard Ramm has noted: "In approaching any parable we must ask ourselves: how does this parable relate to Christ? Are any of the persons in the parable Christ?"[5] The Lord purposely etched the protagonists of that struggle into the fabric of this masterpiece.

Jesus' obvious purpose was to give a graphic portrayal of the leaders' delinquency. They were derelict to duty on a central command of the Law—the very Law on which they based their merit and salvation. As Jesus later said to the lawyers, "you weigh men down with burdens hard to bear, while you yourselves will not even touch the burdens with one of your fingers" (Luke 11:46). Some six months earlier, the Pharisees had called Jesus a "Samaritan" (John 8:48). In ministering healing and cleansing to Israel, He was indeed the embodiment of this Samaritan, doing what the religious leaders failed to do.

The Wider Significance. Besides the obvious overtones of Jesus' ministry, this parable also spoke volumes concerning the disciples' ministry. Notice the significant progression of effective service traced in Luke 10. When the seventy exulted over their success in doing miracles, Jesus reminded them of what really mattered—having their names written in heaven and knowing the Father. Their touted miracles were only transitory; they were to keep their eyes on eternal goals. When the lawyer challenged Jesus on the law of love, He reminded him that true love is not merely reciting the shema, but also actively serving the needy. True religion is not mere temple or synagogue ritual, but also showing mercy on the highways and byways (James 1:26–27).

Immediately after the parable of the Good Samaritan, Luke recounted the story of Martha's zealous service in order to show that sacrificial service is not the whole story. As Martha feverishly rushed around to get dinner, Jesus gently slowed her down to get her attention. She had overlooked something. In her sincere desire to serve, she forgot that fellowship with the Lord is even more important than service. The point stressed is that in order for service to be effective, listening to Jesus' Word must precede it. Both are necessary, but there must be a balance. Worship comes before service (Luke 10:38–42).

PARABLE OF THE BORROWING FRIEND AT MIDNIGHT (LUKE 11:5–13)

In the following chapter, Luke continues to stress Jesus' principles for effective service. Here the movement goes from the need for active service and worship in chapter 10, to the need for proper prayer in chapter 11. Christian service is effective only as a cooperative effort with God.

Having watched the Lord pray, the disciples requested a lesson on how they could pray effectively. They discerned their need for divine help in service. Jesus then repeated His "Prayer Instruction 101," which He had first given in the Sermon on the Mount in Galilee

(Matt. 6:9–13). These two passages give the only specific teaching in the Bible on how to pray. Though the Lord here omitted several phrases previously given, the basic outline is the same: (1) Address God as Father; (2) Worship Him as holy; (3) Seek His interests first—His kingdom and His will; (4) Then seek your own interests of daily bread, forgiveness, and guidance. Though short in construction, the prayer is long in content. Jesus simply repeated it here as His model for effective communication with God.

The Problem Addressed. For the Jews who often recited Old Testament prayers, this approach was a bit revolutionary; rarely had they addressed God as Father. Appropriately, it was God's Son who introduced the Almighty as "Father" and then invited their approach to Him also as a loving Father.

In this instruction Jesus gave new meaning to prayer as an intimate Father-child relationship. However, it also invites a more casual and persistent approach, which might seem a bit irreverent in coming to the Almighty. The question apparently arose as to how confident one may be in bringing small personal matters to God. Perhaps the disciples thought about many unanswered prayers. That, of course, is a universal problem for believers of all ages. How bold and confident should a believer be in making specific requests of God? Why, then, doesn't the Lord answer all our requests?

The Story of Begging Bread. These were some of the queries that Jesus addressed in this parable. The brief pericope is linked with two similar analogies in the following verses (Luke 11:11–12). They move from requesting food from a friend to requesting food from a father. The three are given together with a brief interpretation in the middle and should be treated together. Though this parable and discussion on seeking bread is often related to that of the Unrighteous Judge in Luke 18, they are quite different. They differ in both setting and purpose. Directly following this saying of 11:5–13 is a contrast of the power of the Holy Spirit with that of Satan, summarizing the basic point Jesus is making.

It should also be noted that the comparisons Jesus uses here are different from other parables; they make their points by contrast, rather than similarities. God is not like the givers in these stories, but unlike them. The story of the unexpected guest depicts a familiar but embarrassing scene in that culture. A hungry traveler arrives at the home of a friend late at night, catching him with his cupboards bare. Since showing hospitality was an ego issue in that eastern culture, the friend would feel shame not to feed him. With no late night stores to run to, he hastily sought help from a neighbor. This, of course, was the worst of times to come, and the neighbor was ready to tell him to "bug off" until morning.

We can better appreciate this man's dilemma if we recall the eastern sleeping arrangement of a home. Nathan Levison, who grew up near Nazareth, describes such a home:

> The house consists of one large room which serves the whole family. The bedding is kept in a recess in the wall, and at night is taken out and spread on reed mats on the floor. The father and mother sleep in the centre of the room, the youngest children on the father's right-hand side; but if there is an infant, it is in a cradle next to the mother. The older male children sleep next to the youngest children, with their heads next to the wall and their feet toward the youngest children. The girls occupy the mother's side of the room. With an average family, the father's getting up would certainly disturb the household, especially the children sleeping next to him.[6]

Despite this inconvenience, however, the aroused man gets up and gives his neighbor, not just three loaves, but "as much as he needs" (Luke 11:8).

The Central Truth. The point of this parable revolves around the Greek word rendered "persistence" *(anaideian)* in verse 8. The neighbor grants the request, not because of their friendship, but "because of his persistence." The meaning of this word is greatly debated (used only here in the New Testament). Arndt and Gingrich give two possibilities, "persistence" or "impudence," saying it literally means "shamelessness."[7] N. Levison and G. C. Morgan deny its connotation of persistence here, opting also for the literal "shamelessness." Jeremias likewise takes the meaning "that he may not lose face in the matter."[8]

The Eastern culture of the story also supports this as the probable meaning. The neighbor gave the man as much bread as he needed, not because he was a friend or that he kept hammering on the door, but because it would have been a shame to his friends and community to commit such a breach of hospitality.

How, then, does it relate to persistent prayer? Notice that the three sayings are presented as ridiculous suppositions, asking, "which one of you?" (vv. 5, 11). Jesus asks rhetorically how anyone could possibly respond in the following way, or, "Did you ever hear of such a dumb response as this?" Jeremias has captured the idea in his paraphrase: "Can you imagine that, if one of you had a friend who came to you at midnight and said to you, 'My friend, lend me three loaves, because a friend has come to me on a journey, and I have nothing to set before him,' you would call out, 'Don't disturb me . . . ?' Can you imagine such a thing? The answer would be— 'Unthinkable!'"[9] This also fits the Lord's answer in verse 8: "I tell you, even though he will not get up and give him anything because he is his friend, yet because of his persistence [or shamelessness] he will get up and give him as much as he needs."

What truth about God, then, does this portray? Surely not that "God hates to get up at night," or that He will eventually answer if you keep pestering Him, but that He will answer as a loving Father. G. C. Morgan puts it bluntly:

> Often expositors and preachers have said this teaches importunity in the matter of prayer. It teaches nothing of the kind. It teaches that there is no need when we are dealing with God, to hammer and hammer at His door. God is not . . . a sleepy man who does not want to be troubled, and therefore refuses, and is only persuaded to get up in order to escape trouble for Himself by getting rid of the seeker. That is not the picture of God. God does not need to be importuned or shamed into answering, for He is a loving Father.[10]

As the Lord immediately explains, we only need to "ask," "seek," or "knock" (vv. 9–10). There is no reluctance on God's part or reticence to answer until we grovel sufficiently. Nor is He waiting for us to "storm the gates of heaven," or mutilate ourselves to show we really mean it, for He is not like the Canaanite Baals on Mount Carmel. The Father simply waits for us to make our requests as children, and then He answers at the most appropriate time.

What point, then, does Jesus make about persistence in prayer? Is there not a proper place for waiting on God in prayer? There is, indeed, and that is the point of the parable of the Unjust Judge in Luke 18:1–8. Though not primary here, it is suggested in the two sayings that follow, which are intricately related (11:11–12). As this one contrasts God with a neighbor who gave to prevent being shamed, the others contrast Him with an earthly father. If an earthly father wouldn't give something bad when his children request food, how much less will the heavenly Father. He answers because He cares intensely for His children, far more than an earthly father.

These principles suggest a reason for many unanswered prayers and the need for patience in waiting on God. We often ask for things that appear good, but might bring sorrow in the long run. The "fish" we request may be a camouflaged "snake." Prayer, in other words, is a serious business that needs the screening of the Holy Spirit (Rom. 8:26–27). As Eta Linnemann put it, "God is not a slot-machine in which one only needs to insert the coin of persistent prayer to get what is wanted!"[11]

God forbid we should insist on "fifteen more years," as King Hezekiah did, after which he produced a wicked son (Manasseh), who brought down the kingdom (2 Kings 20:5–6; 21:1). When prayers are not answered, it is still an occasion for thanks. Such prayers call for patience and persistence in waiting, certainly not a "name it and claim it" insistence just because we asked. Persistence does not mean insistence.

The Happy Ending of Praying to the Father. Jesus concluded this instruction by noting that through such prayers the heavenly Father will "give the Holy Spirit to those who ask Him" (Luke 11:13). Does this mean that God gives the Holy Spirit only to those believers who request Him? Many have wrongly drawn from this text the idea of a delayed coming of the Spirit. That, of course, would contradict

Romans 8:9, "If anyone does not have the Spirit of Christ, he does not belong to Him." Every true believer is indwelt by the Holy Spirit as a seal of his or her redemption (Eph. 1:13).

To appreciate Jesus' point here, it is important to keep it in its context of effective prayer, for He stressed that God gives good things to those who ask. Luke 11:13 appends the guarantee. In the parallel passage of Matthew 7:11, Jesus states the same principle in a different way: "How much more shall your Father who is in heaven give what is good to those who ask Him!" Putting the two together, it might be rendered: "How much more shall your heavenly Father give good gifts *through the Holy Spirit* to those who ask Him." The Luke 11:13 passage uses the figure of metonymy (putting cause for effect) to emphasize the work of the Holy Spirit, a strong emphasis of Luke throughout his gospel.

Jesus' point, then, was that simple prayer to the Father (asking, seeking, or knocking) is so effective that it will draw the limitless power of the Holy Spirit to fulfill God's purpose for His children. The Father doesn't need to be badgered. Then, in the following passage, Luke records the blasphemous charge of the Pharisees that Jesus worked in Satan's power (Luke 11:14–22). In response, Jesus stressed that He not only had power to cast out demons, but also would destroy Satan's kingdom. How? By the "finger of God," the Holy Spirit. Such is also the power available for believers today—through prayer.

PARABLE OF THE RICH FOOL (LUKE 12:13–21)

Jesus had more to say about money or possessions than any other subject. From beginning to end (His temptation by Satan to His betrayal by Judas), money, the god of mammon, figured prominently in His warnings. That was also true of Jesus' parables, for He dealt with life as He found it, a struggle to maintain the necessities of life. That tension is often seen as a constant scrimmage between the god of gold and the God of glory. Jesus will later accuse His enemies of capitulating to this "golden calf" (Luke 16) and will illustrate the consequences of it.

The parable of the rich fool especially focuses on that issue, highlighting the problem of property divisions. As Kenneth Bailey has noted, this parable touches on a most sensitive problem of justice in the Middle East today; namely, the division of the land according to heritage rights.[12] Who is the proper arbiter for this age long struggle, and what counsel does the Lord have for its settlement? The world is waiting for an answer to this problem, similar to that which Jesus dealt with in this setting.

The Hostile Setting. This parable of Luke 12:13–21 is an oddity, for it doesn't appear to fit in its context. Does that mean it needs rearranging to make it fit elsewhere? Not at all, if we recognize its context, which shows the motivation for it and Jesus' reason for discussing it at this time.

Following the previous parable on effective prayer, a rather vicious struggle ensued between Jesus and the leaders (11:37–54). Strangely, the conflict began at a lunch to which a Pharisee invited Jesus, during which He showed a lack of "good table manners." Jesus failed to wash (lit. *baptize*) His hands, as the traditions of the Jews dictated. Reading the host's mind and being aware of the shady business dealings of the group, Jesus gave one of His most sultry attacks on the leaders' whole system of pretended piety (vv. 39–52). He described them as "full of robbery and wickedness," while playacting the role of saints.

When one of the lawyers objected, Jesus accused them of religious tyranny in league with the prophet-killers of old (v. 46). They had prostituted their sacred offices for personal aggrandizement. Seldom has such a sophisticated group of the pious elite experienced such a rude dressing down. The Lord purposely initiated it to expose their blatant pretensions before the crowd that had gathered.

When Jesus left the dinner, He was jostled and badgered by these "men of the cloth" in a way He had not experienced before in the south (v. 53). In the aftermath, however, the massive crowds continued to grow as He further cautioned His disciples concerning religious hypocrites. He warned that their further assault might mean death for His followers (12:1–12).

The Parable Provoked. As the Lord stressed the disciples' need for spiritual strength in the coming conflict, He was interrupted by a man with a personal problem (Luke 12:13). The man urged Him to come arbitrate a family squabble over finances. That event admittedly seems unrelated to this context, but that is why it is so significant. The gruffness of Jesus' response reflects that (v. 14).

The man was not interested in the spiritual issues about which the Lord spoke, but rather in his personal welfare. He rudely broke into the Lord's address to solicit help for a petty quarrel. Perhaps his family's inheritance was being divided by an older brother who acted as executor for the estate. As the younger, he may have objected to the older brother getting the double share, as the Mosaic legislation directed (Gen. 48:22; Deut. 21:17). Oesterley confirms this, adding, "this, according to the Law, a younger son had no right to do."[13] The man may have been exploiting Jesus' concern for the underdog to his own advantage.

To this Jesus replied with neutrality, denying His authority to judge matters pertaining to property rights. If that seems strange for the One who had claimed messiahship (Ps. 72:1–2), it should be noted that Jesus no longer pursued that program after the Jews' rejection (Luke 9:20–21). His reply in 12:14 was, "Man, who appointed Me a judge or arbiter over you?" To have arbitrated the matter would have only further enraged the rabbis, who generally claimed this jurisdiction.

The Problem Addressed. Though the man's demand was a selfish intrusion and unrelated to Jesus' serious discussion, He responded to it to deal with the insidious problem of greed. Allowing such intrusions was part of His teaching method, a practice also of the rabbis. Jesus' counsel to the man and the crowd was: "Beware, and be on your guard against every form of greed; for a man's life consists not in the abundance of the things which he possesses" (Luke 12:15 RV). Though Jesus had mentioned covetousness (greed) once before among other sins (Mark 7:22), this was His first specific warning of its dangers.

What specifically is covetousness and how does it relate to riches? William Taylor notes the distinction: It is "neither the having of money, nor the desire to have it for the uses to which it may be rightly put; but it is the desire of having it simply for the sake of having it."[14] The poor can be as greedy as the rich, if that is the ambition of their lives. Covetousness is the desire to have what is not your own for its own worth, thus diminishing your trust in the Lord.

Christ responded here with a clarification of *life*. What really is life? He warned that it does not consist in the abundance of possessions. That, of course, ran counter to the prevailing philosophy of the Pharisees, who saw health and wealth as evidences of the Lord's blessing. "No good thing does He withhold from those who walk uprightly," wrote the psalmist (Ps. 84:11). The Mosaic covenant, in fact, promised these blessings (Deut. 7:12–15; 28:1–6). The problem Jesus evidently addressed in this parable, then, might be stated: Since riches and possessions are so much a part of life and were promised to the righteous in the Old Testament, why is it now wrong to pursue those things?

A "Successful" Farmer Described. This parable is one of four example-stories Jesus told (besides the Good Samaritan, the Rich Man and Lazarus, and the Pharisee and Publican Praying). They are unique in that they simply exemplify the truths they teach in the same realm, leaving no doubt as to their basic meanings.

This story in Luke 12:16–21 could apply to any culture. A man had a piece of real estate that brought large returns in grain and other products. Having just reaped a bumper crop and filling his barns to capacity, he saw the need for more storage space and resolved to build larger barns. As he reconnoitered about his upward mobility, he congratulated himself on his good fortune and decided to retire early for pleasure and relaxation. He could live in the lap of luxury with what he had accumulated. That night, however, God dropped in and said to him, "You fool! This very night your soul is required of you; and now who will own what you have prepared?" (v. 20).

The rich man's nicely planned retirement suddenly collapsed. Yet, as an energetic, forward looking entrepreneur, he sounds like an ideal businessman. We might expect that God would compliment him for his business acumen and award him a gold medal. His personal success is what most people live for. Nor is there any indication of cheating, money laundering, or illegitimacy. The man just reaped the bountiful fruit of the land. Yet God called him a "fool" as He announced his soul's departure. What did the man do to deserve that kind of censure?

Why did God issue this harsh judgment for being successful?

The Central Truth. Jesus' brief explanation pinpoints His lesson and the man's Achilles' heel. The ambitious fellow had worked and laid up treasures "for himself," rather than "toward God" (Luke 12:21). The man was completely self-centered. His thoughts were on "I" six times, and "my" five times: "my crops," "my barns," "my grain," "my goods," "my soul." He had factored God out of his world, forgetting that where there is no rain, there is no grain. Such a person, in God's sight, is a "fool" *(aphron).* This is the same term describing the atheist "fool" in Psalms 14:1 and 53:1 (LXX), who said in his heart, "There is no God." *Fool* literally means "without sense."

The man in Jesus' parable, having provided richly for this life, had no thought for the next one, which is eternal. *Life* for him was the accumulation of riches for his own pleasures. He was oblivious to his coming rendezvous with God. He had a classic case of spiritual myopia.

The point Jesus made, then, was that real life is not the accumulation of things for this life, but rather using what God gives for the next. The Lord rarely announces beforehand when He calls an individual for accounting. As Joachim Jeremias put it, the man failed "to see the sword of Damocles hanging over his head."[15] He was so busy "making a living" that he forgot his need for "life."

The Wider Significance. Besides forgetting God and his own spiritual future, this fool also forgot his social responsibilities as a prosperous man. He ignored the claims of the poor for his help. He stored his wealth in the wrong barns. As Ambrose, Bishop of Milan, once said, "Thou hast barns—the bosom of the needy, the houses of widows, the mouths of orphans and of infants."[16] These are the true storehouses for surplus wealth, with the promise of immense interest (Mark 10:21, 30). One of God's banks is called *Benevolence.*

In the following passage, Jesus continued this theme of "smart banking" by repeating part of His favorite sermon (Luke 12:22–24). Reminding the disciples about the simple trust of birds and flowers (who don't have barns or banks to trust in), the Lord again spoke about the Father's tender care for His children. Though unbelievers are like orphans who must fend for themselves, believers have a heavenly Father who cares daily for His own. He is not a delinquent Father.

Jesus followed this in verse 32 with a forgotten reminder as His punch line: "your Father has chosen gladly to give you the kingdom." In effect, He plans to share with us, not just a small inheritance, such as this man was grasping for, but rather the whole kingdom. It is for eternity! The wealth God entrusts to believers in this life is given to check their stewardship and then to develop it for handling eternal wealth (as the next parable will illustrate). As a careful investor, the Father seeks trustworthy stewards to manage His eternal treasures.

This concept of real life is admittedly a strange notion for our generation. The myopic view of this man in hoarding wealth is so prevalent today that we tend to marvel that the Lord didn't commend him. What constitutes *life* for the average person today? For the average businessman? What is the measure of success for entertainers? For advertisers? For TV? For sports? For politics? For almost anything? Extract money from the equation and much of what we call *life* almost loses its meaning.

However, we need to note that Jesus never disparaged the propriety of riches. That will be evident as we examine several later parables on the subject. The "root of all sorts of evil" is not money, but rather the "love of money" (1 Tim. 6:10). Riches themselves are gifts from God to be used for His good purposes (James 1:17). The danger is that wealth so easily usurps the role of master and becomes a destroyer. Jesus' preventative was to place all surpluses possible in His banks. Missionary Jim Elliott put it succinctly: "He is no fool who gives what he cannot keep, to gain what he cannot lose."[17] To reverse that, Jesus said, is to play the classic "fool."

PARABLE OF SERVANTS AWAITING THEIR MASTER (LUKE 12:35–48)

This section of Luke contains several brief sayings as a follow-up to the previous instruction on wealth. Hardly in parable form, they are a string of metaphors on the theme of servants awaiting their Lord's return. Since Jesus later gave several parables on this theme, we will not lengthily develop this one. Each of the others will stress a specific responsibility.

We should notice, however, several emphases Jesus makes at this time. Flowing from His counsel on the use of wealth, He shows also the great temptations and rewards of stewardship. A steward might browbeat his fellow servants with his particular gifts, but will suffer losses and lashes at the Lord's return (Luke 12:47–48). That sounds harsh, and Peter responded with a question that we also ponder: "Lord, are You addressing this parable to us, or to everyone else as well?" (v. 41). Would true believers resort to such a thing? Would the Lord then apply lashes to His own?

Jesus did not really answer that query, but rather left it as an open question. Some of His true servants do at times get drunk with power and become guilty of abuse, as church history sadly testifies. What those stripes will be we can only guess, but the principle He enunciates is an all-time classic: "And from everyone who has been given much shall much be required; and to whom they entrusted much, of him they will ask all the more" (v. 48).

On the other hand, Jesus promised enormous rewards for those servants who remain faithful in stewardship. As the returning Bridegroom, "He will gird himself to serve, and have them recline at table, and will come up and wait on them" (v. 37). In an amazing portrayal of servanthood, Jesus pictures Himself as a waiter or chef donning a uniform to take dinner orders for each of His servants! This is a seven-course dinner with all the trimmings, no doubt! Jesus often served gourmet meals for His disciples, and He looks forward to hosting this special awards banquet for His faithful stewards.

Chapter 10

LUKE'S TRAVELOGUE

Parables on Human Responsibility and Divine Concern

THE ISSUE OF ENTERING THE kingdom was especially emphasized in Jesus' last year of ministry as He dealt more and more with outcasts. His turning from Jewish messianic expectations to worldwide redemption called for many explanations. This provided the setting and opportunity to further clarify His offer of grace. It enabled Him to relate it solidly to human responsibility.

PARABLE OF THE BARREN FIG TREE (LUKE 13:6–9)

Luke 13 continues this instruction to Jesus' disciples as they traveled in Perea. Large crowds followed as He taught in many villages and synagogues. Stressing stewardship, He noted that great privilege brings great responsibility (12:47–48). Israel's failure here would only increase worldwide distress. Though Jesus came as the Prince of Peace, He here announced a radical turn around; His coming would actually bring divisions rather than peace. What is the reason? His role as the Prince of Peace was being rejected by the privileged nation.

Turning to the multitudes, the Lord then rebuked them for their failure to recognize the prophetic significance of that time (v. 56). Though they could accurately forecast the weather, they were blind to spiritual things. They failed to discern the Messiah and to recognize that His presence called for personal repentance. Though the nation's leaders were spiritually blind, the Lord still pressed His ministry to individuals, stressing the need for heart repentance.

The Setting of Two Tragedies. Luke 13 continues this discourse after someone brought word that Pilate had slaughtered a number of Galileans at the temple (v. 1). This occurred as these worshipers were offering sacrifices, probably at Passover when large numbers of Galileans would gather.[1] As Josephus notes, Pilate (the "Javelinman") had threatened and slain numbers of Jews on several occasions, being especially intolerant with zealots from Galilee.[2] This atrocity was reported to Jesus perhaps to provoke Him to denounce Rome. Jesus, however, refused to make it political and turned it into a personal, theological question. Was this a divine judgment on the victims, He asked? Were they "greater sinners than all other Galileans?" (v. 2).

Jesus' answer to this was a definite no (v. 3; in a place of emphasis in the Greek text). God doesn't normally work that way with sinners. To broaden the question, the Lord reminded the people about another recent disaster in Jerusalem, in case some thought the Galileans were spiritually and morally beneath them. (This was an oblique reference to Himself.) Eighteen people were accidentally killed when the tower of Siloam fell on them. Was this natural misfortune also God's judgment for sin? The Lord strongly denied it for either case (vv. 4–5).

Jesus' purpose in this was to refute a long-held superstition that tragedies are necessarily due to the personal sins of individuals. Job's three friends took that view (which God refuted), and somehow it became a doctrinal plank of the Pharisaic system. Even the disciples reflected that notion in John 9:1–2 (some six months earlier), requiring the Lord's correction. Here He clarified it for the multitude. Its great danger is what it implies about survivors—they must be righteous! The healthy and wealthy supposedly need no repentance. This inevitably spawns a massive division between the "have nots" and the "have lots." Jesus strongly refuted it as a heathen invention.

With that clarification, Jesus then made a sharp personal and prophetic application: "but [strong adversative], unless you repent, you will all likewise perish" (Luke 13:3, 5). This He stated twice. *Likewise* means "in the same way" *(homoios, hosoutos),* not just "also," and the

Greek word rendered "perish" *(apoleisthe)* speaks of a violent death (vv. 3, 5, 33). This information will help us to understand His point.

The Problem Addressed. Having twice stressed the people's need to repent or face destruction, the Lord perhaps sounded like a miffed prophet of doom, an Amos or Jonah. Why all this fuss about repentance when everything was going so well? The world was in comparative peace for the first time in centuries; the temple rebuilding by Herod (of all people) was well under way; pilgrims were traveling to the feasts from all countries; and the priests' coffers were being filled. Though Rome ruled, the Jews had gained a degree of freedom to carry out their ritual system. Having suffered much at the hands of Rome and other nations, they felt they were hardly the ones who needed to repent.

Besides, hadn't Jesus just declared that the two recent calamities were not due to divine judgment? That being the case, why all this talk about repentance or coming doom? Though the parable has other applications, this appears to be the basic problem Jesus here addressed. What was the great sin for which this good people needed to repent or face certain destruction?

The Story of a Fruitless Fig Tree. To make His point, Jesus portrayed another familiar scene in Palestine. A farmer had a vineyard in which he also planted a fig tree. Vineyards often included a fig tree at one end and an olive tree at the other as insurance against vineyard failure.[3] This farmer employed a vineyard-keeper to tend the fig tree along with the vineyard.

For three years, the owner came with his fruit basket looking for fruit, but found none. Therefore, he commanded the keeper, "Cut it down! Why does it even use up the ground?" (Luke 13:7). But the keeper responded by saying, "Let it alone, sir, for this year too, until I dig around it and put in fertilizer; and if it bears fruit next year, fine; but if not, cut it down" (v. 8–9). Fair enough and evidently granted. The tree not only was unproductive, but also wasted the ground as well as the sunshine and rain that other crops might use.[4]

The Central Truth. For His Jewish audience, the lesson Jesus taught was painfully obvious. The prophets had often portrayed Israel as "the vineyard of the Lord of hosts" and "the men of Judah His delightful plant" (Isa. 5:1–7; cf. Ps. 80:8; Jer. 2:21). Isaiah had lamented the fact that Israel produced wild fruit, rather than good fruit; looking for justice and righteousness, the Lord found bloodshed and cries of distress (Isa. 5:7). Hosea 9:10 and Jeremiah 24:1ff. also used this figure, portraying the leaders as *figs*, some good and some bad, both in times of judgment. Micah experienced similar grief as he mourned over Judah, finding "not a cluster of grapes to eat, or a first-ripe fig which I crave" (Mic. 7:1).

Jesus then borrowed this familiar imagery to alert the people to God's woeful assessment of the nation. He needed something familiar and gripping, and Isaiah's ancient critique was well known. The similarity to Jesus' time is hard to miss. In this story, the Lord pictured Himself as the Keeper who had tended the vineyard for the Father for three years, seeking fruit. John the Baptist had warned, "the axe is already laid at the root of the trees; every tree therefore that does not bear good fruit is cut down" (Matt. 3:10). Jesus continued that search for fruit with meager results.

What specifically was the fruit the Lord sought from this tree? It was obviously the fruit of repentance issuing in righteousness and justice. The context makes that clear. Malachi's final prophecy, in fact, showed Elijah returning to "restore the hearts of the fathers to their children, and the hearts of the children to their fathers" (Mal. 4:6). Heart repentance was the key to their problem. Though both John and Jesus found early enthusiasm in the nation, they also found scant awareness of sin. The fruit of repentance was hard to come by in Israel.

Think forward to the following spring before the final Passover (Mark 11:13–22). Just before Jesus cleansed the temple, He performed His only destructive miracle—cursing the fig tree. Though it wasn't time for figs, this tree bore leaves, normally coming when the figs were ripe.[5] Finding nothing but leaves, Jesus cursed the fig tree, which quickly withered by the next morning.

Was this an act of anger and frustration because Jesus was hungry? No! It was an acted parable that illustrates His coming judgment on the temple leaders later that morning. The leadership had luxurious leaves of profession—lots of pious ritual; but they were barren of the fruit of repentance.

Jesus followed this with a lesson to the disciples on faith and prayer: "If you say to this mountain, 'Be taken up and cast into the sea,' it shall happen" (Matt. 21:21). That later cursing of the fig tree brought this fig tree parable full circle. Its fulfillment would also remove a mountain of opposition to God's work; like the conniving Samaritans in Zechariah's time, the Pharisaic system had degenerated into a mountainous obstacle to God's spiritual program (Zech. 4:7). As Jesus said in this parable a year before, "If it bears no fruit, cut it down" (Luke 13:9).

Does history bear out this parabolic judgment on Israel? How well we know it does, and almost with a vengeance! At the crucifixion, her priestly system came to an end as the veil of the temple split in two, signifying its demise (Matt. 27:51). Her law-covenant ended also, "For when the priesthood is changed, of necessity there takes place a change of law also" (Heb. 7:12).

After an additional period of thirty-five years of grace, the "axe" of Rome was laid to the root of the nation. Generals Vespasian and Titus besieged the city for three terror-filled years. Jerusalem and the temple were leveled, and the blood of the zealot worshipers at the temple was "mingled with their sacrifices" (Luke 13:1). That brings us back to what Jesus had said before giving this parable: "Unless you repent, you will all likewise [in the same way] perish" (vv. 3, 5).

In recalling this "cutting down" of that evil generation, we should note a necessary disclaimer. The nation was not destroyed as a people, only cut down as a nation and scattered. Paul reminds us that the covenant promises to the fathers were irrevocable (Rom. 11:29). The covenant that ended at the cross was the conditional Mosaic covenant, not the Abrahamic. That Law was ordained as a covenant system, "until the seed should come," whom Paul identified as Christ (Gal. 3:19). It ended as a "covenant system" with Israel, but not as the elementary principles of God's law, which are eternal (Matt. 5:18). The Abrahamic covenant, being everlasting, guaranteed the land and seed to Abraham, Isaac, and Jacob in perpetuity (Gen. 13:15; 17:8; 35:12), and was irrevocably guaranteed by God's oath (Gen. 22:16; Heb. 6:13).

This figure of the fig tree being cut down is similar to Paul's analogy of cutting off the olive branch so that the wild branch (Gentiles) might be grafted in (Rom. 11:17). That arrangement, however, is only temporary, awaiting the Jews' turning to Christ in faith. Then, "how much more shall these who are the natural branches be grafted into their own olive tree?" (v. 24). The fig tree and olive tree symbolize God's channel through which He blesses the world with prosperity (1 Kings 4:25; Mic. 4:4). That special privilege was forfeited by Israel until the day of the Messiah's return when the Jews will see His wounds and turn in national repentance to Him (Zech. 12:10).

This parable, then, had the character of a solemn warning of God's impatience with continued non-response. He would briefly allow another period of grace as Jesus gave His final appeal, failing which, the nation would be cut down. The self-righteous, religious system would no longer "cumber the ground," distorting both the character of God and true righteousness.

The Wider Significance. The application of this parable to the world at large is that the Lord not only is a God of patience, but also of judgment. His patience with sin is really a marvel of His grace. The only explanation for it is that He "is patient toward you, not wishing for any to perish but for all to come to repentance" (2 Peter 3:9). That patience, however, has a limit. As in the days of Noah, "My Spirit shall not strive with man forever" (Gen. 6:3). God's longsuffering has an end. Following a time of grace in which His special ultimatum is spurned, He brings judgment. Such was the judgment of the great flood, the destruction of Sodom and Gomorrah, and Israel's destruction in 586 B.C. by Babylon. And such, also, was the Roman destruction and dispersion of the Jewish nation in A.D. 70.

This, then, demonstrates the principle Jesus enunciated in Luke 12:48: To whom much is given, of them will much be required. If it was demonstrated in the case of Israel, how much more for our generation with its massive doses of God's grace and the ultimatums of His Word.

PARABLE OF THE GREAT SUPPER AND EXCUSES (LUKE 14:16–24)

Like many parables, this story moves from God's kingdom program to His redemptive program, blending them together. It first deals with the concerns of God to "fill His banquet hall," then the needs of sinners to avail themselves of His gracious offer. Though it gives no plan of salvation, as such, it emphasizes both God's provision and man's need to respond. It also moves from the Old Testament invitation for Israel to enter the Messiah's banquet, to the New Testament extension of that offer to Gentiles and outcasts. It has a transitional character. The previous parable (namely, the Barren Fig Tree) dealt with the national need of Israel for repentance; this one deals with the need of all people to respond to God's call.

Since this parable is so similar to that of the Wedding Feast in Matthew 22:1–14, many modern interpreters relate them as two versions of the same story.[6] Matthew, they say, used the story for one purpose, and Luke for another. Besides casting doubt on their veracity as the words of Jesus, this manipulation fails to notice the progress of each in the movement of His ministry. Though their basic frameworks are similar, their settings, figures, and purposes are entirely different. This will become apparent in the message, or second part, of each, showing their basic points to be just the opposite. Each has a unique truth of its own.

Let's first note the movement of the biblical text from the previous parable in order to pick up the story in Luke's travelogue. The parable of cutting down the fig tree concluded with the promise of the vine-keeper to "dig around it and put in fertilizer" (Luke 13:8) for an additional year. This Jesus continues to do in the remainder of chapter 13 by healing a woman and "digging" at the Pharisees.

As Jesus traveled in Perea, Herod's territory, the Pharisees taunted the Savior by saying that Herod was liable to kill Him. Jesus' dry reply was, in effect, "what a shame it would be for the Messiah not to perish in Jerusalem, the slaughterhouse of prophets!" (vv. 31ff.). Calling Herod a "fox," Jesus said He would have gladly protected the "hens" of Jerusalem under His wings, but they would have none of it. Now their "chicken house" would be left desolate—not because of the Herodian fox, but because of the Jerusalem wolves. The Glory of their house was about to depart.

The Historic Setting. In Luke 14, Jesus again found Himself in strange company in Perea, having lunch on the Sabbath with a chief Pharisee. This was His third recorded dinner with the Pharisees, each filled with tension (7:36; 11:37; 14:1). Many other Pharisees and lawyers were also present, perhaps invited after the morning synagogue service.

This gathering, however, was evidently a trap, allowing a man with dropsy to enter and sit in front of Jesus (a violation of rabbinic rules of defilement). Yet Jesus, aware of the plot, accepted the challenge and healed the man with divine aplomb. He graciously lavished God's mercy on the destitute outcast. But He then challenged the leaders with a moral problem: would they pull their own son out of a well on the Sabbath (14:5)?

That question left the leaders speechless and foiled in their obvious plot. Even the great Rabbi Hillel had been healed on a Sabbath. Having tactfully put them in their place, Jesus then used the occasion to teach them some needed "dinner etiquette" (vv. 8–14). Squirming, these elite squires of Jerusalem seethed under the instruction of this "country rabbi" about proper manners at the table.

The importance of this session on proper hosting was obviously not to instruct the leaders on social grooming, but rather to stress some forgotten theological truths about God's kingdom. As they closely scrutinized Jesus, He also observed their conduct as they entered.[7] He noticed how they all scrambled for the choice seats (usually three spots in the middle of the couches), a habit so juvenile that we blush at their antics, which they practiced to a fine art. The Lord first addressed the discourteous guests, then the boorish, conniving host.

Jesus' advice to the honor-seeking guests was to allow the host to honor them, rather than jockeying for places of honor themselves. Though the Old Testament often emphasized this principle (e.g., Prov. 25:6–7), the Talmud so stressed the merits of being a Pharisee as to reverse it.[8] Hillel, of course, was a grand exception. Taking the place of honor is always risky, for it invites humiliation should the host have a special guest to honor. Humbling oneself, on the other hand, always leads to honor (Luke 14:11; Rom. 12:10; Phil. 2:3). This reminder was a grand put-down for these guests, as well as a novel and forgotten route to social status for everyone.

For the host, Jesus also had some revolutionary counsel on giving a dinner (more radical, in fact, than the former counsel). Rather than inviting your friends and relatives, "invite the poor, the crippled, the lame, the blind" (Luke 14:13). In other words, entertain those who can't repay you. This doesn't forbid the common courtesy of showing hospitality to one's friends, but it does discourage entertaining the affluent with selfish, ulterior motives. Such a practice cuts the nerve of true hospitality. To invite those who cannot return the favor serves a higher spiritual purpose, one that reserves a grand recompense for the time of resurrection. Jesus sees even social graces (or disgraces) as objects of remembrance in the resurrection (v. 14).

To summarize Jesus' counsel on entertaining, He advised that guests avoid self-aggrandizement in coming, and the host guard against ulterior motives in inviting. Humility and unrepaid generosity will be richly rewarded in God's time. Were people to practice these principles today, it would revolutionize social graces.

The Problem Addressed. So impressed was one of these guests that he bubbled with excitement: "Blessed is everyone who shall eat bread in the kingdom of God!" (Luke 14:15). Why this sentimental outburst? Did the man discern the ideal about which Jesus spoke as a foretaste of that new social order in the resurrection? All would have good manners then, perhaps? Or did the man presume and revel in the fact that they would all be in attendance at that supper because they were Israelites? He does seem to have assumed that he, at least, would be at that great eschatological feast. Whatever his intent, it led the Lord to give this parable on the Great Supper.

The unspoken question Jesus dealt with was whether this elite, contemptuous group of Pharisees would be at that resurrection supper, inasmuch as they had practically repudiated Jesus as the Messiah. Many of the Jews believed they would inherit the kingdom by virtue of their being children of Abraham (Matt. 3:9; John 8:39).

Did that automatically reserve them a place at that inaugural banquet? In question form the problem might be stated: How will God fill His kingdom or banquet hall, now that the leaders of Israel have shown disdain for His invitation through the Messiah? In giving this parable, a corollary problem was dealt with concerning individual response: What constitutes rejection of the gospel and what constitutes proper reception?

The Story of a Boycotted Banquet. Responding to the exuberant guest, Jesus told the story of another banquet (Luke 14:16–24). A certain man of means planned a grand dinner and invited many of his acquaintances. They apparently RSVP'd with enthusiasm, and the preparations were finalized. At the appointed time he sent his special agent to contact those invited, saying the dinner was now ready. In their responses, however, each gave a cool reception. They refused, saying, "Please accept my apologies." One had purchased some real estate that needed to be checked. Another had obtained five teams of oxen he was anxious to test. A third had just married and felt obliged to stay with his bride. The rest made similar excuses, leaving the agent aghast.

When the generous host heard about this, he was enraged and resolved to fill his banquet hall with others (v. 21). He therefore dispatched his messenger to the slums and skid rows of the city to bring in all who would come. Hearing there still was room after this offer, he sent his messenger into the country highways and byways to strongly urge in any stranger whom he met. The last word of the master was that none of the rejecters would taste of his supper (v. 24).

The Central Truth. Though this parable suggests many truths about the gospel, its primary point relates to the contemptuous Pharisees and lawyers to whom Jesus spoke. They are the obvious counterparts of those in the parable who declined the invitation.

The idea of a lavish banquet for the faithful of Israel was prophesied in Isaiah 25:6, which also constituted the nation's great resurrection passage. Jesus related these two to remind the people about that coming feast. But the Lord's invitation required a positive response, and they gave Him a "busy signal." The shock of the parable is that this negative response appears to have been almost universal— "they all alike began to make excuses" (Luke 14:18). This was becoming more and more true as Israel's leaders—Pharisees, Sadducees, scribes, and Herodians—all united in rejecting Jesus as the Messiah.

Ironically, the three excuses given were all quite respectable, not nefarious. One wasn't holding up a bank and the other running a brothel, and therefore couldn't come. The Pharisees were fastidious to a fault.

Jesus recognized this and tactfully reminded the leaders that the supreme good is often missed by an unhealthy devotion to a lesser good. As McFadyen has noted, the refusers all found themselves fascinated with something *new*: new land, new oxen, and a new wife.[9] Who would cavil with such worthy causes as making a living and caring for a new bride?

Each excuse was legitimate, but not when given the wrong place of priority (as Jesus notes in v. 26). The culpability of each excuse was that it robbed the leaders of their sense of need for that which was the grand goal of life. The Pharisees, in fact, spent most of the time Jesus ministered among them defending themselves and concocting excuses to justify their rejection. Such defenses were also the excuses they used to finally nail Him to a cross (John 11:50).

The primary point of this parable relates also to the purpose for which the invitation was given. In his final statement, the master notes that the invitation was given "that my house may be filled" (Luke 14:23). We would expect his purpose to be that as many poor, crippled, blind, and outcasts as possible might be fed. Being humanitarian, we tend to see God's whole program as man-centered, rather than God-centered. The human dilemma is usually uppermost in our thinking. Isn't the meeting of human needs more important than filling God's house? Our human instincts tend to demand preeminence. The theological question haunts us: Is God only interested in "filling seats"?

The answer is that God certainly is concerned with the human dilemma, but that is not the point of this parable. Jesus' point here is that His kingdom will not suffer loss by the insolence of sinners. Their sardonic willfulness will not derail God's program. No indeed, for the God who "is able from these stones to raise up children to Abraham" (Matt. 3:9), will now proceed to fill His kingdom with outcasts and Gentiles who respond to His invitation.

The parable, then, deals with a radical change in God's kingdom program. It is presumptive and futile to deny the actual refusal of these pre-invited guests, as some critics have done, proceeding then to reinvent the parable in terms of rabbinic literature.[10] If we fail to see God's grace in this story as Jesus emphasizes God's outrage at pious insolence, be patient. The following passage will more than make up for that. The Lord never gives His whole theology in any one passage, and to force every parable to cite John 3:16 is to distort both the parable and theology.

The central truth of the parable, then, is the fact that the Pharisees' rejection of the Messiah would be their eternal loss, not God's; their loss would be the great gain of the ones they despised, the outcasts of Israel and the Gentile world. Jesus used this dinner and contrived trap of His enemies to colorfully display their demise. The pious leaders who used Jesus as a target for insolence at dinner, Jesus declared, would be excluded from God's great banquet. But the outcasts, such as the man just healed, would be the very ones invited to that joyous feast. Jesus was a master at irony as well as at showing mercy.

TWO PARABLES ON COUNTING THE COST (LUKE 14:28–32)

The following two parabolic sayings are intricately related to the previous parable and should be treated with it. They complement and explain each other. Though the addressees are entirely different, Luke linked them together in his presentation (Luke 14:25). The story of the Great Supper was given to the Pharisees alone to emphasize their *exclusion;* these two sayings were addressed to the multitudes that followed Jesus to emphasize and clarify their *inclusion.* As the previous parable stressed the *invitation* to outcasts, these stress the *responsibilities* of outcasts—those to whom Jesus was now turning on the highways and byways. The movement between them is quite dramatic.

The Problem. The problem and central truth of these short sayings are handily seen in the context. The previous parable stressed God's new program of bringing in the outcasts: "Bring Me your poor, your sick, your strangers, and unwanted" (ironically similar to modern Israel's call to its dispersed children among the nations). The invitation was wide open, seemingly to all outcasts, tramps, emaciated, and disenfranchised. Did that mean that being poor and sick qualified them for the kingdom? Was there no need for preparation or commitment on their part? Is God only interested in the poor and always disenchanted with the rich?

The Central Truth. With the problem highlighted, its central truth is painfully obvious. Anyone who comes to Christ must make proper preparation. He must "hate" all his relatives and even his own life (Luke 14:26–27). He must shoulder his own cross, if he is to be Jesus' follower. The Lord insisted three times that only such could be His disciples.

This is strange copy for our generation, with "Amazing Grace" jazzed into the hit parade, and trivialized grace almost flaunted as a personal right. But how does this demand for stringency by Jesus' followers harmonize with the many statements of free grace in the New Testament: "For by grace you have been saved through faith; and that not of yourselves, it is the gift of God" (Eph. 2:8; cf. v. 9)?

It should first be recognized that the term for *hating* one's relatives and one's life is not vicious but rather a Hebrew idiom for secondary love (Luke 14:26; cf. Gen. 29:31; Deut. 21:15). A parallel passage in Matthew 10:37 also says, "He who loves father or mother more than Me is not worthy of Me." Christ demands unquestioned priority and loyalty from His disciples. He declares that principle in striking, categorical terms and, as Geldenhuys put it, "he who is not willing to die the most hideous death, by crucifixion, for the sake of his love and loyalty to Christ, cannot be His disciple."[11] It's hard to read it any other way.

These two parabolic sayings, then, were given to enlarge on this principle. To begin building a great tower on mere enthusiasm without counting the cost and planning its completion, Jesus says, is sheer folly. Such building inevitably leads to shame, and how many monuments to this folly we see (Luke 14:28–30). In the same way, how foolish it is for a king to blunder into a war without checking his manpower and artillery (vv. 31–32)! King Amaziah of Judah foolishly blundered into this stupidity in his attack on Israel. Unprepared, he suffered defeat and ignominy in Jerusalem's destruction in 790 B.C. (2 Kings 14).

Jesus' point was simply that becoming His disciple is no minor commitment, but a life-changing decision. It is not a mere reflex of the emotions; it is a resolve of the heart and mind. His two illustrations stress the wisdom and necessity of such commitment. He Himself was initiating such a building project and battle, having recently announced that He would build His church and battle the "gates of Hades" (Matt. 16:18). Therefore, Jesus said, "If anyone wishes to come after Me, let him deny himself, and take up his cross daily, and follow Me" (Luke 9:23).

The Wider Application. The Lord here stressed that though He invites outcasts, He is not looking for mere "freeloaders." He is not soliciting lazy "deadbeats." He arms His disciples with a trowel and sword—to lay building blocks and handle the sword of the Spirit. For any who just come along "for the ride," He forewarns, "It's a battlefield, brother, not a recreation room. It's a fight and not a game."

Jesus Himself had counted the cost in commencing the building, and He insists that His disciples also make that strong commitment. Failure to make that commitment produces followers like the masses who fed on Jesus' bread by Galilee, but deserted Him the next day when that bread was denied (John 6:66). He stressed, however, that He can accomplish far more with a few committed men and women than with a crowd of curious, self-indulgent observers.

PARABLES ON THE SEEKING FATHER: THE LOST SHEEP, COIN, AND SONS (LUKE 15)

In this final year, Jesus' quest for true followers was pressed further into the highways and hedges. Having emphasized the importance of human responsibility in Luke 13–14, He then stressed the heavenward side of salvation in the parables of Luke 15. Repentance and commitment are important for this life, but their consequences reach beyond the grave to eternity. These are especially portrayed in the concern of the Father in chapter 15 and the forward look of chapter 16.

The flow of these chapters follows from Jesus' previous challenge to the multitude in chapter 14. From that crowd were heard grumblings by the Pharisees and scribes, who continued to dog Jesus' trail, seeking to build their case against Him. In Galilee, they had chalked up His "sins" of working on the Sabbath, violating traditions, and claiming Godhood by forgiving sins. They now detected another flaw in His armor—He associates with sinners. This they saw as outright slumming with the riffraff. The leaders had made that charge against Jesus in Galilee when He chose Matthew, but now they see Him as making the outcasts His parish. "Birds of a feather flock together." Jesus defended this ministry to the outcasts in the north by His proverb of the sick needing a physician. He will now unveil a new perspective—the view from heaven.

The Unique Portrayal of the Father. Few parables have so complete a gospel message as the three on seeking the lost in Luke 15. The chapter has been called "the gospel within the Gospels."[12] Though the three stories are separate pictures, they form a composite portrayal of God's seeking activities—in three dimensions. Luke, in fact, saw them as singular, namely, "this parable" (v. 3).

Together these three parables present one of the most unique pictures in the Bible of God as a loving Father. As the Old Testament portrayed Him as King, ordering His kingdom by law, the New Testament portrays Him as Father, directing His household by love. Both pictures, of course, are true, but the latter emphasizes God's personal relations with people. The story of the prodigal, in fact, describes a boy's journey from rebellion (imagining himself in servitude to a king) to his return and rejoicing under the loving care of a father. What a striking Synoptic picture of the Father!

The Setting and Problem Addressed. The setting of these stories follows directly from the story of the Great Supper and its aftermath. There we saw the Father's invitation to outcasts after the Pharisees' rejection, and the need to count the cost and make a personal commitment. The Lord's conclusion was that, without such commitment, one soon becomes like tasteless salt and useless (Luke 14:34–35). The crowds that followed Jesus, in fact, were not deflected by that stringency, for chapter 15 finds the same outcasts surrounding Him, clamoring for more. They had found a friend in Jesus.

We may then state the same problem for all three parables. Why does Jesus consort with outcasts and sinners if He is, indeed, the Messiah? Why doesn't He kowtow to the religious leaders of the nation and join them in despising the outcasts? Since the Pharisees had stood for God and righteousness for two hundred years, often decimated by the heathen, shouldn't they expect the Messiah to dash to their side and uphold their cause? Why was Jesus such a friend of sinners?

The Three Stories Compared. Though the three parables teach basically the same lesson, they have a progressive movement. None could be omitted without harming their logic and persuasive power. All speak of something lost, but for different reasons.[13] The sheep was lost because of its curiosity or stupidity; few animals are so easily misled as sheep. The coin, or drachma, was lost because of no fault of its own, but rather due to the woman's carelessness. It's not that she intended to be careless, for the coin was probably a precious part of her dowry, perhaps as part of her headdress or necklace. It might be equivalent to a modern wedding ring. The younger son was lost because of a deliberate choice, a declaration of independence. The lad chaffed against his background and wanted the liberty to "find himself." Though lost for different reasons, all were lost.

A significant difference also appears in what the three lost. The shepherd lost a sheep; the woman lost a coin; and the father lost a son. It is often noted that Jesus included both a man and a woman in this search to catch the attention and sympathy of both genders. Each lost something of great personal value, seemingly increasing in the three incidents.[14] The shepherd lost one among a hundred;, the woman lost one of ten, and the father lost one of two. They go from the loss of property to the loss of a marriage symbol to the loss of one's kith and kin. The three parables show a progressive movement toward the greatest loss of all, God's loss of His crown of creation. Though some of the church fathers also saw the losers representing the Trinity, the point of the parable speaks specifically to the loss of the Father.

We may note that each parable also has three movements: a dreadful loss, a careful search, and a joyful discovery. In the first two parables, the shepherd and the woman do the searching; but in the last, the father seems to just wait and watch. He patiently waits until the son comes to himself and then returns to his waiting father. It is important, however, not to draw wrong conclusions from this of a Pelagian sort.[15] The parable does not teach the whole of redemptive theology, but rather seeks to emphasize the special concern of the Father for outcasts.

Notice finally in relating these stories how Jesus brings them to a climax in the last part of the third parable—the attitude of the elder son. The first two solicit the sympathy of men and women concerning a dire loss, leading to the deepest loss of any family, the baby boy. Who wouldn't grieve deeply for that and rejoice at his return! Then with the crowd applauding these happy endings and celebrations, Jesus artfully focuses on the response of the elder brother. All would expect even the gruffest of brothers to join the party and welcome his lost brother, even embracing him. But, surprise! Like the last book of the Old Testament, this story does not have a happy ending. The brother was unmoved.

Yet this brings the movement full circle back to Jesus' detractors. The Pharisees and scribes had grumbled in the background, "This man receives sinners and eats with them" (Luke 15:2). In His end stress, Jesus brought the mirror up to the leaders so that they could see themselves in full color. And that is where this story ends—dramatically so.

The Central Truth Being Stressed. The common lesson of all three stories is the concern of heaven for those who are lost. The "joy in heaven" (v. 7) or "in the presence of the angels" (v. 10) describes the great relief of all heaven at the penitence of one sinner or outcast coming to Jesus. Heaven is more excited over one harlot repenting than all the host of self-righteous Pharisees dutifully doing their rituals or fondling their phylacteries. The Lord would gladly leave ninety-nine such Pharisees in order to search for an outcast

He can salvage. Such was the concern of the Father for the lost, and this was the reason Jesus associated with the "tax-gatherers and the sinners" (v. 1).

A second part of the central truth is the deliberate scorn of the Pharisaic leaders for the strays coming to Jesus. The Lord reserved this painful truth for the climax of the series to show its stark contrast with the joy of heaven. While heaven celebrated, the Pharisees castigated. The elder brother, in his utter disdain for his philandering brother, typifies this. If the younger brother took a slow boat to China and never returned, it would be too soon for the elder brother. The parable colorfully portrayed the religious leaders as being out of touch with heaven, in contrast to Jesus, who made heaven rejoice in salvaging sinners.

The Story of Two Rebellious Sons

We need to look more carefully at the parable of the Prodigal Son, which A. M. Hunter calls the Pearl of Parables.[16] Besides emblazoning the central truth of all three, this story stresses several related lessons that may be summarized by looking at each of the three figures involved (Luke 15:11–32).

The Prodigal Son. The younger son is often called the Prodigal from the description of his "loose living" *(zon asotos)* in verse 13. Used only here in the New Testament, the Greek word means "profligate" or "spendthrift."[17] Like many young bucks coming of age, the younger son wanted to "fly the coop" and be independent, though everything he had came from his father. The lad wanted to "find himself" as a man of the world. Strangely, he didn't find himself until he lost himself and all he had in the world. When he hit bottom in a pigpen "he came to his senses" (v. 17). Only then did he think about his father and home, and only then did he seek his father's forgiveness and mercy.

This frisky lad typifies many young people who come to resent parental restrictions; but he does not represent all youth. The path to clear thinking about God and righteousness does not have to go through the cesspool of profligacy. It is not necessary to taste poison and nearly die to understand its dangers; reading the label will suffice for many.

But this lad does represent many in Jesus' time who had erred from the way and had no place of refuge. The salvation Jesus offered extended not only to respectable Peter and John, but also to Matthew the tax collector (whom the Jews thought to be an embezzler); not only to worshiping Mary and Martha, but also to the immoral woman of Samaria and the Magdalene.

Nor was this lad's reception by his father necessarily normal, one that every stray might expect. A. M. Hunter tells of a "modern prodigal who, on turning up in the far country of a neighboring parish, was advised by the local minister to 'go back home and his father would kill the fatted calf for him.' The prodigal did so and, months after, meeting the minister again, was asked hopefully, 'Well, and did he kill the fatted calf for you?' 'No,' was the rueful reply, 'but he nearly killed the prodigal son.'"[18] The problem often is that too many prodigal sons have prodigal fathers (or perhaps "elder brother" fathers). But Jesus' description here is an exceptional case to describe the exceptional love and concern of the heavenly Father for all who go astray.

The Elder Brother. The "end-stress" on the elder brother carries the point of the Father's concern a step further by making a striking contrast. Though it appears anticlimactic, it is itself the climax. It brings the Pharisees into the picture to see themselves. It also speaks to every age of self-righteous onlookers, who tend to gloat as scavengers over the carcasses of the fallen, rather than seeing them as strays who need saving. In the elder son we see reflected a little of the early church when Saul of Tarsus, for instance, was saved, but was shunned at first by the disciples.

Bringing it closer to home, it also presents a challenge to our generation in which traditional norms of religious and moral behavior are being overturned. The young products of our culture (street people and other deviants) have arisen to challenge the church with its lauded claims of justice and mercy. With whose eyes do we view them, those of the Father or of the elder brother? And how are forgiveness and restoration to be offered to those who respond? It is really a challenge to all who claim godliness, testing whether their attitude toward the repentant best relates to that of the Father or that of the elder brother.

The basic problem of the elder brother is that he had never really met or known his father. He never called him "father," as did the returning brother. Though the unhappy brother became the sole inheritor of his father's "farm," he saw his parent as a master for whom he worked, rather than as a father. Therefore, the elder brother viewed him as a biased master in showering kindness on his renegade brother. To the disgruntled brother it was inconceivable that the fallen should be seen as anything but a horrible example and a subject of derision. The reason was that he himself was a stranger to the father's love, having never received and embraced it.

Two Lost Sons. This brings us to the crucial issue of the story. The Lord's concern was not just for one lost son, but rather for two. Both were lost, but in different ways. One was lost in the world, and the other was lost in the house. The previous stories of the Lost Sheep and the Lost Coin reflect this twofold lostness in that one was lost in the wilderness and the other in the house.

The fact that the father reminded the elder son that "all that is mine is yours" (Luke 15:31) did not mean he was a true believer or son of the Father. Rather, he represents the Pharisees, who had inherited all the accoutrements of divine fellowship the Lord had given Israel. They had the Law, the temple, the priesthood, the offerings, and the covenant land (Rom. 9:4–5). Yet their rejection of the Messiah showed they were not true sons of the Father (John 8:42–44). Like the parable of the Lost Coin, they were lost in the house of Israel.

The question naturally arises as to who was the worst off, the one lost in the world or the one lost in the house? The story strongly suggests the latter, who represented the Pharisees. Why? Because they didn't know they were lost! Their religious busyness and self-righteousness deluded them into thinking they had no need of repentance or justification. They were squeaky clean in their own thinking. That, of course, is one of the Devil's sliest tricks in distorting the gospel. The truth is that no one can be saved without first recognizing that he or she is lost.

The Prodigal Father? At first glance we are baffled at the father's actions in this story. He appears almost "wimpy" in indulging the younger son. Why didn't he put him off at least until the lad's passions had subsided a bit? Then, when the rascal returned, the father seemed too ready to receive him with open arms—like a returning hero. Why didn't the father have the servants "set up another pad in the servants' quarters" and put the son on probation for a while? Why accord him the "best robe" (Luke 15:22; signifying honor and reconciliation), the "ring" (signifying restored authority), and the "sandals" (a symbol of sonship rather than servanthood)? Why kill the "fattened calf" (v. 23) for the vagabond (an honor reserved for worthy guests)?

The father seems carried away with his sentiment and generosity. For this reason some have called this story the "Prodigal God."[19] Whatever happened to payment for sin and punishment here? Even Joseph in reconciling his long-lost brothers didn't let them off the hook immediately (Gen. 44:1–16). He put them "through the wringer," making them sweat out a confession before reconciliation. Wouldn't this quick reception and celebration by the father tend to invite another fling in the world when his son again got the urge to splurge and vent his passions?

This problem has long been wrangled over and needs frank assessment. For liberal theologians, such as Julicher, it suggests that the one thing separating God and man is the recalcitrance of the sinner.[20] The whole idea of the gospel is to break this down so that the strays will come home. According to this view, the doctrine that "Christ died for our sins" (1 Cor. 15:3) becomes a mere mystification introduced by Paul. God is totally forgiving and is willing to forget the past, if the sinner will just do the same. In other words, liberal theologians seem to assume that Jesus presented the whole doctrine of salvation in this parable. That, of course, overlooks the hermeneutical principle of the analogy of faith (harmony of Scripture); it smacks of ancient Pelagianism or modern humanism. It takes the heart out of the gospel and the doctrine of the atonement.

As with all parables, the central point of this story must be kept in mind. It addresses a specific problem in the context with a specific answer as the central truth. That problem concerned Jesus' policy of consorting with sinners and outcasts, and the answer was that the Father Himself was greatly concerned to seek and save the lost, in contrast to the Pharisees. The parable does not presume to outline a whole course on soteriology, or the plan of salvation.

Jesus' point, then, is that He was seeking sinners because the Father was seeking what He had lost from His kingdom. The emphasis is more on what the Father lost than on what sinners have lost. When the shepherd found his sheep, for instance, it was the shepherd and his friends who rejoiced, not the sheep (Luke 15:4–7). When the woman found her coin, nothing is said about the joy of the coin in having a "jingle party" (vv. 8–10). Jesus put the stress more on the kingdom program and what God had lost than on the redemptive program. Jesus says nothing here about redemption, for instance, or about propitiation, expiation, regeneration, or justification. Not that He denied these in the least, but rather that He stressed the great concern of heaven and the Father for what He had lost.

To make this a plan of salvation is to follow the path of liberalism, suggesting the younger son practically saved himself. He picked himself up "by the bootstraps" after coming to himself, and then wound his way back home. Surprisingly, his father doesn't journey to the far country to search for him, buy him out of the slave market, or pay any penalties he might have accrued. The parent just stood ready to receive his son back when he turned up down the road. The story is not concerned with those issues. Jesus simply highlighted the Father's great concern for the lost, which was also Jesus' concern in ministering to outcasts.

This picture of the Father is really one of the grandest of all Scripture. The earthly father portrayed is certainly not a passive, pampering papa. Knowing his son's nature and need to "try his wings" to appreciate home, the father released him to his own desires—and obviously to the care of a sovereign God.

Though risky for some fathers, it is necessary for others. The parent was not indulgent, but rather patient and deeply prayerful, longing for the day of his son's return. As in Abraham's offering of Isaac, the pain for this father was no doubt greater than that of the straying son. At the lad's return, the father didn't wait for him with a switch or require him to grovel in the dust before showing compassion. He unceremoniously dashed down the road to meet the lad, and upon his confession, took charge of an unprecedented reception, restoring him to unrestrained favor and fellowship.

If the father seems almost beside himself in lavishing such love on his son, the occasion required it, as Jesus notes (Luke 15:32). Likewise, the return of just one sinner is cause for all heaven to rejoice.

Several years ago such a joyous event occurred in the rescue of a little girl from a narrow well in Midland, Texas. Having fallen twenty-two feet into the shaft, she lay immobile for fifty-eight hours while crews drilled through rock to get under her, and the world watched and waited. When the paramedics finally were able to follow the drillers to bring her up, all the major TV networks interrupted their programming to show the completion of the heroic effort and the "resurrection" of the little tot. She instantly became the adopted little darling of every home. The whole world rejoiced at her safe return, and congratulatory gifts inundated the home from everywhere. That is what happens in heaven every time a lost sinner is returned to the Father through Jesus. All heaven celebrates!

The Wider Significance. The tragedy of a father losing a son in sin is really the story of both the Old and New Testaments. Isaiah, the great evangelical prophet, began his prophecy with the Lord's lament and sorrowful admission to both heaven and earth of such a divine tragedy (Isa. 1:1–4). God Himself had raised a son, Israel, who not only revolted against Him, but also disowned and abandoned Him as Father.

In his "far country," this son became not only destitute and prostitute, but also totally sick in head and heart (vv. 5–6). Yet the Lord declared the ultimate return and restoration of this son, Israel, to be one of the grand goals of His mercy and grace. His long persistence in waiting for that return is another demonstration of His unbelievable patience. The joy of that return and penitence will be unprecedented (Isa. 61–62). But that scene occurs in heaven today each time a sinner is brought back to the Father's house.

Chapter 11

LUKE'S TRAVELOGUE

Parables on Living Life in View of the Coming Kingdom

THE SUBJECT OF WEALTH and its pursuit is continued in Luke 16. Its glamour and allurements not only affect the young and impatient, but often the so-called mature and successful. Pursuing riches easily becomes an end in itself, almost religious in nature, and believers are not immune to its temptations. To deflect His followers from this Pharisaic preoccupation, Jesus here portrays the experiences of two men mesmerized by wealth.

PARABLE OF THE CRAFTY STEWARD (LUKE 16:1–9)

The first story comes as a bit of a shocker at first, for the Lord seems to commend a slick shyster. An aggressive business agent gets caught with his "hand in the till," so to speak, and then uses the same chicanery that got him into trouble to get himself out of it. Rather than repent, he devised other shady deals with his boss' money to pad his own future and avoid the consequence of his evil past. For this the unscrupulous entrepreneur received praise and commendation. Ethics seem to take a back seat in this little story. How Jesus could tell this story with anything but scorn for the rascal's conniving is often seen as its biggest puzzle.

For this reason the parable has long been considered one of the most difficult to interpret (next to the Laborers in the Vineyard; Matt. 20:1–16).[1] Its variety of interpretations is seemingly endless. Warren

Kissinger notes there are about 36 different interpretations of it on record, and lists more bibliographic entries for this parable (133) than any other, except for the Prodigal Son (254).[2]

All the experts have wrestled with it in search of its meaning. Theophilus of Antioch saw it as a picture of the apostle Paul being forced out of a Jewish ministry to make friends and minister to the Gentiles. Luther called it a good sermon on the need to "help poor and needy people."[3] Walter Rauschenbusch saw it as a warning to the dishonest rich to show kindness to the children of the kingdom so they might get "some sort of borrowed shelter" when the tables are turned and they are at the mercy of the pious poor.[4] Joachim Jeremias felt that Luke 16:9 had to be deleted from the story in order for it to make sense.[5]

The parable's oblique and subtle lesson is most intriguing, but often missed. How could Jesus possibly congratulate an unscrupulous steward, holding him up as a model for emulation? And how are the "sons of this age" more shrewd than the "sons of light" (v. 8)?

This sampling of interesting and diverse opinions on this story suggests the need for great care in determining its meaning. We believe, however, that this shocker of Jesus has a powerful message for every age, especially ours, if it is properly seen in its own context. Let's look for the problem in the historic setting and then pinpoint the central truth being taught.

The Setting and Problem Addressed. Jesus spoke this parable directly after that of the Prodigal Son in Luke 15. The two chapters actually run together as parts of one message. Luke 16 simply continues Jesus' conversation with the disciples and the Pharisees concerning His associating with sinners.

After replying to the Pharisees' grumble in chapter 15, Jesus then turned more directly to instruct the disciples. In both sections He deals with various hang-ups or misconceptions of the sniping Pharisees. As chapter 15 dealt with their wrong attitude toward outcasts, chapter 16 warns against their wrong view of money or wealth. Having noted that the prodigal son squandered the wealth given him by his father, Jesus now refers to an unjust steward who squanders the wealth entrusted to him by his master. Both were enticed and nearly destroyed by riches. The Lord also commends (though in different ways) the manner in which each resolves his dilemma.

Jesus' point in these stories, of course, was scorned by the Pharisees as puerile and unacceptable to their way of life. Recognizing that, Jesus seems to have used these ubiquitous adversaries, always stalking in the "accusative case," as stooges to emphasize by contrast some important principles for the disciples concerning servanthood.

The problem Jesus addressed in the first story relates to the Pharisees' greedy view of riches and their attitude of superiority toward the poor (Luke 16:14). As previously noted, they championed the sanctity of riches on the assumption that the Lord always blesses the righteous (Deut. 7:12–15; Ps. 84:11). Therefore, the accumulation of wealth demonstrates that one is righteous, suggesting also that poverty demonstrates the opposite. That view gave the Pharisees the best of both worlds, supposedly with the Lord's blessing. Recognizing this carnal view of riches and "righteousness," Jesus spoke the two parables in Luke 16 on the use and significance of acquiring riches.

The problem in the first parable concerned the proper use of riches by the godly. Inasmuch as wealth is called the "mammon of unrighteousness" (v. 9), how should the faithful regard earthly riches, and how should they properly use it? If Jesus considered "mammon" an idol, how can one use it for God's kingdom without being defiled or drawn into idolatry? To press the issue closer to home, should true believers concern themselves with money or bother with good money policies for home or business? How about wills, estates, and insurance? Or should this "mammon of unrighteousness" be considered filthy lucre for believers and left for the world to wrangle over?

The Story of Shrewdness in Business. Jesus then told about a certain rich man who employed a steward in whom he had great confidence to manage his business enterprise. The rich man's major business was oil and wheat farming, involving distribution and loans of large sums to customers. Having complete charge of the business, this steward in the course of time began a secret operation of embezzlement and theft. Wind of this came to his master, and the crook was ordered to submit his books, for he was about to be dismissed from his job. The steward pondered, "What should I do?" Recognizing that no one would hire someone convicted of embezzlement, he knew that he would either have to dig or beg, neither of which appealed to this pencil-pushing plotter.

The crook's scheming mind, however, was equal to the challenge, and he came up with a diabolical plan. Quickly calling his master's debtors, he offered to change the books and reduce their debts before submitting his accounts to the owner. To one he gave a hefty 50 percent discount on his oil bill, oil perhaps having a large markup. To another owing 100 cors (over 1,000 bushels) of wheat, the steward granted a 20 percent rebate. Many other "good deals" were made at the expense of the master's bank account.

The steward's plan in this "midnight madness" was to make some quick friends who would treat him with kindness after he lost his job. In effect, he sought to disarm his enemies and enlist their generosity for a future time of need. What he did ethically, however, was to bring others into his fraudulent operation by embezzling his master's goods on a new and grander scale.

The biggest surprise of the story comes when the Lord seems to give His OK to the shady operation. One would expect such an R-rated yarn to be followed by a lecture on the perils of dishonesty. Instead, Jesus stunned His audience by commending the bum. Not only did the owner who was defrauded in the story commend the shrewdness of this embezzler, but Jesus also commended it as something to be emulated by the "sons of light" (vv. 8–9). He, in fact, commanded it by using the Greek future imperative verb tense: "make friends for yourselves by means of the mammon of unrighteousness." There's a puzzler for you! How could the Lord possibly have complimented this rogue?

The Central Truth. It goes without saying that Jesus was not giving His endorsement to pilfering or dishonesty in business. If the Pharisees had heard it that way, they would have nailed Him immediately for promoting lawlessness. They would have found the flaw they were looking for to crucify Him. The Lord, however, immediately gave a rather lengthy explanation to make sure they got the point (Luke 16:10–13).

Jesus declared that the "sons of this age are more shrewd in relation to their own kind than the sons of light" (v. 8). Like the defrauded rich man who praised his scheming manager for his ingenuity in turning the tables by putting all his clients in debt to him, the Lord commended the "shrewdness" of the sons of this age. It wasn't the ethics of this scalawag that Jesus praised, but rather the crook's "shrewdness" *(phronomos)* or sharp thinking in regards to the future. Unlike the "sons of light," this worldling was no dullard in planning for tomorrow. He made the best of a bad situation by using the means he had to prepare for the time when he would no longer have command of his master's money. In this way he turned his former enemies into future friends for the profit of both.

That decision, we have to admit, represents some sharp thinking. Though the Pharisees prided themselves on their mental gymnastics, they met their match in the shrewdness of this entrepreneur as he outflanked his master. The point Jesus made was so shaking, in fact, that they hardly noticed the anomaly of His reference to underworld tactics.

This might be illustrated by the annual celebration in memory of the infamous skyjacker, Dan B. Cooper. On November 24, 1971, he boarded a plane in Portland, Oregon, held the plane hostage for $200,000 in Seattle, then as the plane headed for Reno, parachuted with his loot into the dark somewhere over southern Washington. The man was never seen again, though a small part of the ransom money washed onto the shores of the Columbia River.

Since then, the search for D. B. Cooper has become a legendary ritual, and the thief has become a folk hero because of his slick escapade. The town of Ariel, Washington, celebrates the event annually with ballads, skydiver stunts, and partying in honor of the mystery man—as if he were some kind of Robin Hood. The celebration, however, is not in honor of his thievery or violence in threatening to blow up the plane, but rather for his ingenuity in the massive fraud and escape from authorities (though he may have drowned in the Columbia River). Like the foxy rascal in Jesus' story, D. B. Cooper has become a legendary hero for his calculated shrewdness, despite the infamy of his thievery.

Unfortunately, Jesus' point in this story is too often missed. The "sons of light," Jesus said, should take a lesson from the worldlings in their preparation for the future (v. 8). The ungodly are often quite shrewd in preparing for their earthly future. They work to save and insure themselves splendidly for every exigency until the time of their death, which the Lord, of course, doesn't disparage. But "sons of light," ironically, seem to be dullards by comparison in laying up treasures for their future. We tend to make more preparation for this short life than for that endless life ahead. Jesus' disappointment can almost be heard as He bemoans this drowsiness and complacency on the part of His people.

Making Friends for Eternity. To further clarify His point, Jesus spelled it out in Luke 16:9, "Make friends for yourselves by means of the mammon of unrighteousness; that when it fails, they may receive you into the eternal dwellings." Here He related several parts of His parable to show how believers can overcome that dullness or lethargy concerning eternity.

First, put the "mammon of unrighteousness" to work for eternal purposes. The Greek word rendered *mammon* has a vague background, but refers in Scripture to riches that the ungodly serve and practically worship (Matt. 6:24; Luke 16:13). Though the world idolizes wealth as a god, believers should harness and utilize it as a servant of God. As a god, it is deceptive and unstable, and will "fail" for everyone at death; but riches can be used as an effective tool to fulfill God's purposes.

Second, Jesus urged believers to use that mammon, or money, to "make friends" for eternity (Luke 16:9). This He related to the rogue in the parable who made friends by winning his enemies with the money committed to his charge. Jesus obviously did not mean "buying" friends with gifts as might a shrewd politician, but rather bending every effort to make them friends of Jesus and, thereby, personal friends for eternity. This can be done by using earthly resources to bring the lost the gospel. The result, Jesus said, will be that at the eternal dwellings, those friends will greet and forever thank you for the sacrifices you made to get them to the Father's heavenly home. It will bring an eternal bond of friendship!

The Wider Significance. Though Jesus often spoke about money, He here refers to it as an idol that easily takes the place of God in one's life. Pursuing it can become so demanding as to usurp all of one's time, talent, and energies. Ironically, most of these perish with the using. The wise use of money is to convert it into eternal currency before its value plunges to zero at the grave. "Making friends for eternity" preserves their values and dividends forever.

PARABLE OF THE RICH MAN AND LAZARUS (LUKE 16:19–31)

This famous story is known as the classic "poor man's parable." It makes many contrasts in favor of the poor. Like Nathan's parable of the Ewe Lamb (told to David in 2 Sam. 12:1–4), this story boldly strikes at the pompous rich in defense of the powerless poor. To draw the lesson that it condemns the rich, however, completely misses the point. As the second of two parables on the use of riches, they must be seen together as complementing each other. Both begin with "a certain rich man" (Luke 16:1, 19) and lead to truths about the eternal dwellings. Both also address the question of how the use of riches relates to eternity. The bottom line in each is that final day of accounting.

For various reasons some expositors have denied this story is a parable. One group contends that because Jesus specifically named the man Lazarus, it must relate actual history. (Jesus rarely named anyone in His parables.) Naming characters in a story, however, does not make it actual any more than "Mary had a little lamb" has to be actual history. The name *Lazarus* means "God has helped," similar to Eleazar in the Old Testament, a name most befitting the point of this story. It was the early church, of course, that named the rich man *Dives,* Latin for "rich." Naming characters and places is a common practice in all kinds of stories.

We should note, however, that this is one of Jesus' four "example stories," making their point by a specific example.[6] Rather than referring to two realms of reality that have to be interpreted, they simply exemplify their truths in the one realm described. Being fictional does not minimize their being true to life, for every true parable has this true-to-life feature to preserve its persuasive power.

In an effort to preserve the story's veracity in describing consciousness after death, others have denied that it is a parable. They do this because some have used its parabolic form to mythologize the scenes portrayed, especially the graphic scenes of the flames of Hades. Since it is "only a parable," these contend, it does not have to be interpreted literally, but can be understood symbolically. Reacting to this, other conservatives have sought to make the story an actual event, rather than a parable. They do this with the assumption that a parable is somehow less trustworthy. Thus, they seek to rescue its veracity by claiming that it literally happened. Each view seeks to defend its dogmatic position by the literary character of the story. Which view is the most credible?

The answer to this dilemma lies in the recognition of what is a parable. One of its basic features, as previously noted, is that though it is fictional, it is always true to life. In contrast to a fable or allegory, the parable must be true to reality, for that is what gives it its convincing power. Being so true to life, it can't be argued with. Properly interpreted, its doctrines are always true to reality.

That leads to one of the unique features of this parable. In the second part or end-stress, Jesus opens the curtain to the reality of the afterlife as rarely done elsewhere in Scripture. Though the doctrine of the afterlife is taught in many places, only here is it described in specific terms. This brief opening of the veil was essential for Jesus to make His point on the ultimate meaning of riches, for the Pharisees were challenging Him. Only in this glimpse beyond the grave could the outcome of living for riches be demonstrated.

The Setting and Problem Addressed. When Jesus finished explaining His first parable on the Unjust Steward, the Pharisees had loudly guffawed His put-down of wealth. Luke describes them as avaricious or "lovers of money" (Luke 16:14). In self-defense, they then derided Jesus' doctrine by scoffing His person. The Greek word rendered "scoff" *(ekmukterizw)* means "to turn up the nose," as in spiteful derision (Ps. 2:4 LXX; Luke 23:35). The Pharisees regarded Jesus as hopelessly naive in declaring, "You cannot serve God and mammon" (Luke 16:13). Having heard His previous parable on the need to invest for eternity, they scoffed at Him, defending their love of money. They had made God and mammon to be one, and they loved the union.

The purpose of this extended parable of the Rich Man and Lazarus was to show that God and mammon are not necessarily one. Jesus began by noting that the Pharisees "justify [themselves] in the sight of men" (v. 15). How does that fit into this discussion on money? He also made several other statements that seem to be out of place here, as many commentaries have noted (vv. 14–18).[7] How do these statements about "justify[ing] yourselves" (v. 15), the perpetuity of the Law, and committing adultery fit between these two parables on the significance of riches?

These statements relate to Jesus' central charge that the Pharisees sought to "justify" themselves before people. How does that fit? They construed their accumulation of wealth as a sign of righteousness. What they forgot was that God looks on the heart, rather than the wallet. The things people highly esteem (such as health, wealth, position, and so on) mean nothing to God, and may be detestable (v. 16).

To further demonstrate that charge, Jesus reminded the Pharisees about the Law and Prophets for which they had substituted the traditions of the Elders (vv. 16–18). Though those rabbinic traditions allowed divorce for practically any excuse (even a bad breakfast), the first law of the second table of commands (in the LXX) declared such casual divorces to be adultery and deserving the same penalty as the high crime of murder (v. 18). That Law, Jesus said, is so firm and unchangeable that it will outlast heaven and earth. Therefore, to justify oneself on the supposition that riches is an outward sign of God's blessing, while violating God's Law in the heart, is pure sham and demented thinking.

The problem Jesus dealt with in this parable, then, concerned the Pharisees' misconception of wealth. Like the three friends of Job, these Pharisees had developed a "fat cat" theology that linked health and wealth with being righteous, and sickness and poverty with being wicked (an error even the disciples reflected in John 9:2). In this dialogue, Jesus confronted that question head on: "Does the possession of riches or human comforts have any bearing on a person's standing before God?"

The Tragic Comedy of a Rich Man and a Poor Man. This story might be called, "The Great Reversal of Death." A certain rich man, Dives, lived sumptuously in the highest style and splendor. His life was a continual feast of good health, much wealth, and high entertainment. While living in a palace of splendor with a magnificent wardrobe, he daily feasted on gourmet food and gaiety. His was the ideal life about which many dream.

In the same town lived a beggar named Lazarus who had neither health nor wealth. To help keep body and soul together, some friend carried him each day and flung him down at the gate of the rich man's mansion. There Lazarus spent his time begging and nursing his sores. His only companions were stray dogs who licked his sores and shared the crumbs or crusts used for napkins that were swept as garbage from the rich man's table. Those crumbs were Lazarus' main fare as hunger and starvation daily stalked him.

This tragic comedy came to an end one day when both of these men died. The rich man was buried, no doubt with great eulogies and a grand procession of friends and mourners. His five brothers probably erected an elaborate monument in his honor and perhaps a memorial drive was begun to rid the town of beggars who are such an eyesore to respectable society. ("They become such a nuisance when banquet guests are arriving.") Fortunately, the beggar died on the same day. However, he had no burial, his remains probably being sacked and thrown out with the garbage to the fires of the southern dump called "Gehenna." Though the beggar was hardly missed, the prestigious rich man was no doubt memorialized in the many elite clubs of the town.

On the other side of the veil, however, a strange thing happened. The death angel seems to have made a horrible mistake in deliveries. The soul of the rich man was thrown into hades, the place of anguish awaiting all those who will one day go to the "lake of fire" (Matt. 25:41; Rev. 20:14). Lazarus, on the other hand, was gently carried to "Abraham's bosom" (Luke 16:22), otherwise known as "Paradise"

(23:43). In Pharisaic thinking, the two men were earmarked for just the opposite destinations.

Dives made an impassioned appeal to Abraham, whom he could see afar off. Calling him "Father" (16:24), the former rich man reminded Abraham of his ancestry and good standing as a Pharisee, having acquired wealth and all the touted credentials of Pharisaic "justification." Abraham himself had been a rich man and would surely understand and at least seek to bring Dives some relief. Noticing that Abraham was comforting the former beggar named Lazarus, Dives decided to cash in on the paltry crumbs he had let Lazarus scrounge at his gate. He therefore begged Abraham to send the former beggar with a drop of water to at least cool Dives' tongue.

To this Abraham responded with a most solemn reminder of the finality of one's destiny after death. Unimpressed by the former rich man's credentials, Abraham gave two reasons for which neither Lazarus nor Dives could cross over or communicate in any way to each other. First, they had each made their choice on earth. Dives had basked in wealth and pleasure, while Lazarus found help in God (as Lazarus' name suggests). Second, death constitutes a great chasm that makes it impossible for any to cross over, either one way or the other. There was an awful finality in Abraham's tone.

It should be noted that hades is not the lake of fire, nor is Abraham's bosom heaven. They are rather a kind of "holding zone" for the dead as they await the resurrection of their bodies. At the resurrection of the just, the righteous will bodily ascend to heaven (1 Thess. 4:16–17); and at the resurrection of the unrighteous, the wicked will be judged for disposal in what Jesus called "the lake of fire" (Rev. 20:13–14). Hades and paradise, however, appear to give a foretaste of the final estate of each group.

In desperation, Dives then made another request of Abraham. Again calling him "Father" (Luke 16:27), Dives begged him to send Lazarus on a mission of mercy to his "father's house," to warn his five brothers lest they also be sent to hades. Dives' plea was that such a reappearance and warning by Lazarus would surely shock the five into repentance. Abraham's solemn response, however, was that if they did not heed the Scriptures of Moses and the Prophets, nothing else would move them, not even a resurrection from the dead.

The Central Truth. Jesus told this parable to further explain His word to the Pharisees, "who justify yourselves in the sight of men" (v. 15). The central truth revolves around that misconception. Jesus' lesson is really two-pronged, with the emphasis being on the second part. The first point was the fact that the rich man went to hades and the beggar went to paradise, defying conventional expectations. That great reversal controverts a basic premise of Pharisaic theology; namely, that health and wealth are a certain sign of one's favor with God.

Jesus deftly portrayed the two men with minimal details, showing that the exact opposite often takes place. Nothing is said about the rich man being wicked, for instance, nor about Lazarus being righteous. Dives is not described as a thief or drunkard necessarily; nor is Lazarus portrayed as a devout saint who reads his Bible, prays, or goes to the synagogue. We may assume that the rich man failed to keep the law of love by refusing to share with the beggar, but Jesus says nothing about that in the story.

Jesus' first point is that the rich man died and went to hades, and that the poor man died and went to Abraham's bosom. Though riches or poverty had nothing to do with where they went, Jesus told this story to show that humanistic expectations are often false. The highly touted prize of riches is no guarantee of heaven, and the condition of poverty is no guarantee of hades or of God's disfavor toward a person.

Grasping for riches, then, was one way the Pharisees sought to justify themselves in the sight of men, failing to realize that the things highly esteemed by people are "detestable in the sight of God" (v. 15). Not that those things are inherently wrong, but rather that God looks deeper than mere earthly success to the heart where pride and self-righteousness lie.

The second point of this two-pronged lesson concerns the rich man's request to send Lazarus back to evangelize his five brothers (vv. 27–31). On the surface that suggestion sounds like an excellent, innovative way to win the lost. Why didn't Abraham award Dives some kind of kudo for this brilliant idea? His earnest plea and concern for others seem to suggest his experience in hades had produced a change of heart. The fires *(phlogi)* of "purgatory" appear to have mellowed Dives into a flaming evangel. When told that there was no escape from hades, he pled for his brothers that they might be spared coming to "this place of torment" (v. 28). Such evangelistic zeal seems to equal that of the apostle Paul (Rom. 9:3). Abraham, however, was not impressed and, almost with a wave of the hand, asserted the futility of Dives' grandiose scheme.

That picture appears to put God and Abraham in a rather repulsive light. The former rich man supposedly repented in hades and was willing to take his punishment, but Abraham was unmoved and refused to even consider an alternative that might save Dives' brothers. The grand patriarch appears cold and adamant, while pathetic Dives pleads mercy for others. The former rich man sounds like a converted Scrooge, ready to mend his ways after a trip to the netherworld. Did "purgatory" really change this opulent sinner into a vibrant saint?

Let's look a little closer at what Dives suggested. "If God would just send missionaries from the dead, most people would repent. Maybe all would repent, and there would be no need for hades!" Notice the cynicism. "If God would just do it my way. . . . If only God had an effective plan of salvation. . . . What a pity that God didn't think this thing through more carefully!"

Dives' response doubtless had further implications in defending himself: "If I myself had been warned by someone arising from the dead, I would not have come to this place of torment." He practically impugns God for his being in hades, implying that the Almighty failed to properly alert him. In other words, God's plan of salvation was faulty. In this light, the pretended penitence and evangelistic fervor of Dives turns out to be more of a smoke screen to cover his deeply impenitent heart. Rather than repenting in hades, this former rich man struck at the heart of God, accusing Him of hard-heartedness in failing to show mercy to sinners.

The major thrust of this parable is enshrined in the response of Abraham to this proposal by the former rich man: "If they do not listen to Moses and the Prophets, neither will they be persuaded if someone rises from the dead" (v. 31). Strange as it may seem, people are not moved to repentance by miraculous acts of sensationalism. It just doesn't happen. Witness Pharaoh's hardening his heart after the first Bible miracles performed by Moses; or Ahab's non-response to the miracles executed by Elijah; or Israel's non-response to the mighty miracles enacted by the Messiah Himself. To further drive home this truth, Jesus later raised a man by the name of Lazarus from the dead at Jerusalem's backdoor (John 11:43). The result was hardly a great revival, but rather a new determination by the chief priests and Pharisees to murder Jesus (v. 53).

This final point was that God does not convict and convert sinners by miraculous interventions of mighty winds, earthquakes, or fires. More often, He uses a "still small voice" (1 Kings 19:12 KJV). That still small voice is His Word. Jesus here emphasized the total adequacy of the applied Word of God. By that Word He created heaven and earth, and by that same Word He brings redemption to people (Ps. 19:1, 7; John 1:4, 9, 12–13, 29). Though often impugned by people today as too narrow or inadequate, the gospel is seen as the "power of God for salvation" (Rom. 1:16) to every generation.

How, then, does this relate to the Pharisees' error of justifying themselves in the sight of people (Luke 16:15)? Having reduced God to the size of mammon, they measured spiritual things by physical phenomena and achievements. The rich man's health and wealth became the Pharisees' measure of spirituality. Why? Because it was "highly esteemed among men." Dives' notion of winning his brothers by sending Lazarus back from the dead reflected this same naturalistic approach. The Pharisees sought to justify themselves in the sight of people by humanistic measures. They substituted the "tradition of men" for the Law and the Prophets (Mark 7:8).

The Wider Significance. The rich-man stories of Jesus often had sad endings, for He stressed the perils of mammon and materialism. Those warnings, however, should be put in their proper perspective for our age. Jesus fought a system that saw riches as an indication of one's blessing and, therefore, good standing before God. The problem today is often the reverse. We tend to see the rich as having pulled some shady deals to become wealthy and the poor to have been cheated along the way. Thus, the rich supposedly must be wicked and the poor pious.

However, that was never Jesus' point. The peril He warned against was *trusting* in riches and its wrong use. That is also a peril for the poor, if they see their poverty as something meritorious before God (as we will notice in a later parable). Covetousness is not confined to either the rich or the poor, though the advantage of the poor is that God chose the "poor of this world to be rich in faith" (James 2:5). Both riches and poverty are gifts from God to prepare people for eternity, each affording its special long-term blessings.

A Final Word. In the course of his lecture to the rich man, Abraham made one of the most solemn declarations of the Bible. He underscored the fact that there is no crossing over after death (Luke 16:26). Though many assume that some kind of a second chance awaits the sinner after death, no warrant is given for such a hope in all the Scripture. All crossing over must be done in this life by way of the Cross, a truth that Jesus also stressed in His final warning in the book of Revelation (22:11–14). A finality attaches to death that irrevocably seals one's eternal destiny. Though these are strong and terrifying words, who would be so brash as to question the Son of God, the One who spoke them?

Chapter 12

LUKE'S TRAVELOGUE

Parables on Effective Service for the Kingdom

PREPARING THE DISCIPLES for ministry was all-important to Jesus as He moved toward Jerusalem and the Cross. Following His departure, they would face a myriad of roadblocks and testings in a hostile environment. Though much of that would come from the world, their most immediate problems would come from within.

The disciples could easily become their own worst enemies. Impatience, pettiness, and desires for prominence often arise to put in jeopardy even one's relations with the Lord. Recognizing the inevitability of those traps, Jesus pressed home the danger of several on this final journey south (Luke 17–18). As with other difficult lessons, He again resorted to parables to rivet His truths on their minds.

PARABLE OF THE UNPROFITABLE SERVANT (LUKE 17:7–10)

The next parable in this series of instructions in Perea is a curious little saying that has also suffered at the hands of interpreters—mostly by neglect. It is certainly not one of Jesus' popular stories. Several reasons for this benign neglect might be noted.

First, the parable appears to portray God as a slave driver with little compassion for His working crew. That inclines some to relate it to the Old Testament, but not to the New Testament. Second, this parable doesn't seem to fit its context, with some suggesting that Luke had this story left over and randomly placed it here.[1] Third, the story of a servant working long hours in the field and then asked to do further service in the kitchen, all without thanks, is hard to relate to Jesus. It seems to controvert His teachings about compassion (Luke 12:37). It certainly doesn't fit well with modern labor and management principles. Labor unions would picket this farm as a "sweat shop." The story seems to promote thankless slavery.

Those views are unfortunate, for they miss the point of the parable. Properly understood in its context, this story presents some of the most essential principles for Christian service. It bluntly illustrates a theology of service.

The Parable's Background and Problem. In Luke 17, Jesus turned from lecturing the Pharisees on the perils of avarice to warning His disciples about the pitfalls of Christian privilege. Having emphasized many times the greatness of their position and rewards in the kingdom, He here alerted them to an attendant danger. They could become stumbling blocks instead of stepping-stones. The blessings of grace and high position can also lead to presumption and disregard for others who are weak in faith (Rom. 14:15; 1 Cor. 10:32; 2 Cor. 6:3). Great blessings have a way of making one vulnerable. How can the blessings of effective service be enjoyed without falling prey to this trap of the Devil?

Jesus' counsel for this problem was twofold: neither give nor take offense (Luke 17:1). Guard against becoming a stumbling block, and be quick to forgive an offender who repents—seven times a day if necessary (vv. 2–4). Rather than casually dismiss sin, Jesus required the interaction of both parties to bring about repentance and forgiveness. This was a big order, but most essential for Christian service.

Overwhelmed by this counsel, the apostles then made a strange request: "Increase our faith" (v. 5). We might wonder how this fits and why they didn't ask for *increased love* to forgive seven times a day. Evidently, they saw true faith in God as the ground and inspiration of love.[2] Only faith in God can instill such love and forgiveness.

That request brought the Lord's famous statement on "mustard seed" faith (v. 6). The smallest faith has the power to move mountains or mulberry trees (Matt. 17:20). Jesus' point was that the strength of faith is not in its quantity; it is in its quality or its object. Faith is not measured by its own greatness, but rather by the greatness of its God. Such faith handily moves mulberry trees. The mulberry (sycamore) tree is significant here, for its roots were extraordinarily strong, being able to sustain the tree to the age of six hundred years.[3] Irreconciliation heads the list of such obstacles to effective service, but it is helpless before this kind of faith.

The Problem Addressed. That brief sermon on the power of faith led to the problem Jesus dealt with in this parable (Luke 17:7–10). With such power available, how can God's servants avoid the pride that easily attends such success, thus creating more offense? Samson was mighty, but offended everyone. David was mighty, but that might led to his great downfall and scandal. How can that be avoided? What attitude should believers have when they achieve great success in serving the Lord? And why should anyone say after such success: "We are unworthy [unprofitable] slaves; we have done only that which we ought to have done"(v. 10)?

The Story of an Unthanked Servant. To personally involve the disciples, Jesus solicited their judgment in His story. He put them in the shoes of a farmer who had a bond slave working for him both in the field and the house. Though hired servants worked by the day, bond servants had no specific hours, serving whenever or wherever needed (called "double the service" in Deuteronomy 15:18).

When such a servant completed his work of plowing or shepherding in the evening, he wasn't free to go his way reveling in his great accomplishments. Nor did his owner invite him to sit down to a prepared meal and kick off his sandals for a round of fellowship. Rather, the owner expected him to put on a chef's uniform and prepare a gourmet dinner, after which the servant could fix his own meal. Clearly, the bond servant wore many hats. He moved from one task to another and was not necessarily thanked for each.

Jesus' portrayal of this heartless slave owner is admittedly rather disgusting when viewed from our culture. He hardly sounds civil. It was, however, strictly in line with the culture of Jesus' time as He presents it in this story. Other compensations such as security, provisions, and belonging made up for some of the managerial courtesies we think the owner should have shown.

The Central Truth. Jesus had no compunctions about representing God here by this brusque owner, for His focus was not on the owner, but rather on the servant. A servant of the Lord is a bond servant who serves out of love, not for compensation or even thanks. The Old Testament bond servant allowed his owner to pierce his ear as a sign of continual service. This he did "because he loves you and your household, since he fares well with you" (Deut. 15:16–17).

Jesus' first point here was that a servant of the Lord does not serve by a time clock or for wages, but rather because of his love relation as a bond servant. He or she is not hired by the day, but for life in a covenant relationship. That arrangement might sound scary to some, but not for true servants who know their Master. The designation "bond-servant" was how Paul described himself, as did Peter, James, Jude, and John (Rom. 1:1; James 1:1; 2 Peter 1:1; Jude 1; Rev. 1:1). They had learned the lesson of this parable, and gloried in their bond servant relation to the Lord.

Second, servants of the Lord do not serve primarily for thanks or praise; rather, they serve for the satisfaction of pleasing the Lord. They do not wait for a gumdrop or a pat on the back after each task. Instead, their interest is to move on to the Lord's next assignment. They recognize that this is not a "time to receive money and to receive clothes and oliveyards," which too often brings "the leprosy of Naaman" when wrongly appropriated (2 Kings 5:26–27). Not that God's servants despise rewards, but like Abraham and other heroes of faith in Hebrews 11, they look "for the city which has foundations, whose architect and builder is God" (v. 10). They admit that despite all their service to the Lord, they may retire to a chopping block like Paul, or an inverted cross like Peter. But they defy and confound the world by thanking God for the privilege.

This attitude of not expecting praise is especially essential for those who have experienced success. People who move mountains tend to expect praise. When we have successfully plowed straight and deep furrows or reaped large harvests, the pride factor easily crowds in. What, then, should our attitude be toward success when we have slain our Goliaths, moved multitudes down the sawdust trail, or served the Lord in other ways? How do we properly handle success?

Jesus' application thundered home His answer: "So you too, when you do all the things which are commanded you, say, 'We are unworthy slaves; we have done only that which we ought to have done'" (Luke 17:10). The Greek word rendered "unworthy" *(achreios)* always means "unprofitable" in its other usages (Matt. 25:30; Rom. 3:12; Philem. 11) and should be so understood here as well. Why, then, did Jesus exhort His servants to confess they are "unprofitable" after they seemingly have been very effective in moving mountains? Isn't this a bit tacky or put-on?

Jesus' point was not to pretend humility, but rather to recognize that any real success we enjoy comes from God. Our greatly touted talents are almost incidental to success. God can speak eloquently through a mule, if He has to, or raise up children to Abraham from the stones. But, He has chosen to use us as instruments to fulfill His will.

Billy Graham was once asked why he was so successful in his evangelistic campaigns. Wherever he preached throughout the world, multitudes flocked to the altar. His classic reply was, "I just happened to be in town when God was working." That is doubtless part of the reason for Graham's continued success, and speaks volumes concerning the short-lived success of others. God will not share His glory with another (Isa. 42:8; 48:11).

The reality of this "unprofitableness" is not easily grasped. We may give a tongue-in-cheek confession of it early in life, but gradually succumb to pride as success mounts and we forget that He's pulling on the other side of the yoke. A homely illustration once drove this home for me. While I was building a cabinet in our garage, our seven-year-old son Dave wanted to help. So finally I marked a board I planned to cut (with plenty of margin) and let him saw as best he could. After long effort he finished the cut with some interesting curves. I thanked Dave for his fine job, and he went into the house to proudly tell Mom how he had helped Dad build the cabinet. After he left the garage, however, I re-marked the board, took it out back, and cut it straight while he wasn't looking.

As I reflected on that incident, I wondered how many times the Lord has had to take our proud successes out back somewhere to straighten them out while we gloat over *our* great success. By themselves, even our best efforts are quite "unprofitable," and that is the little secret the Lord helps us to grasp in this parable.

That secret, however, is not just interesting doctrine; it also has great practical applications. It first helps to guard against the big head when success comes, thus stifling the plague that always follows pride, namely, destruction (Prov. 16:18). But it also helps to prevent breakdown and disenchantment when things go awry, simply recognizing that it is God who gives success and who also withholds it at times. This gives stability in service, whether in success or seeming failure. As servants of the Lord, believers are not obligated to always ring up so-called triumphs, but simply to do "that which we ought to have done" (Luke 17:10). The mountains we move are not ours, but the Lord's, and we are not to fret if our best efforts don't seem to move them.

The Wider Significance. Though the Lord's servants are not to expect praise, that does not mean they are not to give it. Rather, they should be profuse in giving thanks and praise to others who serve. The very next story in Luke describes the healing of ten lepers where Jesus carefully noted who returned to give thanks. Only one did, and he was a Samaritan. This, by the way, is the only instance in the Gospels where anyone thanked Jesus for anything (cf. Luke 18:11). What a sad commentary on the state of Israel at that time when God was giving His best! Paul's writings, however, are characterized by constant giving of thanks to God and people.

This exhortation to confess "unprofitableness" should not be confused with the notion of personal denigration. Jesus never downgraded personal worth, but rather elevated the eternal value of every individual (Mark 8:36). As Paul declared, "I can do all things through Him who strengthens me" (Phil. 4:13). The Bible everywhere elevates man's personal dignity as created in God's image. Jesus' point here is that great personal worth and dignity are unable by themselves to accomplish God's work. As Jesus Himself exemplified, every disciple must depend entirely on the Spirit's power.

Though this parable exhorts servants to faithfully serve without seeking thanks or praise, Jesus did not imply that such service would be without reward. Many times He spoke about the greatness of God's rewards for faithful service, giving a specific illustration of it in Luke 12:37. That picture of the Master serving the slaves is just the opposite of this parable of the seemingly thankless master. There Jesus portrayed Himself as putting on a chef's uniform to serve His faithful servants as they recline to dine on His specially prepared gourmet dinner. The difference in the two pictures is that this parable requires faithful service without promise of praise in this life, while the other describes the Lord's profuse praise and banquet for those at the resurrection who have served faithfully here. The two stories give a balanced view of Christian service with respect to rewards in God's kingdom.

TWO PARABLES ON UNANSWERED PRAYER (LUKE 18:1–14)

Prayer was always central in Jesus' life, and He often stressed its vital importance for disciples. Three such exhortations were given before His final emphasis in the Passion week: in the Sermon on the Mount (Matt. 6:5–15); in response to the disciples' request for instruction (Luke 11:1–13); and on this occasion in Perea (18:1–14). Though this parable of the Unjust Judge in chapter 18 is similar to the one of the Borrowing Friend at Midnight in chapter 11, their emphases are different. The circumstance of urgent prayer is much more pronounced here. The next time Jesus asks the disciples to pray will be in the Upper Room and at Gethsemane where that urgency will be sorely demonstrated (22:40).

At this time (Luke 18), Jesus gave two parables as a pair, dealing with two different problems in prayer. The first concerns *unanswered* prayer and the second *unheard* prayer. One emphasizes the need for persistent prayer, while the other the futility of proud and self-righteous prayer. In each story Jesus portrays a disgusting character, one contrasting God and the other representing certain men. Only Jesus, of course, could have properly done that. In both parables the Lord's purpose is declared before the story to indicate its relation to the context. Let's look at that background to see the specific problems that brought forth these parables.

The Background and Problem Addressed. The specific point of the first parable stems from the emphasis Jesus had just made concerning the kingdom. Upon being asked by the Pharisees as to when the kingdom of God would come, He first disabused them of a classic misconception they fondled (Luke 17:20ff.). The kingdom is not primarily an outward display of earthly powers to be observed; rather, it is a spiritual reality to be experienced. It is basically internal *(entos humon),* as opposed to external (Rom. 14:17).[4] It was, of course, already "in your midst" (Luke 17:21)—in the Person of its King (Mark 1:15)— but not presently observable in terms of political movements or marching armies.

That brief explanation to the Pharisees was what triggered Jesus' first description of His second coming to the disciples. To them He declared that He will yet come in great power (Luke 17:24). The time of that glorious coming, however, will be preceded by a period of great sorrow. Jesus Himself will "suffer many things and be rejected by this generation" (v. 25). For the faithful dark days also lay ahead in which they will long for His coming, seemingly without response.

Rather than be preceded by signs, however, that glorious kingdom will eventually come like lightning. As Geldenhuys says, "In general the spiritually alert will probably discern when the time of the second advent is approaching, . . . nevertheless, the actual moment of the advent will arrive suddenly and unexpectedly."[5] If self-proclaimed prophets arise to set dates for its coming, they are not to be heeded as true prophets (v. 23). Just as the judgments in the days of Noah and Lot had no signs to herald their coming, so it will be when Christ returns in judgment to usher in His kingdom.

For those looking for signs, however, Jesus gave some clues. The world in the days preceding His coming will be completely engrossed in material and worldly things (vv. 26–28). As in the days of Noah and Lot when materialism was rampant—home building, marketing, and pleasure—so it will be in the end times. The best preparation for that day, Jesus said, is to "Remember Lot's wife" (v. 32). Why remember her? (She is the only person Christ told us to "remember.") She had set her affections on this world, oblivious to coming judgment. Ending up as a pillar of salt, she became a tragic memorial of the danger of misplaced affections in a world of selfish planning.

Parable of the Unjust Judge and Persistent Widow (Luke 18:1–8)

That announcement of dark and tragic days ahead led to Jesus' emphasis on the believer's place of refuge. This He did with two parables in Luke 18:1–14. The problem addressed might be stated in question form: In the difficult times ahead when justice seems to go begging (as in the times of Noah and Lot), how should the faithful deal with injustices that will abound? Should they fight, desist and play dead, compromise with the world, or what action should they take?

Jesus then told about a certain judge who refused any responsibility to God or people. He might have been an appointee of Herod whose character he reflected. In the same city lived a poor widow who came seeking protection from her adversary. Perhaps she was about to lose the land she inherited from her husband or an only son in military service. Though defending widows and the defenseless was the judge's primary job (Ps. 82:2–4), he heartlessly shrugged her off. Priding himself on being independent and obliged to no one, he used his office for his own selfish ends.

In this widow, however, the judge met his match, for she was relentless in plaguing him for judicial help. That persistence finally broke him down, impelling him to reluctantly bring her justice. His motivation was, "lest . . . she wear me out" (Luke 18:5). The word for "wear me out" *(upopiadze me)* literally means "give me a black eye."[6] Not that the judge expected violence from her, but rather that he feared her constant bugging him would drain and drive him to distraction. She won her case by persistence and refusal to accept injustice.

The Central Truth. Jesus portrayed this odd couple to describe God's great concern for His elect who suffer unjustly, especially those who cry to Him day and night, seemingly without avail. The relationship Jesus describes, however, is one of contrast rather than direct comparison (as in Luke 11:5–8, Borrowing Friend at Midnight). It is another "how much more will God" parable. God is the true Judge and Avenger, not only for widows and orphans (Deut. 10:17–18), but also for all His elect who cry for justice.

Jesus' argument here is classic. If a base, pigheaded, earthly judge will finally succumb to the urging of a defenseless widow for whom he couldn't care less, how much more will the Righteous Judge speedily come to the defense of His own who persistently cry to Him for justice. This rare usage of the term "elect" in Luke 18:7 emphasizes God's care. A greater contrast could hardly be made to stress the Father's great indignation against any adversaries who would afflict His chosen ones.

The statement about God bringing justice "speedily," however, seems to conflict with the elect crying out "day and night." How can both be true? That seeming delay is related to His longsuffering (*makrothumei,* "delay long") in verse 7. God's delay is not due to reluctance, but rather to His longsuffering and desire to fulfill all His purposes concerning His elect (2 Peter 3:9).

God's delays often mean He is planning something better than the deliverance requested. When Jesus delayed coming to the struggling disciples on the raging sea, for instance, He later came at the fourth watch to show Himself Master of the sea. In delaying to come to the sickbed of Lazarus, allowing him to die, Jesus fulfilled His grander purpose of resurrection for a witness to the nation. Likewise, the Father often delays His answers until the most propitious moment, at which time He brings about justice with great speed and thoroughness. He doesn't leave His children in the fire of affliction a moment longer than necessary, but allows time and patience to fulfill His perfect will in their lives.

The Application and Appeal. That central truth, as Luke states it in his introduction (Luke 18:1), has a broad application. It relates to the coming of difficult times between the suffering of the Son of Man and His return in judgment. When believers suffer injustice, their primary recourse is to be persistent in prayer to the Father, the heavenly Judge. If His answers are delayed (as He appears slow to respond), in all probability He is preparing a greater blessing while building one's faith and maturity. His answers are never late. Even when justice seems to go begging, it is not a time to lose heart, blame God for unconcern, or attempt to force justice on our own. It is rather a call for persistent prayer, knowing that "the Judge of all the earth" will indeed "deal justly" (Gen. 18:25).

In His conclusion, Jesus emphasized this urgency of prayer by leaving the disciples with a question. "When the Son of Man comes, will

He find faith on the earth?" (Luke 18:8). His implication was that, like the days of Noah and Lot, so massive will be the unbelief of the time that persistent faith will be rather scarce. Not that there would be no faith or that perfunctory prayer would cease, but rather that the costly, agonizing prayer about which Jesus spoke and later exemplified in Gethsemane would be hard to find. Like Lot's wife, many will be so engrossed in worldly interests that lackadaisical faith will be more fashionable than daring, persistent trust. But those that persist like this woman will find God's answer to overwhelm injustice, even in an unjust world.

Parable of the Pharisee and Publican Praying (Luke 18:10–14)

The second of these parables on prayer is one of Jesus' better known stories, perhaps because of its satirical portrayal of the "holier-than-thou." That pretension is today held in quite universal contempt, especially by the "smarter-than-thou's." Few that disdain it, however, fail to catch a glimpse of the sly fellow in the mirror now and then. This anecdote of Jesus is a classic put-down of self-righteousness, a fault that easily afflicts all of us on occasion.

To make His point, Jesus called onstage another odd couple representing two prominent segments of His audiences. Rather than using a symbolic parable with strange figures to interpret, He called the two men by their professions, a Pharisee and a tax collector. In these example-stories (as the Good Samaritan), the lesson is quite evident, for the story exemplifies its truth. Here Jesus is as direct as an arrow. The Pharisee, of course, represents the professional religionists of the day who had made prayer and religion a "performing art." The contrasting figure is a tax collector (publican), who, because of his connections with Rome and the notoriety of his craft, was regarded as a traitor to the nation. The name was synonymous with "sinner." But again, the most startling point of the story is Jesus' assessment of them after they prayed. For His listeners, the story was like a religious bomb.

The Setting and Problem Addressed. Having stressed the need for a faith that persistently waits on God in times of trial, Jesus noticed some of His ever-present "friends," the Pharisees, tuning in (Luke 18:9). Though others were included, Jesus' special target here was the Pharisees. Self-righteousness to them was a prized virtue they felt they had dearly purchased.[7] For two hundred years their fathers defended their religious heritage, and recently they had seen many of their own crucified by Herod.

During this long battle with the "*goyim*" or heathen Gentiles, the Pharisees developed a code of religious regulations and a sanctimonious lifestyle to preserve that godly heritage. The pious prayer of this Pharisee, in fact, was not unusual, but typical of a Talmudic prayer for those who were strict Law-keepers *(habarim).*[8] They shunned defilement and bristled with "godliness." One would think they had a continual entrée to the divine throne at all hours. Their every move had a religious rhythm.

It would be wrong, however, to imagine that Jesus had only these Pharisees in mind in this instruction on prayer. The problem He addressed was far more universal. He had detected in His own group a growing pride and cynicism toward the less "spiritual" or those who were not privileged to be with Jesus. His own were certainly not immune to this bug of self-righteousness.

That background brings us to the problem Jesus dealt with in this moving picture: With what qualifications or attitude should one approach God in prayer? What kind of righteousness does He require of those coming to His throne of mercy? Inherent in this problem are also the dangers that often plague the righteous, who strive to live lives of separation. How should the virtues of godliness affect one's attitude and demeanor toward other people, as well as toward God?

Two Men Praying in the Temple. Jesus described a common scene in Jerusalem of two men going into the temple to pray. One was a pious Pharisee and the other a penitent tax collector (Luke 18:10). The part of the temple they entered was the outer court, since only the priests were allowed into the inner court. The time of day was probably 9 A.M. or 3 P.M., the scheduled times for prayer at the temple. Standing apart from others, the Pharisee prayed with his head lifted up to heaven. The phrase rendered "praying thus to himself" (*pros;*

v. 11) could be "about," "for," or "to" himself, all three of which would be apropos.

The Pharisee's prayer was all thanksgiving, but he focused on his own virtues. He thanked God that he himself was "such a lovely fellow." Obliquely, he congratulated the Almighty for having the good judgment to choose such a fine specimen of mankind as he. His prayer was both an exposition of what he was not (namely, the common herd of sinners around him) and what he did (namely, fasted and tithed; vv. 11–12).

By these two religious activities the Pharisee reminded God of his surplus of virtues, for neither were commanded in the Law. The Law commanded tithing of all the Israelites produced, but not of what they acquired (Lev. 27:30; Num. 18:21; Deut. 14:22–23; Matt. 23:23), a feature over which the rabbis often quibbled. The Pharisee reminded God of his super-sainthood. His recital practically put the Lord in his debt, in case the Pharisee might think of something he needed, which he didn't (fortunately).

Besides reminding God of his surpassing greatness above "other people" (Luke 18:11), this Pharisee also called the Sovereign's attention to the depth of the sins of some people among whom this saint was obliged to live his life of perfection. Halos so easily tarnish among the riffraff! Observing a stray tax collector that had wandered in and was "beating his breast" (v. 13), evidently for some great sin, the Pharisee had occasion to again point out his own great superiority over the common herd.

This tax collector was the second figure Jesus wanted us to observe. Going to the temple was for him a strange experience, indeed, but his load of sin was apparently so great that he was impelled to find his way there, if only to stand in the back. There he made his confession. Far from lifting up his head or his hands, as the Pharisee no doubt had done (Ps. 28:2), this penitent would not even lift up his eyes. Rather, he beat his breast as a gesture of guilt, and began quoting David's penitent Psalm 51, "God, be merciful to me, the sinner" (Luke 18:13). Perhaps the tax collector had learned this psalm long ago at Sabbath school in the synagogue. Certainly no Old Testament passage could have been more apropos as he sought mercy from the Lord.

The Central Truth. Jesus followed this portrayal with His own evaluation of the two prayers and a principle that summarizes His point (Luke 18:14). Both of these men received what they requested—only because the Pharisee asked for nothing. The penitent tax collector went home justified, while the Pharisee went home proudly self-satisfied. One was "blood-washed," the other, "white-washed." Jesus summarized His point by applying a principle He had used several times: "Everyone who exalts himself shall be humbled, and he who humbles himself shall be exalted" (Luke 14:11; cf. Matt. 23:12).

Both of these men sought justification, but in two different ways. The Pharisee touted his own justification, while the publican sought the Lord's. One pled on the basis of merit, the other on the basis of mercy. The Greek word rendered "be merciful" (*hilastheti;* Luke 18:13) means "be propitiated" or "be satisfied" (used only here and in Hebrews 2:17 in verbal form). This aorist passive imperative form asks God to "be propitiated" or satisfied concerning one's sin on the basis of an appropriate sin offering, so that reconciliation might be effected, as Jesus the High Priest does in Hebrews 2:17. Not that this publican would have understood all that, but Jesus here introduced the concept. The man acknowledged himself as "the sinner" (Luke 18:13; perhaps a chief of sinners, as Paul in 1 Timothy 1:15), humbling himself in penitence. For this, Jesus said, the tax collector went away justified, rather than the Pharisee.

The principle with which Jesus concluded this story helps to pinpoint the central truth (Luke 18:14). The proud inevitably face humiliation, but the humble, exaltation. That principle is a key to prayer as exemplified in this parable. Not that the publican was "justified" for his humility, but rather that his prayer was heard because he humbly acknowledged himself as "the sinner" (v. 13), seeking God's mercy. The Lord does not hear those who plead their own righteousness, for "God is opposed to the proud, but gives grace to the humble" (1 Peter 5:5; cf. Prov. 3:34). He gives His righteousness to those who humbly confess their sin and seek His mercy.

The Wider Significance. Jesus' pronouncement of the publican being justified was an outrage to many of His listeners. He seemed to be turning religion upside down, as Linnemann has noted.[9] Isaiah had warned against justifying the wicked and depriving those in the right of their rights (Isa. 5:23). For the Jews justification was the judicial recognition of the righteous, not the judicial pronouncing of sinners as righteous. Thus, Jesus' pronouncement of justification by faith was seen as sheer heresy.

At best the tax collector might have been forgiven, had he made restitution plus one-fifth, and brought his offering to the priest (Lev. 6:4–7). But Jesus turned that around, justifying the sinner on the basis of the Savior's own impending sacrifice. This allowed the man to then make restitution to others because he was now justified, not to become justified. That doctrine would soon be demonstrated in the salvation of Zaccheus (Luke 19:2–9), and later thoroughly developed by Paul in Romans 1:17ff. Its introduction here by Jesus, however, is most striking. It colorfully contrasts one who was denied it because he tried to claim it on his own merit.

The concept of being "holier-than-thou" has thoroughly soured many today on what we call "Pharisaism." People are more apt to pray, "God, I thank Thee that I am not like this Pharisee. . . . I resist any kind of 'legalism' and 'let it all hang out.' . . . I am not a prude. . . . I thank Thee that I am not a hypocrite, but am transparent and respond to my inner urgings, since they are the real me. . . . I thank Thee that I am not like this Fundamentalist, . . . this Holiness Arminian, . . . this straitlaced Calvinist!"

Pharisaism has been so lampooned by our generation that much of its good has been forgotten and thrown out with the bathwater. It is well to remember that the Pharisaic movement was rooted in a glorious past as their fathers valiantly stood for godliness when it cost them dearly. Many of the virtues this Pharisee extolled were exhorted in the Old Testament.

The problem with the Pharisee's prayer was not so much what he said, but the fact that he said it. Righteousness, like beauty, turns sour when it becomes self-conscious and forgets its purpose to glorify God. Likewise, championing Christian liberty in the wrong way can become proud and egotistical. Our generation is not so much in danger of becoming "super saintly" as it is of throwing out the virtues for which the Pharisees stood. Those virtues, of course, were not the subject of Jesus' satire; instead, it was the error of the Pharisees' parading them as a garment of righteousness.

Summary. These two parables exemplify two grand principles of effective prayer—how a believer, by prayer, can procure God's justice in times of trial, and how anyone can secure God's mercy for salvation. The first illustrates God's great concern to bring justice to those who wait on Him for His timing. Even a helpless widow can procure it by persistent prayer. The second illustrates how anyone can receive God's justification by the humble prayer of faith. Even a jaded publican can receive it—not by producing a dossier of merit over a long life of striving—but rather by seeking God's mercy with a sincere heart of humility.

Chapter 13

FINAL PARABLES ON REWARDS IN THE KINGDOM

ON THIS LAST JOURNEY TO Jerusalem, Jesus continued to minister grace and healing, especially to the common people of the Transjordan. The leaders' animosity only enlarged His ministry of showing mercy to these outlying areas. Anticipating His final departure at the cross, He also stressed in these last months some vital issues of discipleship.

After holding and blessing little children in Matthew 19:13–15, Jesus was challenged again to clarify how one might obtain eternal life. This led to several other questions about the afterlife and God's reward program. The first discourse took place here in Perea (as recorded by Matthew) and the other in Jericho (as recorded by Luke). Both discourses followed conversations with rich men that provoked Jesus' counsel on receiving eternal riches.

PARABLE OF LABORERS IN THE VINEYARD (MATT. 20:1–16)

The parable Jesus tells in Matthew 20:1–16 again zeros in on employer-employee relations and their constant haggle over wages. Jesus was always concerned for the common working class, being one of them. Many of His stories were built around their struggles. Though this story deals with activities peculiar to that time, it has a unique message for every age. Wages are always important to working people and not less so to God's workers.

The spiritual problem Jesus deals with in this parable concerns the principles of God's reward program. The passage and its context are, in fact, perhaps its classic treatment in the Bible. Yet the subject is seldom taught from this passage. The probable reason is that it has been interpreted so many ways that there is a general haziness as to its meaning. Some call it "the most vexing and irritating of all for present day readers."[1] One of the parable's biggest problems is what Jesus meant by all the workers receiving the same wage, whether they worked all day or one hour. The owner seems irrationally generous on the one hand and coldly unfair on the other. Justice again seems to go begging.

This then has generated a surplus of interpretations (as in the Unjust Steward). Augustine and A. M. Hunter saw the story as teaching the equality of all believers in receiving the gift of eternal life.[2] Blomberg echoes this popular view in saying "he makes plain that there are no degrees of reward in heaven."[3] Others (e.g., Chrysostom) say the parable teaches that strenuous effort in a short time can make up for the shortness of the time one serves.

For some (Calvin) the story is a warning to those who have run well to beware lest they let down and be outrun by others, as the "turtle and the hare."[4] Some (Henninges, Linnemann) see it as a contrast between the long, grudging service of the Pharisees and the quick response of outcasts and tax gatherers.[5] Still others see the parable as a contrast between the covenant of the Jews and the grace given to Gentiles.[6] It has even been used by some Muslims to validate their late coming on the scene (after the Jews and Christians), making them superior as the "last" made "first."[7]

The emphasis the story makes on sovereign grace, however, is generally recognized. Oesterley sees it as another instance of God's grace applied to rewards. Taylor relates it to the spirit in which one serves, and Morgan saw it as rewarding fidelity to opportunity. For Jeremias, the whole emphasis of the parable is God's generosity. The list goes on and, though the emphasis on grace is quite obvious, a general vagueness persists as to the parable's specific point.

What does it teach? Again the key is found in discerning the problem raised in the context.

The Historical Setting. This parable forms the conclusion to Jesus' discussion on two questions in Matthew 19:16–30, dramatizing His final point. The chapter division here is unfortunate. The two questions concern eternal life and eternal rewards—certainly the most profound anyone could ask. The first was posed by a rich and devout young ruler in Perea: "Teacher, what good thing shall I do that I may obtain eternal life?" (v. 16).

Strangely, the Lord did not answer as we might expect. He replied in Jewish terms, stressing two requirements: (1) keep the Law by giving up all your riches (the man's idol), and (2) follow Jesus (v. 21). It's not that keeping the Law would earn the man eternal life, but rather that its purpose was to convict him of sin, for riches had become his god. The man's response in walking away shows he didn't recognize his real need or his problem of being lost. He appears to have been looking for a pat on the back from this traveling Rabbi, rather than seeking eternal life. Clutching his riches, the man preferred them to following Christ and accepting the corresponding risks and sacrifices.

The sad response of this young man brought Jesus' statement of how difficult it is for the rich to be saved (v. 23), another shock to Pharisaic theology (Prov. 10:22). As previously noted, even the disciples still harbored the notion that wealth was an outward sign of God's approval. They also reflect that attitude in their next question: "Then who can be saved?" (Matt. 19:25). To this Jesus replied that though it is humanly impossible, the rich can be saved, but only by trusting God alone, not their riches (v. 26).

It was then that Peter posed the second question concerning rewards. Noting the rich man's refusal to give up riches and recalling their own great sacrifices, he asked the personal question: "Therefore what shall we have?" (v. 27 NIV). To put it bluntly, what rewards are in store for believers? This triggered Jesus' discussion on rewards, a subject all would like to have clarified. Having received salvation, what further benefits are there for a believer in making the many commitments the gospel requires?

Some regard this question as reflecting Peter's carnality and therefore unworthy of discussion. The Lord rebuffed a similar concern by the sons of Zebedee, James and John, shortly after their mother had negotiated for them (Matt. 20:20). When we recall the rabbis detailed doctrine of works leading to salvation and rewards, we might suppose the subject of rewards itself was alien to Jesus' doctrine.[8]

That, however, does not appear from Jesus' immediate response (19:28–30). Rather, He used this question as an opportunity to summarize for all of us the broad principles of God's reward program. Peter's question simply reflects the Jewish mode of thinking in concrete and practical terms.[9] As Jesus and the apostles had often discussed rewards, Jesus used this occasion to outline its basic principles. They are twofold.

The first is given in verses 28–29: Every sacrifice for Jesus' name's sake will be greatly rewarded. This was meant for both the disciples, who will "sit upon twelve thrones," and everyone forced to leave relatives or possessions for Him. Those sacrifices, He said, will bring immensely rich dividends.

The disciples needed that incentive, then, as they were giving up so much for the gospel. But it is equally needed in our day of many solicitations for time, talent, and money. The remuneration Jesus promised was "one-hundred fold," (Mark 10:29–30). Such a promise should make any enterprising businessman pant and want to pawn all his assets to invest in these "futures." Jesus painted them as strictly "blue-chip" stocks. The tendency for most, however, is to respond with surprised awe, muttering piously what a great idea it would be for someone else. It is, however, brutally important for all in God's reward program.

The Problem Addressed. The Lord then added a second principle in Matthew 19:30 that led to the parable: "But many who are first will be last; and the last, first." That statement He repeated in 20:16 in reverse order. Mark 10:31 gives the same principle in the order of Matthew 19:30, and Luke 13:30 gives it in the order of Matthew 20:16 (though in another discourse). Only in Matthew 20 is it illustrated by this parable. How, then, does this reversal of expectations relate to the following parable of the Laborers in the Vineyard?

Though the statement by itself is a bit puzzling, it capsulizes the problem and point of the parable. Who, then, are the first that will be last and the last that will be first in God's reward program? Is Jesus talking about the Pharisees and the disciples, Israel and the church, the rich and poor, the lost and saved, the talented and untalented? If He spoke only about believers, does He teach that all believers will receive the same reward at the bema judgment? What specifically is this principle that Jesus adds to the crucial issue of rewards?

The Story of a Landowner Paying His Workers. This story portrays another common scene in Palestine, the hiring of workers for the grape harvest. Extra seasonal workers were required for this work. One fall a certain landowner went to the marketplace early in the morning to hire a crew into his quickly ripening field. Following the usual haggle over wages, he agreed to pay them a denarius each for the day's work and sent them into the vineyard. This was the normal wage for field workers at that time, working a shift of twelve hours from sunrise to sunset.[10]

Sensing the need to speed the harvest (perhaps before Sabbath), the landowner sought additional workers at nine o'clock, noon, and again at three in the afternoon. With these, however, he made no agreement for wages, but rather promised to give them "whatever is right." Again at 5:00 P.M., as the crop ripened in the hot sun, the landowner went to the marketplace and hired all he could for one hour. When he asked why they were standing idle, they replied, "Because no one hired us" (Matt. 20:7).

At six in the evening the workers were paid, following a custom of the Law (Lev. 19:13; Deut. 24:15). For some reason, however, the owner had the paymaster pay those hired last, first, and those hired first, last. To their delight and the others' chagrin, these latecomers received a denarius, a full day's pay for one hour's work. That, of course, excited everyone, suggesting to the twelve-hour vets that they would receive a similar bonus of generosity. To their dismay, however, they also received a denarius, the wage they had bargained for.

At this scrupulosity these tired workers grumbled and became haughty at the owner. They felt cheated and demanded an explanation. Having endured the toil and heat of the day, they were baffled at not receiving more than those that loitered most of the day and worked but an hour. Their beef seemed legitimate. To this the owner replied that he had kept his bargain with them and had a perfect right to be generous to those who faithfully worked the last hour. Having shown justice to the first group, he was perfectly free to show mercy to the others. He was, after all, the owner. His final word to them was a challenge as to whether his generosity had evoked envy in them, hardly a trait of the godly (v. 15).

The Central Truth. Though the parable has received many explanations, its intended meaning must relate to the context of Peter's question. That eliminates a number of very attractive options that have been suggested. The view that takes the story as a prophecy of the Jewish leadership being replaced by that of the Gentiles is provocative, but has nothing to do with the question. Nor is it a picture of the Pharisees' and publicans' position being reversed, though that argues some interesting analogies; it doesn't relate to the problem. Likewise with the popular view that all believers will receive the same reward—eternal life.[11] Though well-intentioned and true to salvation theology, that also is foreign to the discussion at hand. The parable was obviously given to elucidate Jesus' second principle of rewards in which the "first will be last, and the last, first" (19:30). The lesson must relate to this and Peter's question about believers' rewards.

An obvious clue to the central truth is given in 20:7, where the landowner asks the latecomers in the market why they were standing idle. Their reply was, "Because no one hired us." They were not producing simply because they had not had the opportunity. That excuse might sound frivolous and inappropriate, since they failed to be at the marketplace at hiring time; but Jesus' story ignores that. He simply gives it as their adequate reply for which they were sent into the vineyard. The point stressed is that they worked diligently and faithfully while they had opportunity and were rewarded with pay similar to the daylong workers. Their reward was obviously a gift of the owner's grace, simply because of their faithful service when hired, rather than because of their production or longevity.

The central truth, then, concerns God's plan to reward His people, not only for their sacrifices, longevity, or production, but also for their faithfulness to opportunity. The implication is that though many believers are limited by impossible circumstances, their case will not go unnoticed by the Sovereign Lord. He ministers both justice and grace. Having encouraged the disciples that their many sacrifices will be richly rewarded, the Lord then reminded them about this extension of His grace to the less fortunate. He has a plan of "affirmative action" for those who have had fewer opportunities, but have faithfully used what they had while they could.

In essence, Jesus' answer to Peter's question was: "Yes, Peter, your sacrifices for Me and the kingdom will bring immense rewards. But there are many others who are not of this flock, many who will follow Me in the years to come from distant lands and different races, many whom you would not even notice; they may receive as great rewards as you." These rewards will not be determined by one's position as an apostle or preacher, the amount of "splash" made in kingdom work, evangelistic statistics compiled, or long years of service. Jesus will also factor in the underlying circumstances of each believer and how faithful he or she has been to opportunities afforded.

Corollary to this is the Lord's condemnation of the "hireling spirit" in service.[12] That is the attitude of serving the Lord on a bargain basis of so much reward for so much effort or sacrifice. Jesus stressed in a previous parable that His servants are not hirelings or mercenaries on contract, but rather are bond servants for life. They serve because of love rather than to stack up merits for rewards. Though productive service will be richly rewarded, that is not the whole story. Jesus warns against any spirit of bargaining with the Almighty, for all His gifts are due to His grace.

The Application. At its conclusion, the parable shows many of the workers surprised at their wages. In a similar way there may be many surprises in heaven when the Lord bestows His honors, crowns, and rewards. Some who have labored long, acquiring grand credentials and statistics—perhaps swaying multitudes by their oratory—or have gained high positions in Christian work may be standing first in line, so to speak, with their impressive lists of kudos. To these the Lord may have to say, "Stand back here," while He ushers forward many who have been "last."

It may be the poor widow who gave her last two mites, or a tongue-tied boy who radiated the Lord's love, or a church janitor who quietly served behind the scenes, or a faithful Sunday school teacher, or . . . or . . . who served the Lord to the best of their abilities. To such He may say, "You have been faithful in a very little thing, be in authority over ten cities" (Luke 19:17). Their rewards may be similar to that of the apostles.

In His sovereignty, the Lord will measure greatness on a higher scale. He will evaluate all circumstances of each believer to bring both justice and mercy into play in His grand awards program. Fidelity to opportunities will be the prominent factor. David used a similar principle in awarding his troops in 1 Samuel 30:24: "For as his share is who goes down to the battle, so shall his share be who stays by the baggage; they shall share alike."

The Wider Significance. Those two principles have immense overtones. They stress an often-forgotten fact about the believer's life to come. Though we had no choice in picking our genes or chromosomes for development in this life, that will not be true for the life to come. No one asked us before we were born, for instance, what we wanted to be like. We were not given a list of options to check off: rich or poor; tall or short; handsome or homely; red, yellow, black, or white; talented, musical, artistic, or "just plain vanilla." We simply took what we were given without personal choice.

If that seems unfair, the Lord shows that it will not be so for the life to come. The choices we make in this life will largely determine the character of our life to come. Every individual is entrusted with the personal decision of not only their eternal destiny, but also their eternal character. That is certainly part of the message of Matthew 20:1–16.

In 2 Peter 1:1–11, the apostle gave this lesson an interesting sequel. He reminds believers to continue preparing their souls, or personalities, for that new life to come. He begins by stressing our need to add seven virtues to our faith, which he calls partaking of the "divine nature" (v. 4).

Some might ask, however, "Why be bothered inasmuch as all believers will be like the Lord in the resurrection?" Peter supplies the answer: "For in this way the entrance into the eternal kingdom of our Lord and Savior Jesus Christ will be abundantly supplied to you" (2 Peter 1:11). Peter used the Greek word rendered "supplied" *(epichoregethesetai)* only here and in verse 5, where he exhorts believers to "add" (NIV) to their faith.

The apostle's point is that if we "add" these virtues to our faith, the Lord will "add," or supply, a rich and abundant entrance into His eternal kingdom. These virtues are moral excellence, knowledge, self-control, perseverance, godliness, brotherly kindness, and Christian love (vv. 5–7). Interestingly, when we add these virtues to faith, they make a perfect octave. Adding these will enlarge our capacity to enjoy the riches of God's eternal kingdom; but we must appropriate them in this life. We do this by being faithful to the opportunities God provides.

The apostle Peter had learned that lesson well and reflected it in his final words to the church: "But grow in the grace and knowledge of our Lord and Savior Jesus Christ" (3:18). Why bother to add these virtues to faith? It's because they will greatly enhance our capacity to glorify God and enjoy Him forever.

PARABLE OF THE POUNDS ENTRUSTED (LUKE 19:11–28)

Following Jesus' extended ministry in Perea, He moved toward Jerusalem for the final Feast of Passover. Like Joshua before Him, Jesus crossed the Jordan shortly before Passover and on the way brought a taste of salvation to Jericho. There He healed two blind men and brought salvation to the house of Zaccheus, attesting again His messianic mission to both the down-and-out and the up-and-out (Luke 19:1–10).

Jesus' main ministry, however, in the fleeting hours before the cross was to prepare the Twelve and His other followers. Having just reminded them about the greatness of God's reward program,

Jesus again had to emphasize the immense stringency that lay ahead (Matt. 20:17–19). Even His most explicit statements about impending crucifixion were not accepted as literal, so intent were the disciples on immediate glory.

The Problem in the Historical Setting. With Passover approaching, the road to Jerusalem was filled as pilgrims came early to prepare for the Feast. Increased tension filled the air as Jesus and His disciples also approached the city where the Sanhedrin had ordered His arrest. Despite this, many of His followers still expected Him to turn the tables, zap His enemies, and set up the Davidic kingdom. Passover season seemed an ideal time to break the tension and launch His political career.

It was in this setting of expectancy that Jesus had to puncture the disciples' balloon of imminent ecstasy. How do you gracefully deprive children of candy and whet their appetite for what appears to be more like sauerkraut, especially after Jesus had just blessed the outcasts with healing and salvation? To impress these difficult truths, Jesus again reached for a parable. The problem He dealt with was really twofold. First, would Jesus now set up His kingdom in Jerusalem and vanquish His enemies, or what new direction would the kingdom take? Second, what would the role of the disciples be in this new program? Already they were jockeying for positions of glory in an earthly reign of His kingdom (Mark 10:37).

The Story of a Nobleman Seeking a Kingdom. To counter such self-centered thinking, Jesus then told about a nobleman who went to a far country to receive a kingdom. The journey was necessary to validate his rulership and squelch the hatred of his citizens who spurned his rule. To maintain his affairs during his absence, the nobleman commissioned ten of his servants, giving each a pound with which to trade.[13]

When the nobleman later returned with kingly authority, he first rewarded his servants, each according to his productivity. The rewards the ruler gave were various positions over the cities of his realm. The greater part of the story, in fact, concerned this awards program, seven verses of which deal with the negligent servant. Then, in accord with the custom of oriental princes, the noble-man ordered the destruction of his enemies who had rebelled against his rule.

This parable in dialogue style struck familiar chords in Jewish memories, especially around Jericho. Most of the Herods had gone to Rome to secure from Caesar their right to rule. At the death of Herod the Great (4 B.C.), his son Archelaus, whom his father had appointed to the throne, had traveled from Jericho to Rome to obtain investiture from Caesar Augustus. Having already drawn the hatred of the Jews for his brutality, however, Archelaus was trailed to Rome by a large delegation of accusers. These not only prolonged his stay with lawsuits, but also finally influenced the emperor to deny him the kingship and put him on probation.[14] Archelaus then ruled as an ethnarch over Judea, Samaria, and Idumea for ten years. In A.D. 6, he was removed from office and banished for his continued barbarity.

Though the brutal rule of Archelaus is best remembered, that journey was also made by Herod the Great, who had fled to Rome to confirm his right to rule. That sordid memory no doubt lingered and recalled for the disciples a change of government largely dependent on foreign sovereignty. That bit of history Jesus used to remind His followers of a greater change that was about to take place.

We should not confuse this parable with the similar story of the Ten Talents, which Jesus gave several days later during Passion Week (Matt. 25:14–30). Many have imagined the two to be different versions of the same story, artfully rearranged by the Gospel writers.[15] Accepting the Spirit's inspiration of both texts, however, leads us to a more sober evaluation of their uniquenesses. In reality, their differences outweigh their similarities. Jesus gave them at two different times to two different audiences at two different places to resolve two different problems with two different casts of characters. Even their central truths are quite different. The apparent similarities are mainly structural and incidental to their purposes, as we will note in the later parable of Matthew 25.

The Central Truth. In answer to the disciples' first mistaken notion (Luke 19:11), Jesus told this story to clarify what changes were about to take place in God's kingdom program. The pressing throngs were anticipating a crisis, sensing something violent approaching. Yet they were suppressing those dark feelings for the moment. Inspired by Jesus' recent groundswell of acclaim as He moved toward Jerusalem, the disciples eagerly conjured up an immediate fulfillment of David's empire. They found repulsive Jesus' recent revelation of His impending death and resurrection, and they apparently dismissed it as unthinkable (18:31–34).

Yet this parable added a further depressing thought to that of Jesus' coming death; He would not return for an extended period. To give shocking realism to this central truth, Jesus used the haunting memory of the Herods' journeys to Rome to legitimize their reigns. Jesus would also soon leave without establishing His glorious kingdom. But, coupled with it, He gave assurance that He would later return after an extended period to fulfill that Davidic promise. Without that return the very purpose of His departure to obtain the kingdom could not be realized.

Having stressed this central truth of the coming kingdom, Jesus next gave a corollary reminder of stewardship. Most of the parable, in fact, is given over to this truth of individual responsibility during the interim. Commentaries frequently see it as the primary emphasis.

The nobleman gathered ten of his servants to commission them to "do business [occupy, *pragmateusasthe*] till I come" (Luke 19:13 NIV). He gave each of them a small pledge (a *mina*) with which to trade in a hostile environment. Surprisingly, this king-elect did not leave them a cache of swords with which to do battle while he was away, as other claimants might. Rather, he simply gave each servant some money, which they could invest in various ways.

As in the parable of the Laborers in the Vineyard, this awarding event is the heart of the story. Highlighting this awards ceremony serves to make two basic points: the wisdom of careful investing and the folly of neglect. Unlike the previous parable, however, the servants here are rewarded according to their production. All were given an equal amount of money, but the multiplication of ten brought the first one authority over ten cities, and the increase of five gained rule over five cities. The point is that faithfulness and effort in the use of "a very little thing" will bring huge returns in the kingdom (v. 17). That, of course, was not a new revelation, yet it needed constant stress in a world of many attractive options.

The story, however, focuses most of its attention on the negligent servant. That appears to be Jesus' primary caution at this time. Keeping the coin wrapped in a napkin revealed not only his fear and timidity, but also his disobedience and lack of trust. The excuse of hiding it was really a cover-up for refusal to identify with the nobleman who commissioned him (v. 20).

With that excuse, however, the servant also showed malice toward his master by the rationale he used. He blatantly accused his master of being a hard man, able to "take up what you did not lay down, and reap what you did not sow" (v. 21). The servant saw his master as impossible to please and not really in need of his help. In theological terms, he typifies the sluggard who excuses his laziness on God's sovereignty. "The Lord is able to do everything Himself—evangelize the lost, feed the hungry, and establish His kingdom—all without my help."

Interestingly, this nobleman does not deny the statement, but rather simply dismisses the servant without even thanking him for the compliment. In fact, the ruler declared the servant's loss of even what he thought he had (v. 24). Giving that extra mina to the one with ten simply emphasizes the blessings of obedience and the dire consequences of disobedience. It is a drapery detail that lends further realism to the king's disgust. The inference is that those who show such zeal in kingdom service are in line for vastly more.

To distinguish these servants from the ungodly, Jesus concluded the parable with a note on the fate of the enemies of this king (v. 27). They would be slain in his presence at his return. He called them both "his citizens *[politai]*" and his "enemies *[exthrous]*" who refused his proper reign over them. That note rounds out the story that began with the hatred of the countrymen, which made necessary the nobleman's departure. Likewise, this last journey of Jesus to Jerusalem was under the cloud of sinister enemies. They were in hot pursuit of Him, seeking some convenient way to arrest Him.

Summary. This story is another parable with several parts to its central truth. Many modern commentators, of course, disallow more than one basic point to a parable and see this pericope as a fusion of several stories from the "debris" of Jesus' parables.[16] Even Joachim Jeremias, who rejected Julicher's one-point limitation, accuses Luke here of having his stories mixed up.[17] If we accept the text's accuracy as divinely given, however, it is obvious that several points stand out. The twofold problem required this. Concerning the kingdom, Jesus alerted the pilgrims to the fact that He would soon depart without fulfilling the anticipated Davidic kingdom; yet, He would later return to bring those promises to a glorious fruition after an extended period of absence.

Concerning the plight of the faithful, Jesus reminded the pilgrims that each would receive an earnest of the kingdom for which they would be held accountable. At His return, He would reward them in proportion to their individual efforts. His special caution, however, was for those who fail to take Him seriously, those who presume on His gracious sovereignty to excuse their indolence. Jesus nailed that pious tendency with a solemn warning. In this parable, then, He combined those basic reminders to alert the pilgrims on their way to that last Passover. Intense and brutal days lay ahead, but He assured them that the day of kingdom glory would eventually come at the King's return.

The Wider Significance. As the previous parable of the Laborers in the Vineyard encouraged the "least," or "last," by the fact of God's gracious sovereignty in rewards, this parable warns of presuming on that sovereignty. Balance is always needed for effective ministry. Jesus' teaching, in fact, often stressed different facets of a doctrine to make a point, which He usually counterbalanced elsewhere.

The acceptance of outcasts in the parable of the Great Supper (Luke 14:16–24), for instance, is balanced by the following instruction on the stringency of discipleship. Far from calling mere "freeloaders" to salvation, Jesus welcomed all outcasts to come "for free"—but on His terms. That balancing motif is also evident in these two parables on rewards. While we thank God for His gracious sovereignty, we dare not presume on it as an excuse for indolence.

An interesting progression should also be noted in these two parables concerning the environment of Christian service. While the first one stressed faithfulness to opportunities without regard to production, this parable enjoins productive service even in a climate of hostility. Production, of course, is not necessarily a head count or list of statistics, but rather an indefinable fruitfulness that follows faithfulness. Not even a climate of belligerence can squelch such service, for that is its native soil. Though the King is absent and His enemies entrenched, believers are to boldly and wisely use their resources. Failing to put them to work for fear of failure is anathema to God's program, inviting stagnation and an eventual loss of rewards.

The pity is that this tendency to inaction or complacency is often the norm rather than the exception. As Paul declared in 1 Corinthians 3:15, some will be saved "as through fire," having no rewards. Mere good intentions will count for nothing. Jesus' word to the faithful in this parable was not, "Well thought, good and faithful servant," but rather, "Well done" (Luke 19:17). Inaction in the face of need is intolerable in God's program.

Chapter 14

FINAL PARABLES TO REJECTERS ON LOSS OF THE KINGDOM

As Jesus approached that final Passover of A.D. 33, a flurry of events were taking place. The massive gathering of pilgrims for Passover (estimated by Josephus as over two and one-half million in A.D. 70) had spread out in tents around the city.[1] Since the Sanhedrin had an alert out for Jesus' arrest (John 11:57), He went first to Bethany, where He stayed at the home of Simon the leper (probably the father of Martha, Mary, and Lazarus). This had become like a second home for Jesus. That Sabbath evening, Martha served Him a meal and Mary anointed Him for His burial (as Jesus interpreted the latter event).

The following morning, Jesus entered Jerusalem riding an untrained colt as great throngs hailed Him "the Son of David" (Matt. 21:9). This "Palm Sunday" was also the tenth of Nisan, the day Jewish families set aside their lambs for Passover. Jesus, however, called it their special day of "visitation," long foretold by the Old Testament prophets (Luke 19:42–44). As demonstrated by Sir Robert Anderson, Harold Hoehner, and many others, it was the final day of Daniel's sixty-ninth week, after which the Messiah would be cut-off (Dan. 9:25-26).[2] Jesus wept over the people's failure to recognize this and its disastrous consequence for the city.

In the temple that day, Jesus healed the sick and briefly met the chief priests, who chided His "arrogance" in accepting homage from the people (Luke 19:39). They were miffed and outraged. It was the next day, however, that Jesus openly challenged these Sanhedrin leaders by asserting His messianic authority (20:1–8). Prior to that, Jesus had overturned the tables of the money changers and dispersed the crowd. He then cleansed the temple courts and shut down the whole commercial charade (19:45–46). It had become a bazaar (called "Annas' Bazaar") of priestly impudence as the sale of lambs with exorbitant exchange fees lined the high priest's pockets.[3]

This second cleansing of the temple especially kindled the fury of the Sadducees, who had been relatively inconspicuous to this point.[4] They and the Pharisees, of course, were traditional foes, joining forces here only to rid themselves of this One they considered their common enemy.[5] Whereas the Pharisees were Hebraists and rigid legalists, the Sadducees were Hellenist Jews who discarded all traditional writings but the books of Moses. While the Pharisees served among the common people and ran the synagogues, the Sadducees were the aristocrats who ran the temple. Later confrontations with Jesus not only will reveal their differences, but also their common hypocrisies. From this point on, however, it is mainly the Sadducean leaders, under the bigoted rule of Annas and Caiaphas, who orchestrated much of the travesties leading to Jesus' crucifixion.

PARABLE OF THE TWO SONS ASKED TO WORK (MATT. 21:28–32)

For these priestly clerics, this second cleansing of the temple was the ultimate indignity. They regarded the temple as their exclusive domain and were enraged at its disruption during Passover season. This was their most lucrative week of the year as they orchestrated the sale of lambs to pilgrims from far and wide. To answer their rage and defend His actions, Jesus challenged them with three parables, leaving them with a sharp warning.

The Problem Addressed. The following morning (Tuesday), the chief priests and elders confronted the Lord as He taught in the temple. Having nursed their outrage overnight, they wasted no time in asking Him: "By what authority are You doing these things and who gave You this authority?" (Matt. 21:23). For them it was a burning issue, jeopardizing their clout with the people.

In rabbinical fashion Jesus responded with a counter question: "Was the baptism of John from heaven or from men?" (Luke 20:4). If the leaders wanted a game of hardball, He deftly put the ball in their court with a serve they hadn't expected. To say "from heaven" would show them condemned before God (Matt. 21:25); to say "from men" would enflame a riot by the people who still revered John (v. 26). Taking a quick caucus on its implications, they then pleaded ignorant: "We do not know" (v. 27).

That left Jesus with the ideal setting to expose the leaders' dereliction to duty and loss of temple authority. He simply turned their question of "authority" around and put them on the hot seat they intended for Him. If they couldn't recognize the authority of John as the prophesied forerunner—or knew it and failed to respond—they were hardly qualified to sit in the seat of Moses or the prophets. Their temple franchise as God's agents had run out. Sensing this jeopardy too late, they brooded in silence. The Lord then used their frustrated silence to emblazon their delinquency before the people with three common anecdotes. In the first, He prodded them with the basic question: "When God speaks from heaven, how should true priests of the Lord respond?"

The Story of Two Contrary Sons. Jesus' first picture was a drama of real life for many fathers in the audience. Two boys were asked by their father to work in his vineyard. One responded positively, but failed to act. The other said no, but later regretted his impudence and went (Matt. 21:28–30). Jesus then drew these clerics into the plot with another jeopardy question (one they answered this time, but wished they hadn't). "Which of the two did the will of his father?" (v. 31). The leaders' logical response again put them in a convicting noose of their own making.

Many have noted that this story is given differently by various versions of the Bible.[6] Some (KJV, RSV, NIV) give it with the first son saying no, and later repenting and going, and some (NASB, NAB, NEB) with the first saying yes, but not going. Those variations are traced to the ancient Greek codices (Sinaiticus and Vaticanus), which reverse them. It is generally agreed, however, that the basic meaning of the parable is not appreciably affected either way. Using the NASB with the latter rendering relates well to its application, first to the leaders who asked the question and then to the outcasts.

The Central Truth. Jesus' immediate interpretation leaves no doubt as to what He meant, relating it to His question about John's authority. Since the leaders refused to answer that question, Jesus obliged them with it in this parable. To make sure they got the point, He used several loaded metaphors that He immediately interpreted: "tax-gatherers and harlots will get into the kingdom of God before you" (Matt. 21:31). Why did Jesus issue this offensive slur at these leaders? Besides deserving it, they desperately needed it to correct, if possible, their blasphemy of John's authority. The leaders' contempt had gone so far that they were deaf to heaven's call, even after seeing its saving effect on sinners of all classes (v. 32). They were unresponsive to every signal from heaven.

Jesus' central truth, then, was a strong indictment against the leaders of Israel. Claiming to be vice-regents of God, they showed their contempt for God's program by despising one of His chosen agents. The long expected forerunner had come, and they treated him like dirt. How could such leaders be trusted to shepherd God's flock? To follow them would bring disaster, as Jesus' next two stories will show. His purpose here was to answer the question about John, which the leaders refused to answer, and to contrast their pious pigheadedness with the blessing of the Lord on the outcasts who were responding to God's grace.

The Wider Significance. Ingrained in this parable is a principle that runs throughout the Bible: Refusal to be corrected inevitably shuts one off from the blessing of God. Though that applies to both the saved and unsaved, this parable highlights its effect on the ungodly leaders of Israel and the outcasts, both of whom were lost. The principle showed itself also in a previous parable of two sons, that of the Prodigal in Luke 15:11–32. The son least likely to respond, in both cases, was the one who did respond. Why? It's for the simple reason that each came to the end of himself and responded positively to correction. Though the independent, self-sufficient son had good intentions, his pride and rejection of correction cost him the blessing of life.

The principle especially applies to those who are successful or in other positions of leadership. Its perniciousness is that it so easily afflicts the self-sufficient or elders in the faith. David, for instance, fell at the height of his career, requiring a special parable through Nathan the prophet to bring him to his senses (2 Sam. 11–12). Many other good kings of Israel also fell, but unlike David, they refused the correction of the prophets (Asa, 2 Chron. 16:7–12; Joash, 24:20–25; Uzziah, 26:16–21). Each ruler met disaster after early success, reminding us that a special vulnerability attends those who enjoy successful leadership but fail to reckon with its perils and accountabilities.

How, then, can one properly discern the Lord's correction? How is it distinguished from mere acquiescence to others' desires, whether for doctrine or practice? The context of this parable answers that problem in Jesus' question to the chief priests about John's authority (Matt. 21:25). Was it from heaven or from men? Did the leaders have a word from heaven on the coming of such a forerunner who would prepare the way for the Messiah? They did, indeed (Isa. 40:3; Mal. 3:1; cf. Mark 1:2). But the Sadducees had discarded the prophets, and the Pharisees subordinated their message to the "oral traditions" of men. The leaders had lost touch with heaven. The authority of God's Word is always the key to discerning the correction of the Lord. Any pious diversion from it inevitably ends in disaster sooner or later.

Ironically, these temple keepers were fulfilling Malachi's prophecy about them at the Messiah's coming: "He will purify the sons of Levi and refine them as gold and silver" (Mal. 3:3). The leaders represented the house of Levi. That very afternoon, both the Pharisees and Sadducees stood before Jesus in the temple experiencing some of the fire of His cleansing (Matt. 22:15–46). While the vilest of sinners found cleansing and redemption in His words, those refusing correction experienced only the heat of His judgment. Those words, however, were also written for our admonition so that we might constantly be corrected by His Word to serve Him effectively (Rom. 15:4; 1 Cor. 10:6, 11; 2 Tim. 3:16–17).

PARABLE OF THE WICKED TENANTS (MATT. 21:33–46; MARK 12:1–12; LUKE 20:9–19)

Known traditionally as the Wicked Husbandman, this parable followed immediately after the preceding one in Matthew, being recorded also by Mark and Luke. Jesus here continues His dialogue with the chief priests. As the parable of the Two Sons answered the question of John's authority, this one answers the question of Jesus' authority, the real crux of the issue: "By what authority are You doing these things, and who gave You this authority?" (Matt. 21:23). Its inclusion in all three Gospels shows how central it was to the whole conversation. In it, the person of Christ comes center stage as the owner's "son" who was sent and slain.

This parable neatly ties together many features of God's kingdom program from the Old Testament to its capstone in the ministry of Christ. His following quotation from Psalm 118:22–23 rounds it out by showing His final exaltation as the "chief corner stone." It is almost a history of the kingdom in capsule form. Beginning with Isaiah's well-known "song" of the "vineyard," it moves from that description of God's planting and tender care of the nation to His later sorrow over her lack of fruit (Isa. 5:1–7).

Inasmuch as the prophet used many metaphors to portray that history, Jesus also peppered this story with symbols to bring that "song" of the "vineyard" up to date. Few of His parables are so resplendent in colorful figures as this one. Yet He gave only broad hints of their meanings, in contrast to His more detailed interpretations of some of His earlier parables (for instance, the Sower, the Tares, and the Two Debtors). The obvious reason is that the "song" of Isaiah was so familiar that these additional figures needed little explanation.[7]

This generous use of metaphors has caused many liberal scholars to reject this parable as the actual words of Jesus. They see it as a reconstruction by the early church, which supposedly had a penchant for allegorizing.[8] A. B. Bruce and Adolf Julicher were especially averse to this use of metaphors by Jesus, seeing it as an attempt to remodel the original in terms of subsequent history.[9] To be authentic the parable must be cleansed of these pious fabrications, they claim.[10]

We have previously noted that metaphors do not necessarily make a story an allegory. Metaphors are common in all speech. An allegory is distinct in that all its parts are symbolic, and they are almost always interpreted within the story. A parable may also use metaphors to present its central truth, but its likeness is not in multiplied symbols, but rather in relationships. Many of its parts are given for realism, rather than as figures. In this parable of the Wicked Tenants, however, Jesus used many metaphors to bluntly portray for the leaders the fulfillment of Isaiah's prophetic parable being enacted before their eyes.

The Problem Addressed. This confrontation of Jesus with the leaders was long in coming. From the time of His first cleansing the temple four years before, He was the object of the leaders' anger and suspicion. Their planning councils often had His destruction on their agendas (Mark 3:6; John 11:47–53). Many charges were concocted for His arrest. As this Feast approached, however, Jesus boldly entered the city with messianic authority, as much of the nation was at hand. In cleansing the temple this time, Jesus laid down the gauntlet to the leaders, summoning them for a confrontation.

The Jewish leaders' questioning of Jesus' authority forms the backdrop for the parable of the Wicked Tenants. Matthew 21:23 records what happened. On Tuesday morning of the Passion Week (the final week of Jesus' earthly life), the Savior arrived at the Jerusalem temple and began teaching and preaching the gospel. The chief priests and elders of the people came to question Him about His activities.

The chief priests were high-priestly functionaries, members of the priestly aristocracy. The elders of the people were heads of the most influential lay families of the nation. Thus both priestly and nonpriestly members of the Sanhedrin approached Jesus. These men considered themselves the true leaders of the people.[11]

In Jesus' day, the Sanhedrin was the supreme Jewish authority. It was composed of religious leaders, mostly upper-class Sadducees. When Judea was made a Roman province in A.D. 6, the Romans granted this council almost exclusive control of Jewish affairs. Following Moses' pattern in choosing elders (Num. 11:16), the Sanhedrin had 70 members, not counting the presiding high priest.[12]

The religious leaders asked Jesus who had given Him His authority. No official of the Jewish government had empowered Jesus to cleanse the temple of its merchants or to teach and heal people in its courts. In publicly questioning Jesus about these matters, the nation's leaders sought to discredit Him and make it appear as if He were a threat to the authority of Rome.

The Savior knew His interrogators had sinister motives. That's why He rebuffed them by asking a question in return about the authority of John the Baptist (Matt. 21:24–25). Since the priests were unwilling to risk an answer, Jesus refused to answer them as well. Rather, He rebuked them for rejecting John's message (v. 27).

Jesus then told the parable of the Two Sons (vv. 28–32). It's a story about one son who said he would not work, but did anyway, and the other son who agreed to work, but did not. The first son represented the social outcasts of Jewish society, such as the tax collectors and prostitutes. At first, they were disobedient to God. Yet when these people recognized the truth that John the Baptist had proclaimed, they believed.

The second son in Jesus' parable represented Israel's religious leaders. Although they pretended to obey God, they had actually rebelled against Him. Despite their pious activities and sophisticated rituals, they were far from genuinely serving the Lord, for they rejected John's message. Jesus saw a close connection between John's preaching and His own. For instance, both men pointed to the same way of righteousness (though entrance into the kingdom of heaven is dependent on Jesus, not on John).

In Jesus' day, the religious leaders were looked upon as paragons of righteousness, while the common people were considered to be further from pleasing God. Jesus did not hesitate to reveal that the situation was actually more like the opposite of that stereotype. This parable, then, reminds us that God is not impressed by our status in society or our religious practices. Only one thing ultimately counts—personal faith in Christ.

The Central Truth. Jesus began by noting that a certain landowner planted a vineyard, built a stone wall around it, dug a pit for pressing out the grape juice, and constructed a lookout tower. Matthew 21:33 is an allusion to Isaiah 5:1–2, which would have been familiar to the Jewish leaders. The Isaiah passage notes how the owner of the vineyard made every conceivable provision for the vine's productivity and protection.

This activity illustrated the Lord's gracious choice of Israel. Though God expected a plentiful yield from His investment, the vine only produced worthless grapes. Such were inedible and thus suitable only for discarding. In verses 3–5, the Lord declared that He would judge His faithless and disobedient people by allowing their nation to become desolate and accessible to any nation wishing to invade the land. This happened, of course, when the Babylonians overran the country in 586 B.C. The unbelief and rebellion that existed at that time mirrored what Jesus encountered among the religious leaders of His day, and the parable of the Wicked Tenants makes that truth crystal clear.

In Matthew 21:33, Jesus said that the landowner leased his vineyard to tenant farmers and then moved away to another country. When it was time to harvest the grapes, the owner sent his slaves to collect his share of the crop (v. 34). Amazingly, though, the farmers grabbed the slaves and treated them abusively (v. 35). Even when the landowner sent a larger group of slaves to collect for him, the outcome remained the same (v. 36).

Mark's gospel contains additional information concerning the owner's slaves. The first slave he sent was grabbed, beaten, and then sent back to him empty-handed (12:2–3). When the owner sent a second slave, the farmers treated him shamefully (v. 4). The third slave the owner sent was murdered, and others he sent were either beaten or killed (v. 5). The owner finally decided to send his son, whom he loved dearly. The owner gave the farmers the benefit of the doubt when he said they would respect his son (v. 6).

Sadly, this was not the case, for when the farmers saw the owner's son coming to the property, they decided to mistreat him, too (v. 7). After grabbing him (an indignity in itself), the malcontents murdered him and tossed his corpse out of the vineyard (v. 8). They assumed that by doing this, the estate would be ownerless, thus enabling them to claim the property for themselves (Matt. 21:38–39).

The details in Jesus' parable accurately reflect the situation as it existed in Bible times. For instance, grapevines covered the hillsides of Palestine and were the backbone of the economy.[13] Also, wealthy people, who lived elsewhere, owned large tracts of agricultural land. They would hire local peasants to cultivate the land, and these tenant farmers often coveted the property for themselves. In fact, the farmers sometimes conspired to take over ownership of the land.[14]

Despite the realism of Jesus' parable, it's not about land ownership disputes. Rather, it's about the religious leaders to whom He had just been speaking. Sadly, they thought they were stopping someone whom they perceived to be a danger to Judaism.[15] Perhaps that's why Jesus asked them what they thought the owner of the estate would do when he returned to his property (v. 40). They correctly surmised that the owner would have the wicked farmers executed and then lease the vineyard out to others who would give him his share of the crop after each harvest (v. 41).

In understanding this parable, it's helpful to keep in mind its central elements. The landowner represents God the Father, the vineyard symbolizes the kingdom of God, the tenant farmers stand for the Jewish religious leaders, the landowner's slaves represent the prophets who remained faithful to God and preached to Israel, the son symbolizes Jesus, and the other tenants stand for the church (v. 45).[16]

We can see from the above that Israel was the nation that God had cultivated to bring salvation to the world.[17] The religious leaders not only repressed their nation's purpose but also killed those who were trying to fulfill it (namely, the Old Testament prophets). The Jewish establishment was so jealous and possessive that they ignored the welfare of the very people they were supposed to be bringing to God. By telling this parable, Jesus exposed the religious leaders' plot to murder Him, and He warned that their sins would be punished (v. 46).

The details of this parable do not correspond exactly with particular spiritual realities. For instance, unlike the owner of the vineyard, God would never be so naive to assume that Israel's religious leaders would respect His Son. Also, few owners would send one slave after another to be murdered by a group of vicious malcontents. The story, of course, illustrates the immense patience that God had with Israel.

Just as the landowner kept giving the tenant farmers the opportunity for repentance, so too God continues to reach out to sinners.

Jesus asked His listeners whether they—the biblical experts—had ever read Psalm 118:22–23. (Imagine the rage that must have welled up inside them when they heard this question!) Perhaps by choosing to quote from this psalm, Jesus sought to reinforce the hosannas of the crowd during His triumphal entry. After all, the crowd had used this same psalm. This passage also validated Jesus' claim that His authority came from God rather than being derived from human institutions.

Psalm 118:22–23 reveals that the stone (the Messiah), whom the builders had rejected, would become the cornerstone. (In ancient times, this stone set the foundation and squared the building, which was critical to the symmetry and stability of the structure.[18]) It greatly pleased the Lord that the Savior occupied such a foremost place in His redemptive plan and program (Matt. 21:42).

Jesus left no doubt as to what He meant (v. 43). The religious leaders, who considered themselves spiritual builders, had examined Jesus and judged Him unworthy of their structure. Though they rejected Him as the Messiah, God would still make Him the most important part of His spiritual edifice, the church (Eph. 2:20; 1 Peter 2:6–7).

Because the Jewish authorities played a key part in the crucifixion of the Messiah, the Lord would judge them (Acts 2:23). For example, in A.D. 70 the Romans smashed a revolt in Jerusalem and destroyed the temple. Also, the kingdom and all the spiritual privileges, which were originally given to Israel, were subsequently given to the church, which is comprised primarily of Gentiles (Acts 13:46; 18:6; Rom. 11:11; Eph. 2:21–22).

It would be incorrect to conclude from this last point that God has forever removed the kingdom from Israel. Such an outcome is impossible, especially in light of the promises God made to Abraham, David, and the prophets. Paul asserts in Romans 11:26 and 27 that in the millennial kingdom Israel as a people and nation will be restored to the land of promise (Matt. 19:28). In the meantime, God has made the church the custodian of the vineyard (so to speak), and He expects Jesus' disciples to "bring forth fruits worthy of repentance."[19]

From the above we can discern the central truth of Jesus' parable. The Savior was exposing the religious leaders' murderous plot and declaring that despite their rejection of Him, He would still become the Head of a new redeemed community, the church (Eph. 1:19–23). His statement in Matthew 21:44 is echoed in 1 Peter 2:8, which refers to Christ as a "stone of stumbling and a rock of offense" (see Isa. 8:13–15). The Savior declared to the religious leaders that anyone who stumbled over Him, the chief cornerstone, would be shattered like a piece of fragile pottery. Similarly, the foundation stone would crush anyone on whom it fell (Dan. 2:44–45).

The Wider Significance. The parable of the Wicked Tenants continues to be relevant. We learn from it that for those who respond in faith, Jesus is their Savior. Oppositely, for those who respond in unbelief (whether through ill will or indifference), Christ is their Judge. Mercy and forgiveness await those who follow Him, while condemnation and disgrace await those who rebel against Him. The only sensible choice is to receive Christ by faith and inherit eternal life (John 1:12; 3:16).

The religious leaders of Jesus' day pretended as if they loved God and did His will. But, as Jesus' parable makes clear, they were phony to the core. Sadly, this problem still exists today. There are people in our churches who claim to obey God, yet their hearts are far from Him. To the unsuspecting they appear to be upright, but the Lord knows the true evil intentions of their hearts (1 Sam. 16:7). From this we see that our actions must match our words. Though we might be able to deceive others with our pious conduct, we cannot fool God.

The parable also touches on another important principle, namely, that everything ultimately belongs to God. Our culture, of course, tells us that we are the owners of such possessions as money, houses, cars, and clothing. And supposedly our significance is measured by how much we own. Jesus' parable, however, makes it clear that we are stewards of what God has entrusted to our care. The Creator and Lord of all expects us, His servants, to use responsibly our lives, our families, and our skills (to name a few things).

Admittedly, maintaining this attitude is difficult in a materialistic society in which people worship material things rather than their Maker (Rom. 1:25). Nevertheless, buying into this hedonistic philosophy leads to ruin (1 Tim. 6:9–10). Thus, we must resist getting so tied up in the things of the world that we are tempted to resort to evil or even violence to keep what we have. (Israel's religious leaders made this tragic mistake.) It is far better to see ourselves as tenants of God's possessions and to understand that He has loaned these possessions to us to glorify Him and serve others.

PARABLE OF THE WEDDING FEAST (MATT. 22:1–14)

The religious leaders of Israel had questioned Jesus' authority to drive out the merchants from the temple (Matt. 21:23). The Savior answered their rage and defended His actions by telling them three parables, two of which we have just finished examining (namely, the parable of the Two Sons Asked to Work, vv. 28–32, and the parable of the Wicked Tenants, vv. 33–45). The third is the story of the Wedding Feast.

Scholars have observed that this parable is similar to the story of the Great Supper and Excuses, which is recorded in Luke 14:16–24. As was noted in chapter 10, this similarity has prompted many modern interpreters to insist that the two parables are slightly different versions of the same story. This line of reasoning not only casts doubt on the veracity of each parable as the words of Jesus, but also fails to notice some key distinctions in each story.

For instance, the settings, figures, and purposes of each parable are entirely different.[20] Also, each story has a unique truth of its own to make. Jesus told the parable of the Great Supper and Excuses to warn that not everyone will enter the divine kingdom. The parable also reveals that God is more willing to save sinners than the sinners are to be saved. In contrast, the parable of the Wedding Feast confronts the obstinacy of the Savior's Jewish opponents. He taught that although many people are invited to put their faith in Him, a much smaller number actually do so.

The Problem Addressed. The Passion Week forms the backdrop for the parable of the Wedding Feast. Having ministered in Perea and the Jordan River area, Jesus then traveled with His disciples to Jerusalem on Sunday. As they drew near the city, He sent a couple of His followers ahead to a village to procure a donkey. In fulfillment of Scripture, Jesus chose to enter the capital riding on the animal. The crowds treated Him like a king entering the city. They sang praises and carpeted His path with their garments and with branches (Matt. 21:1–11).

Despite all the celebration, it wasn't long before Jesus made some people angry. One of His first acts was to go into the temple and drive out those who were selling sacrificial animals and exchanging money. His motivation was to keep the temple a pure place of worship. While there, Jesus healed the sick, and the children sang praises to Him. The Pharisees were critical of this, but Jesus would not compel the children to quiet down. After this incident, Jesus left the crowded city, walked to Bethany, and spent the night there (vv. 12–17).

According to Mark 11:12, it was Monday morning when Christ returned to Jerusalem from Bethany. While walking with His disciples, Jesus spotted a fig tree in full leaf, which was usually an indication that it had fruit. However, upon finding no fruit on the tree, Jesus cursed it and pronounced that it would never bear fruit again. When the tree withered, the disciples asked why it happened. Jesus used the opportunity to teach them about the power of faith in prayer (Matt. 21:18–22).

On Tuesday morning, Jesus arrived at the temple and began teaching and preaching the gospel. In response to the religious leaders' challenge to His authority, He wanted to know what they believed about the authority behind John's baptism ministry: was it heavenly or earthly? The religious leaders discussed Jesus' question among themselves and figured out the safest answer was, "We don't know." Because of their ambiguity, Jesus refused to answer their challenge (vv. 23–27).

The Savior then told the parable of the Two Sons Asked to Work. In it, Jesus likened the religious leaders to the son who made a promise but would not carry it through (vv. 28–32). Jesus next told the parable of the Wicked Tenants in which He stressed that all who rejected Him would be eternally condemned, while all who received Him by faith would be eternally blessed (vv. 33–44).

When the chief priests and Pharisees heard these parables, they realized that Jesus was talking about them (v. 45). This made the religious leaders furious and prompted them to find a way to arrest the Savior. However, they were afraid to do so, for the crowds considered Jesus to be a prophet (v. 46). In contrast, Jesus continued to assert His authority as the Messiah, this time by telling the parable of the Wedding Feast. As 22:14 makes clear, though God invites all (including such antagonists as the religious leaders of Israel) to be part of His kingdom, only a smaller number (such as the people the religious leaders spurned as sinners) turn to Jesus in faith for salvation.

The Central Truth. Jesus used the parable of the Wedding Feast to teach principles and truths concerning the kingdom of God. He noted that a powerful ruler prepared a sumptuous wedding feast for his son (Matt. 22:2). The gala celebration would not be complete without lots of guests, so the host made sure that plenty of friends were invited. In fact, when the banquet was ready, the king dispatched his slaves to notify everyone that it was time to come (v. 3).

In Bible times, Jewish weddings involved several steps.[21] The couple started by being betrothed, and such a contractual arrangement was as legally binding as marriage itself. Before the engagement could be finalized, negotiations took place between the groom and the family of the bride. In addition, the groom paid a dowry (usually money or property) to the father of the bride.

For a virgin, the period of betrothal typically lasted a year and could be terminated only by divorce. If the groom died during this time, the bride would be regarded as a widow. Sexual unfaithfulness during the betrothal was considered adultery (Deut. 22:13–21).[22]

When the period of betrothal had ended, the groom claimed his bride. The wedding celebration usually took place after dark at the bride's house. Prior to the wedding ceremony, the groom and his friends would form a procession and walk to the home of the bride. After the couple was officially married, the procession would return to the home of the groom or his father. As the procession journeyed along a planned route, friends of the groom would join the group and participate in singing, playing musical instruments, and dancing. The bride would wear an ornate dress, expensive jewelry (if she could afford it), and a veil over her face. The groom typically hung a garland of flowers around his neck.[23]

Once the procession arrived at its destination, a lavish feast, lasting up to seven days, would begin. Friends would sing love ballads for the couple and share stories about them. Everyone would consume food and drink in generous quantities. At the end of the first day's festivities, the bride and groom would be escorted to a private wedding chamber, where they would consummate their marriage.[24]

In the culture of Jesus' day, two invitations were expected when banquets were given. The first solicitation was sent far enough in advance of the celebration so that the guests would have sufficient time to prepare themselves for the banquet, which could last as long as a week. Moreover, it took time for the replies to come back. The second invitation announced that everything was ready, and the guests were expected to come right away. To turn down this offer was not merely bad manners, it was considered a rejection of the host family's hospitality and a complete insult to their dignity.[25]

Amazingly, all those whom the king in Jesus' parable had originally invited refused to come to his son's wedding feast. Despite this personal affront to his goodness, the ruler sent other slaves to tell the guests that the feast was ready and the choicest meats had been cooked. Therefore, they needed to come quickly and enjoy the lavish provisions (Matt. 22:4).

Again, the guests the king originally invited ignored his generous and gracious offer. With what appeared to be complete indifference, they went about their daily occupations, whether it was farming or trading (v. 5). What's worse, some of the ingrates seized the king's messengers and treated them shamefully, with a few of the slaves even being killed (v. 6). These atrocities understandably infuriated the king, and so he sent his army to wipe out the murderers and burn their city (v. 7).

In making sense of the parable of the Wedding Feast, it's important to note what each person or group symbolized. The king stands for God the Father, the son symbolizes Jesus, and the slaves represent such people as John the Baptist, Jesus, and His disciples (3:1–12; 4:17; 10:5–42). The guests who spurned the king's invitation stand for the religious leaders of Israel. Despite their obstinacy, God continued to show them patience and forbearance.

The four Gospels reveal that over the course of Jesus' earthly ministry, the Pharisees and scribes grew increasingly opposed to Him. They envied His popularity, resented His challenges to their traditions, and hated His exposure of their hypocrisy. Undoubtedly, the Jewish leaders wondered whether Jesus had political aspirations and worried about how His increasing influence would affect their control over the people. The Pharisees and scribes allowed their petty concerns to blind them to the truth that Jesus was their Messiah.

Regrettably, the Jewish authorities were so preoccupied with the present that they had no concern for God's kingdom. Also, they played some part in the demise of John the Baptist (21:25), they masterminded the crucifixion of Jesus (26:3–5; 27:1–2), and they endorsed the persecution of the early church (Acts 4:1–22; 5:17–40; 6:12–15). God eventually judged the leaders and nation of Israel by allowing the destruction of Jerusalem in A.D. 70 under Titus. Even the impressive stone temple was burned and reduced to rubble in that conflict.[26]

The powerful ruler in Jesus' parable still wanted to have guests at his son's wedding feast. Tragically, those whom he had originally invited proved by their actions that they were not worthy of such an honor (Matt. 22:8). He thus ordered his slaves to go out to the street corners and invite everyone they could find (v. 9). The slaves did just this, and they were able to fill the spacious banquet hall with people from both noble and ignoble backgrounds (v. 10).

The people who subsequently attended the feast represent individuals from all walks of life who hear the gospel and make some sort of profession of faith. It remains true to this day that regardless of a person's condition, he or she needs to respond in faith to the gospel in order to be saved. While the religious leaders of Jesus' day rejected the good news, many others—both Jews and Gentiles—have responded to the invitation.[27]

When the king in Jesus' parable came into the banquet hall to meet the guests, he noticed a man who wasn't wearing the proper clothes for a wedding (v. 11). When questioned about this, the man could offer no excuse for his misbehavior (v. 12). In Jesus' day, it was customary for wedding guests to be given festive attire to wear to the banquet. Also, it was socially unacceptable to refuse to wear these garments, for to arrive in soiled clothes would insult the host. The incompliant guests either arrogantly assumed they didn't need these garments or wanted to have nothing to do with the wedding celebration.[28]

The wedding clothes in Jesus' parable picture the righteousness that people need to enter God's kingdom (Isa. 61:10). It is the total acceptance in God's eyes that believers enjoy through faith in Christ. Jesus has graciously made these garments of righteousness available to all people. Every person, in turn, must choose to put them on in order to be saved (Eph. 4:24; Col. 3:10).

Those who refuse Christ's righteousness are ashamed to admit their own spiritual poverty. They arrogantly believe they are sufficiently good to merit God's favor and forgiveness. Many in New Testament times were guilty of this heinous sin (Rom. 10:3). In light of these truths, we can understand why the king in Jesus' parable had his aides bind the incompliant guest by his hands and feet and throw him into the outer darkness (Matt. 22:13). This is a reference to hell, a place characterized by incessant misery, grief, and torment.

Jesus declared in verse 14 that many are called (or invited), but few are chosen (cf. 7:13–14). In other words, God invites all people through the proclamation of the gospel to repent, believe, and thereby inherit the kingdom of heaven. Those who favorably respond show by their decision (which they freely make) that God has chosen them for eternal life. In contrast, those who reject the Lord's invitation to be saved remain lost and thus excluded from the kingdom. This outcome is perfectly just, for they have willfully rejected Christ (1 Peter 2:7–8).

The Wider Significance. In looking back over the parable of the Wedding Feast, it is clear that the first part of the story (Matt. 22:1–10) continues the theme begun in the previous chapter. To be specific, the original intended heirs of the divine kingdom (namely, the Jewish people) rejected it, and the kingdom has been offered to others. Like the followers of Jesus in the early days of the church, believers today have the privilege and responsibility of offering the kingdom to others. The offer is made through the proclamation of the gospel.

The second part of Jesus' parable (vv. 11–14) reveals that receiving an invitation to God's kingdom does not guarantee admittance. In other words, one must receive by faith the offer of salvation, for apart from faith in Christ no one can be cleansed from sin and imputed with His righteousness (Zech. 3:3–5; Rev. 3:18; 19:7–8). As Paul says in 2 Corinthians 5:21, God "made Him who knew no sin to be sin on our behalf, that we might become the righteousness of God in Him."

It's true that everyone who hears the gospel has been invited to the King's banquet. And while many might claim to be in the kingdom, only those clothed with the righteousness of Christ are actually acceptable to God. They have humbly relied on Him to remove their filthy clothes (their sins) and to provide them with fine, new garments (the virtue and holiness of Christ). They, in turn, demonstrate by their changed lives and upright conduct that they have embraced Jesus by faith. Admittedly, there is a cost to being a follower of Christ, but whatever we give up for Him, it is nothing compared to the marvelous blessings He gives us (Rom. 8:18).

If God were only just, humanity would never have a prayer. Our situation is clear: we have sinned before a holy God. The only just response from God is death. At the same time, if God were solely loving, we would be swept up to His bosom without a glance at the sinfulness of our hearts. Neither happens, however, because God is neither exclusively just nor exclusively loving; He is all of both. He loves us and wants us to join Him in His heavenly kingdom. But He first had to establish a way for our sin to be annulled. That was what He accomplished through Jesus Christ.

In a metaphorical sense, God has sent us an invitation marked RSVP *(répondez s'il vous plaît)*—French for "Please reply." Although our Lord waits patiently for our favorable response, He has set a limit on how long He will tarry. At some point He must say, "Enough!" and the doors will swing shut. Before it's too late, we must say *yes* to His invitation and join His great banquet.

EPILOGUE

Some Concluding Thoughts

We now come to the end of what must be called a monumental work. I think that you will agree with Dr. Bailey's opening remarks, which he expressed in the Foreword. He said that in this work Dr. Ellisen has succeeded in opening "up the mind of our Lord as revealed in the parables."

Our goal in this chapter is to step back briefly and recall the highlights of what Dr. Ellisen has said in his work. We'll do so by making a number of general observations and summary statements.

We begin by first noting that the importance of the parables is evident from both their number and their referent. They account for more than one-third of the sayings of Jesus, and the primary referent is the kingdom of God.

Second, Jesus' parables give us a clear sense of His mind and heart. We see Him to be our Lord and Savior, and our Friend and Guide. Both His holiness and grace, His joy and sorrow are made evident in the parables.

Third, no other teachings of Jesus have been more maligned in their interpretation or have been used to advance more private agendas than the parables. That's why the author has spent so much time clarifying and explaining the proper way to handle this unique body of biblical literature. It is clear that he pursued his study of the parables with enthusiasm, and his love for the Gospels and the life of Christ has been conveyed to us in this book.

Fourth, the parable is a subsection of wisdom genre that contains a range from the shorter one-sentence sayings of Jesus to the more full-length parables. It is important not to confuse the parable with the figurative language of allegory, fable, and myth.

Fifth, a proper hermeneutical approach to the parables must be distinguished from allegorization, moral generalizations, redaction criticism, and the destructive approaches of the Jesus Seminar. Dr. Ellisen was committed to the acceptance of the Bible on its own terms and treating the material as it stands in the finished text. Because he took the gospel texts as authentic material, he believed that both the parables and their accompanying interpretations are the message of Jesus as He gave it.

Sixth, the hermeneutical approach in this book appreciates the delicate balance between the literary, historical, and theological concerns. Ellisen realized that much injustice has been done to the life and teachings of Jesus. That's why, in his work on the parables, he argued that the parables should be understood within both the literary contexts of the Gospels as well as the historical contexts of the life of Christ.

Seventh, the purposes for Jesus' parables are interlocked with the various audiences for which they were crafted. In other words, Jesus used these stories as teaching aids for the disciples, apologetic responses to His enemies, and convicting challenges designed to evoke appropriate decisions from the uncommitted. Jesus also used the parables to reveal more truth about the kingdom program of God to the receptive, while for the rejecting hearts the parables were employed judicially to conceal these new kingdom truths.

Eighth, in light of the above, it is clear that the kingdom of God is the primary referent of Jesus' parables. In fact, Ellisen chronicled the ministry of Jesus in parables by way of chapters highlighting the entrance into the kingdom, servanthood, human responsibility and divine concerns, anticipating the coming kingdom, rewards in the kingdom, warnings to those who would reject the message of the kingdom, and the accountability required by Jesus at His return.

Ninth, though the parables speak about the kingdom, their sphere of revelation is not the whole of God's kingdom. They say very little about the Old Testament kingdom revealed by the prophets, for instance, or about the New Testament millennial kingdom. Rather, the parables outline a new direction for God's kingdom program during the interadvent period. More specifically, the parables describe the operation of that kingdom from the time of Jesus' rejection to His future reception by the nation of Israel.

Tenth, in stressing the chronological order of the parables, the author noted a diabolic movement that gradually increased from a group of local irritants to a final conspiracy of national repudiation. Though ignored by many, this chronological approach serves an essential function in revealing the full impact of the parables.

Eleventh, we can identify four kinds of parables in the Gospels: similitudes, example stories, symbolic parables, and parabolic sayings. Ellisen noted that Jesus intentionally used each of the four styles at a particular time in the chronology of His ministry as warranted by the historical need. Let's briefly summarize each type.

- The *similitude* is a germ parable expanded into a moving picture of drama and seen as a generalization. As such, it portrays a normative action of what a person generally does, rather than a specific incident. The referent of the similitudes is the mystery aspect of the kingdom of God, which would extend from the time of Israel's rejection of the Messiah until the time of the nation's reception of Him at the end of the present age.
- The *example story* is an illustration of a truth that Jesus was presenting. Rather than comparing two realms of reality, it gives a specific example of its truth in a single realm. Jesus used the example stories and full-length parables to describe the drama of life within the present age of the kingdom and the need to be ready for the future kingdom.
- The *symbolic parable* involves two realms of reality. A scene in the physical is portrayed to teach specific truths in the spiritual realm concerning God and humankind. This type of parable may depart from the normal or generally expected. In fact, this unexpected turn in the story often is its major point. In this way Jesus revealed difficult secrets of the kingdom.

- The *parabolic saying* is the one-liner that Jesus used to crisply deliver a sermon in a sentence. He gave these in various ways, as short statements, questions, or commands, each in essence compressing a narrative into a single sentence. Jesus employed these pithy sayings as aphoristic barbs to describe the forecasting shadows of rejection as hinted by the responses of the leaders to His claims to be the Messiah.

Twelfth, Ellisen's goal was to briefly exposit each of the parables to discover its historical interpretation and contemporary applications. The author treated virtually every parable with equal attention to its setting, need, central truth, and wider application. Rather than emphasize literary analyses and structures for specialists, he stressed practical guidelines and balanced expositions for practitioners. He sought to help pastors, teachers, and students discern the basic message of each parable in order to pursue its broader applications.

With this in mind, Ellisen's book suggested five guidelines for interpreting a parable, which are then applied to the parables themselves:

- *First, discover the problem that made the parable necessary.* The problem sought is almost invariably found in the context, often at the heart of the preceding discussion. Any titillating points one might dredge up unrelated to this native problem will soon fade into insignificance when the real problem is discerned.
- *Second, seek the central truth of the parable.* It is the primary lesson being taught, though related truths may also be involved. Everything revolves around it. Its discovery is not really difficult, for clues often appear throughout the context and in the story.
- *Third, relate the details to the central truth.* None of the details are superfluous in Jesus' stories. Each is given to serve one of two basic functions: it may contribute directly to the central truth, or it may contribute to the realism of the story. In considering the various details, though all contribute to the central truth, not all relate in the same way.

- *Fourth, clarify and authenticate the central truth.* Jesus gave His parables specifically to reveal new truths about the kingdom program. One should first press for clarity and unity in the central truth. Then, with a clear understanding of the main point, one should then check its validity with the rest of Scripture. The vital test is whether the central truth is corroborated by its context and in harmony with later revelation.
- *Fifth, discover the intended appeal of the parable for proper application.* Jesus did not tell His stories to entertain, but rather to instruct and involve. He appealed to the mind and conscience to elicit a decision of the will. This appeal is sometimes explicit in the prologue or epilogue and sometimes implicit in the story or context. Proper interpretation should bring this out.

In closing, it is clear that the author pursued his study of the parables with enthusiasm, and his love for the Gospels and the life of Christ has been conveyed to us in this book. The body of Christ owes a large debt of gratitude for what Dr. Ellisen has accomplished!

—Daniel T. Lioy
October 2000

ENDNOTES

Preface

1. As in any story, the various pieces find their overall significance only when seen in their proper places as parts of the whole.
2. Joachim Jeremias, *Rediscovering the Parables* (New York: Charles Scribner's Sons, 1966), 13; and Robert W. Funk and Roy W. Hoover, *The Five Gospels: In Search of the Authentic Words of Jesus* (New York: Macmillan, 1993), ix.
3. Funk and Hoover, dedication page to *The Five Gospels.*
4. Eta Linnemann, *Is There a Synoptic Problem?* (Grand Rapids: Baker, 1992), 209. Compare her earlier work, *Parables of Jesus: Introduction and Exposition* (London: SPCK, 1966). See also recent redating of Matthew in the Magdalen Papyrus by German papyrologist Carsten Peter Thiede with Matthew D'Ancona in *Eyewitness to Jesus* (New York: Doubleday, 1995), confirming "the Gospels' historical truth" and early datings, and the current challenge to Markan priority in Simon J. Kistemaker, *The Gospels in Current Study* (Grand Rapids: Zondervan, 1972), 36–37.
5. Inconclusiveness and almost futility are often admitted by historical-critical authors in their search for the authentic words of Jesus; for example: Kenneth E. Bailey, *Through Peasant Eyes* (Grand Rapids: Eerdmans, 1980), ix–x, xiii; Bernard B. Scott, *Hear Then the Parables* (Minneapolis: Fortress, 1989), 4ff.; and Amos N. Wilder, *Jesus' Parables and the War of Myths* (Minneapolis: Fortress, 1982), 10ff. Some of the existential or structuralist school even find that a plus in promoting polyvalence and open-endedness in application (Warren S. Kissinger, *The Parables of Jesus: A History of Interpretation and Bibliography* [Metuchen, N.J.: Scarecrow, 1979], 218, 227).
6. David Wenham, *The Parables of Jesus* (Downers Grove, Ill.: InterVarsity, 1989), 234–35.
7. Leland Ryken, *How to Read the Bible as Literature* (Grand Rapids: Zondervan, 1984), 31.
8. Linnemann, *Is There a Synoptic Problem?* 114.

9. Ibid., 122.
10. Ibid., 123.

Chapter 1: Jesus' Unique Teaching Aids

1. Hillyer Straton, *A Guide to the Parables of Jesus* (Grand Rapids: Eerdmans, 1959), 11.
2. A renewed emphasis on allegorical features in the parables is prominent today, which is basically a recognition of the wider use of symbolisms in the stories, rather than ancient allegorism. Craig L. Blomberg, *Interpreting the Parables* (Downers Grove, Ill.: InterVarsity, 1990), 23, 29ff.; and John W. Sider, *Interpreting the Parables* (Grand Rapids: Zondervan, 1995), 237ff.
3. Joachim Jeremias, *Rediscovering the Parables* (New York: Charles Scribner's Sons, 1966), 15.
4. Adolf Julicher, *Die Gleichnisreden Jesus,* 2 vols. (Tubingen, 1886, not trans. into English); see T. K. Cheyne and J. S. Black, eds., *Encyclopaedia Biblica: A Critical Dictionary of the Literary, Political, & Religious History, the Archaeology, Geography, & Natural History of the Bible* (New York: Macmillan, 1899), 1:3563–67.
5. So pervasive is this low view of the text by modern critical scholars of the past half century, it is almost universally accepted; for example: John D. Crossan, "Structural Analysis and the Parables of Jesus," *Semeia I* (Atlanta: Scholars Press); Robert W. Funk, *Language, Hermeneutic, and Word of God: The Problem of Language in the New Testament and Contemporary Theology* (New York: Harper and Row, 1966); Bernard B. Scott, *Hear Then the Parables* (Minneapolis: Fortress, 1989); Daniel O. Via, *The Parables: Their Literary and Existential Dimension* (Philadelphia: Fortress, 1967).
6. A. M. Hunter, *Interpreting the Parables* (Philadelphia: Westminster, 1960), 40–42.
7. Siegfried Goebel, *The Parables of Jesus* (Edinburgh: T & T Clarke, 1883), vii.
8. Jeremias, *Rediscovering the Parables,* 15.
9. Ibid.
10. Eta Linnemann, *Parables of Jesus: Introduction and Exposition* (London: SPCK, 1966), 158.
11. Richard C. Trench, *Notes on the Parables* (New York: D. Appleton, 1856), 41.
12. James Smart, "A Redefinition of Jesus' Use of the Parable," *Expository Times* 47 (September 1936): 5511.
13. E. W. Bullinger, *Figures of Speech Used in the Bible* (reprint; Grand Rapids: Baker, 1968), v–vi.

14. F. C. Grant, "A New Book on the Parables," *Anglican Theological Review* 30 (April 1948): 1181.
15. Robert H. Stein, *An Introduction to the Parables of Jesus* (Philadelphia: Westminster, 1981), 27–35, gives an excellent elucidation of contending views of Mark 4:11–12. See also David Wenham, *The Parables of Jesus* (Downers Grove, Ill.: InterVarsity, 1989), 240–45; and Hunter, *Interpreting the Parables,* 110–12.
16. William F. Arndt and F. Wilbur Gingrich, *A Greek-English Lexicon of the New Testament and Other Early Christian Literature* (Chicago: Univ. of Chicago Press, 1957), 378. See also Joseph H. Thayer, *Greek-English Lexicon* (Grand Rapids: Zondervan, 1962), 304.
17. Kenneth S. Wuest, *Mark in the Greek New Testament* (Grand Rapids: Eerdmans, 1950), 86.
18. Floyd V. Filson, *A Commentary on the Gospel According to St. Matthew* (New York: Harper and Brothers, 1960), 160.
19. J. Dwight Pentecost, *The Parables of Jesus* (Grand Rapids: Kregel, 1982), 12–13; and Stanley D. Tousaint, *Behold the King* (Portland: Multnomah, 1998), 169.

Chapter 2: The Kingdom of the Parables

1. John Bright, *The Kingdom of God* (New York: Abingdon-Cokesbury, 1953), 219.
2. Alva J. McClain, *The Greatness of the Kingdom* (Grand Rapids: Zondervan, 1959), 17ff.
3. Alfred Edersheim, *The Life and Times of Jesus the Messiah,* vol. 1 (Grand Rapids: Eerdmans, 1953), 265.
4. McClain, *The Greatness of the Kingdom,* 303.
5. Cf. Warren S. Kissinger, *The Parables of Jesus: A History of Interpretation and Bibliography* (Metuchen, N.J.: Scarecrow, 1979), 145. The distinctions of these various phases of God's kingdom program are often blurred in modern critical analyses of the parables. C. H. Dodd developed the concept of "realized eschatology" (followed by Joachim Jeremias, A. M. Hunter, and many others), which sees Jesus' ministry "as the great eschatological act of God in which He visited and redeemed His people." They view the Old Testament promises of a kingdom of Israel as fulfilled in Jesus' life, death, and resurrection, thus denying any further fulfillment of Israel's kingdom. This they achieve by an allegorical blending of what the prophets foretold and what happened in Jesus' first coming, alleging that the parables were Jesus' special weapons to battle

the kingdom of the Devil and reinterpret the prophets. This, of course, is not far from the allegorism of the early church and many others today who see the church as intercepting the Old Testament promises to Israel on the basis of their rejection. Muhammad used a similar argument to claim those promises for Islam, inheriting them through Ishmael, when he saw the failures of the church in A.D. 610 (*Qur'an,* Surah 2.122–141; 5.15–65).

Chapter 3: The Unique Nature of Jesus' Parables

1. Madeleine I. Boucher, *The Parables* (Wilmington, Del.: Michael Glazier, 1981), 25; and E. W. Bullinger, *Figures of Speech Used in the Bible* (London: Messrs. Myre and Spottiswoode, 1898), v–xii. A rare work on 217 figures used by the Greeks, many forgotten in our day.
2. A. M. Hunter, *Interpreting the Parables* (Philadelphia: Westminster, 1960), 8; T. H. Horne, *An Introduction to the Critical Study and Knowledge of Holy Scripture,* vol. 2 (London: Longman, Brown, Green, and Longman, 1839), 475.
3. Leland Ryken, *How to Read the Bible as Literature* (Grand Rapids: Zondervan, 1984), 91–97; and Robert H. Stein, *An Introduction to the Parables of Jesus* (Philadelphia: Westminster, 1981), 18f.
4. Bullinger, *Figures of Speech,* 48.
5. Hunter, *Interpreting the Parables,* 9–10; and Craig L. Blomberg, *Interpreting the Parables* (Downers Grove, Ill.: InterVarsity, 1990), 43.
6. Boucher, *The Parables,* 28; Bullinger, *Figures of Speech,* 748; and Blomberg, *Interpreting the Parables,* 43.
7. Boucher, *The Parables,* 13; and Stein, *An Introduction to the Parables of Jesus,* 55.
8. Hunter, *Interpreting the Parables,* 8–9; and David Wenham, *The Parables of Jesus* (Downers Grove, Ill.: InterVarsity, 1989), 225–26.
9. For an extended history of parable interpretation, see Warren S. Kissinger, *The Parables of Jesus: A History of Interpretation and Bibliography* (Metuchen, N.J.: Scarecrow, 1979). For an excellent brief summary of that history see Stein, *An Introduction to the Parables of Jesus,* 42–81; or Hunter, *Interpreting the Parables,* 21–41.
10. Bernard B. Scott, *Hear Then the Parables* (Minneapolis: Fortress, 1989), 45.
11. Ryken, *How to Read the Bible as Literature,* 47.
12. Wenham, *The Parables of Jesus,* 19.
13. Hunter, *Interpreting the Parables,* 27.
14. Craig L. Blomberg, *Interpreting the Parables* (Downers Grove, Ill.: InterVarsity, 1990), 162.
15. Hunter, *Interpreting the Parables,* 9–10.

16. Siegfried Goebel, *The Parables of Jesus* (Edinburgh: T & T Clark, 1913), 3.
17. Cf. Boucher, *The Parables,* 16–17; and Scott, *Hear Then the Parables,* 8.
18. Richard C. Trench, *Notes on the Parables of Our Lord* (London: John W. Parker and Son, 1855), 9.
19. Ryken, *How to Read the Bible as Literature,* 145.
20. Leland Ryken, *The Literature of the Bible* (Grand Rapids: Zondervan, 1974), 359.
21. Geoffrey W. H. Lampe and Kenneth J. Woollcombe, *Essays on Typology* (Naperville, Ill.: Alec R. Allenson, 1957), 56.
22. F. W. Farrar, *History of Interpretation* (London: Macmillan, 1886), 27.
23. The *allegoroumena* of Galatians 4:24 is used in the sense of Old Testament types, not the multiple senses of allegorism.
24. Kissinger, *The Parables of Jesus,* 12.
25. Bernard Ramm, *Protestant Biblical Interpretation* (Boston: W. A. Wilde, 1950), 25.
26. James Smart, "A Redefinition of Jesus' Use of the Parable," *Expository Times* 47 (September 1936): 552.
27. Stein, *An Introduction to the Parables of Jesus,* 22–25.
28. Eta Linnemann, *Parables of Jesus: Introduction and Exposition* (London: SPCK, 1966), 3–8.
29. Adolf Julicher, "Parable," in *Encyclopaedia Biblica: A Critical Dictionary of the Literary, Political, & Religious History, the Archaeology, Geography, & Natural History of the Bible,* ed. T. K. Cheyne and J. S. Black (New York: Macmillan, 1899), 1:3566.

Chapter 4: Guidelines for Interpretation

1. J. Dwight Pentecost, *The Parables of Jesus* (Grand Rapids: Kregel, 1998), 15.
2. Contrast the new emphasis on "imagination" by Amos Wilder, *Jesus' Parables and the War of Myths* (Philadelphia: Fortress, 1982), 6, 17ff., which adopts a new allegorism of extremes of mythical speculation.
3. Richard C. Trench, *Notes on the Parables of Our Lord* (London: John W. Parker & Son, 1855), 39.
4. A. M. Hunter, *Interpreting the Parables* (Philadelphia: Westminster, 1960), 27.
5. Joachim Jeremias, *Interpreting the Parables* (New York: Charles Scribner's Sons, 1963), 51ff.
6. Hunter, *Interpreting the Parables,* 94ff.
7. Jeremias, *Rediscovering the Parables,* 63ff.
8. A. T. Cadoux, *The Parables of Jesus: Their Art and Use* (London: James Clarke, 1930), 60.

9. Hunter, *Interpreting the Parables,* 95–96.
10. Pentecost, *The Parables of Jesus,* 19.

Chapter 6: "Mysteries of the Kingdom" Unfolded: Part 1

1. Nathan Levison, *The Parables: Their Background and Local Setting* (Edinburgh: T & T Clarke, 1926), 17–18.
2. H. B. Swete, *Parables of the Kingdom* (London: Macmillan, 1921), 31.
3. Richard C. Trench, *Notes on the Parables of Our Lord* (London: John W. Parker & Son, 1855), 97.
4. Swete, *Parables of the Kingdom,* 30.
5. Warren S. Kissinger, *The Parables of Jesus: A History of Interpretation and Bibliography* (Metuchen, N.J.: Scarecrow, 1979), 9.
6. Ibid., 22.
7. Ronald W. Wallace, *Many Things in Parables* (Grand Rapids: Eerdmans, 1963), 22.
8. Trench, *Parables of Our Lord,* 114.
9. Simon J. Kistemacher, *The Parables of Jesus* (Grand Rapids: Baker, 1980), 55.
10. J. Dwight Pentecost, *Parables of Jesus* (Grand Rapids: Kregel, 1998), 55.
11. Trench, *Parables of Our Lord,* 282.
12. Kistemacher, *The Parables of Jesus,* 31.
13. Swete, *Parables of the Kingdom,* 19.

Chapter 7: "Mysteries of the Kingdom" Unfolded: Part 2

1. Warren S. Kissinger, *The Parables of Jesus: A History of Interpretation and Bibliography* (Metuchen, N.J.: Scarecrow, 1979), 15.
2. G. C. Morgan, *The Parables and Metaphors of Our Lord* (New York: Revell, 1943), 77.
3. J. Dwight Pentecost, *The Parables of Jesus* (Grand Rapids: Zondervan, 1982), 60.
4. Lloyd J. Ogilvie, *Autobiography of God* (Glendale, Calif.: Gospel Light Publications, 1979), 114.
5. H. B. Swete, *Parables of the Kingdom* (London: Macmillan, 1921), 53.
6. Richard C. Trench, *Notes on the Parables of Our Lord* (London: John W. Parker, 1855), 134; and Joachim Jeremias, *The Parables of Jesus* (London: SCM, 1954), 156.
7. Simon J. Kistemacher, *The Parables of Jesus* (Grand Rapids: Baker, 1980), 62.
8. Norval Geldenhuys, *Commentary on the Gospel of Luke* (Grand Rapids: Eerdmans, 1951), 174.

9. Robert W. Funk and Roy W. Hooker, *The Five Gospels: In Search of the Authentic Words of Christ* (New York: Macmillan, 1995), 62.

Chapter 8: Parables on Entering the Kingdom

1. Johnston Cheney, *Life of Christ in Stereo* (Portland, Ore.: Western Baptist, 1969), 231ff.
2. Nathan Levison, *The Parables: Their Background and Local Setting* (Edinburgh: T & T Clark, 1926), 135.
3. See the subsections "The Parable Defined" and "The Parables Distinguished" in chapter 3 of this book, 43–45.
4. Flavius Josephus, "Jewish Antiquities," in *The New Complete Works of Josephus*, trans. William Whiston (Grand Rapids: Kregel, 1999), 12.7.7.
5. G. C. Morgan, *The Parables and Metaphors of Our Lord* (New York: Revell, 1943), 312.
6. See Cheney, *Life of Christ in Stereo,* 231ff.; H. Hoehner, *Chronological Aspects of the Life of Christ* (Grand Rapids: Zondervan, 1977), 45ff.; and A. T. Robertson, *Harmony of the Gospels* (New York: Harper & Brothers, 1922), 276ff., for discussions of these views.
7. See Hoehner's excellent chapter on "The Year of Christ's Death," in *Chronological Aspects of the Life of Christ,* 95–114.
8. Richard C. Trench, *Notes on the Parables of Our Lord* (London: John W. Paraker & Son, 1855), 145.
9. H. B. Swete, *Parables of the Kingdom* (London: Macmillan, 1921), 88.
10. J. Dwight Pentecost, *The Parables of Jesus* (Grand Rapids: Kregel, 1998), 63.
11. Trench, *Parables of Our Lord,* 151.

Chapter 9: Luke's Travelogue: Parables on Servanthood

1. Most Gospel harmonies equate this journey with Jesus' trip to the Feast of Tabernacles in John 7, placing the Feast of Dedication in John 10 at Luke 13:22 (e.g., Robert L. Thomas and Stanley N. Gundry, *Harmony of the Gospels with Explanations and Essays* [San Francisco: HarperCollins, 1986], 128, 146; A. T. Robertson, *A Harmony of the Gospels for Students of the Life of Christ* [New York: Harper and Brothers, 1950], 113, 129). Many of the sayings and teachings in this section have parallels in Jesus' earlier mission in Galilee (for example, the Sermon on the Mount, the blasphemy, and the mysteries of the kingdom, reapplied for the Perean crowds).
2. Nathan Levison, *The Parables: Their Background and Local Setting* (Edinburgh: T & T Clark, 1926), 98.

3. Joseph A. Fitzmyer, *The Gospel According to Luke* (Garden City, N.Y.: Doubleday, 1985), 880.
4. Cunningham Geikie, *The Life and Words of Christ* (New York: Appleton, 1880), 2:312.
5. Bernard Ramm, *Protestant Biblical Interpretation* (Boston: W. A. Wilde, 1950), 258.
6. Levison, *The Parables,* 80.
7. William F. Arndt and F. Wilbur Gingrich, *A Greek-English Lexicon of the New Testament and Other Early Christian Literature* (Chicago: Univ. of Chicago Press, 1957), 54.
8. Joachim Jeremias, *The Parables of Jesus* (London: SCM, 1954), 118.
9. Ibid.
10. G. C. Morgan, *The Parables and Metaphors of Our Lord* (New York: Revell, 1943), 184.
11. Eta Linnemann, *Parables of Jesus: Introduction and Exposition* (New York: Harper & Row, 1967), 123.
12. Kenneth E. Bailey, *Through Peasant Eyes* (Grand Rapids: Eerdmans, 1980), 71.
13. W. O. E. Oesterley, *The Gospel Parables in the Light of Their Jewish Background* (New York: Macmillan, 1936), 169.
14. William Taylor, *The Parables of Our Saviour* (New York: Armstrong & Son, 1901), 262.
15. Jeremias, *The Parables of Jesus,* 123.
16. Richard C. Trench, *Notes on the Parables of Our Lord* (London: John W. Parker, 1855), 334.
17. Paul Lee Tan, *Encyclopedia of 7700 Illustrations: Signs of the Times* (Rockville, Md.: Assurance Publishers, 1979), 1185.

Chapter 10: Luke's Travelogue: Parables on Human Responsibility and Divine Concern

1. Joseph A. Fitzmyer, *The Gospel According to Luke* (Garden City, N.Y.: Doubleday, 1985), 1006.
2. Flavius Josephus, "Jewish Antiquities," in *The New Complete Works of Josephus,* trans. William Whiston (Grand Rapids: Kregel, 1999), 18.3.1–2; and Cunningham Geikie, *The Life and Words of Christ* (New York: Appleton, 1880), 2:531.
3. See Nathan Levison, *The Parables: Their Background and Local Setting* (Edinburgh: T & T Clark, 1926), 115.

4. F. W. Farrar, *The Gospel According to St. Luke* (Cambridge: Cambridge Univ. Press, 1890), 236; and Simon J. Kistemaker, *The Parables of Jesus* (Grand Rapids: Baker, 1980), 185.
5. Geikie, *The Life and Words of Christ,* 2:401.
6. William Barclay, *And Jesus Said: A Handbook on the Parables of Jesus* (Philadelphia: Westminster, 1970), 154; Joachim Jeremias, *The Parables of Jesus* (London: SCM, 1954), 50; and Eta Linnemann, *Parables of Jesus: Introduction and Exposition* (London: SPCK, 1966), 93.
7. Farrar, *The Gospel According to St. Luke,* 244.
8. Ibid., 246.
9. Joseph F. McFadyen, *The Message of the Parables* (London: James Clark, n.d.), 99.
10. Linnemann, *Parables of Jesus,* 160–62.
11. Norval Geldenhuys, *Commentary on the Gospel of Luke* (Grand Rapids: Eerdmans, 1951), 398.
12. Barclay, *And Jesus Said,* 182.
13. Richard C. Trench, *Notes on the Parables of Our Lord* (London: John W. Parker & Son, 1855), 372.
14. Barclay, *And Jesus Said,* 185.
15. Trench, *Parables of Our Lord,* 403.
16. A. M. Hunter, *The Parables Then and Now* (Philadelphia: Westminster, 1971), 59.
17. William F. Arndt and F. Wilbur Gingrich, *A Greek-English Lexicon of the New Testament and Other Early Christian Literature* (Chicago: Univ. of Chicago Press, 1957), 119.
18. Hunter, *The Parables Then and Now,* 60.
19. Lloyd J. Ogilvie, *Autobiography of God* (Glendale, Calif.: Gospel Light Publications, 1979), 10.
20. Hunter, *The Parables Then and Now,* 61.

Chapter 11: Luke's Travelogue: Parables on Living Life in View of the Coming Kingdom

1. Simon J. Kistemaker, *The Parables of Jesus* (Grand Rapids: Baker, 1980), 228.
2. Warren S. Kissinger, *The Parables of Jesus: A History of Interpretation and Bibliography* (Metuchen, N.J.: Scarecrow, 1979), 398–408.
3. Richard C. Trench, *Notes on the Parables of Our Lord* (London: John W. Parker & Son, 1855), 441.
4. Kissinger, *The Parables of Jesus,* 101.

5. Joachim Jeremias, *Rediscovering the Parables* (New York: Charles Scribner's Sons, 1966), 34–35; and idem, *The Parables of Jesus* (London: SCM, 1954), 33, 127.
6. See the subtitle, "Jesus' Four Kinds of Parables," in chapter 3 of this book, 48–51.
7. Joseph A Fitzmyer, *The Gospel According to Luke,* 10–24 (Garden City, N.Y. Doubleday, 1985), 1111–12, 1121.

Chapter 12: Luke's Travelogue: Parables on Effective Service for the Kingdom

1. David Redding, *The Parables He Told* (Westwood, N.J.: Revell, 1962), 144; and Kenneth E. Bailey, *Through Peasant Eyes* (Grand Rapids: Eerdmans, 1980), 114.
2. G. C. Morgan, *The Gospel According to Luke* (New York: Revell, 1931), 195.
3. Norval Geldenhuys, *Commentary on the Gospel of Luke* (Grand Rapids: Eerdmans, 1951), 434.
4. A. T. Robertson, *Word Pictures in the New Testament: Luke* (Nashville: Broadman, 1930), 229. *Entos humon* is used only here and in Matthew 23:26, where it means "within" or internal, as opposed to external.
5. Geldenhuys, *Commentary on the Gospel of Luke,* 443.
6. William F. Arndt and F. Wilbur Gingrich, *A Greek-English Lexicon of the New Testament and Other Early Christian Literature* (Chicago: Univ. of Chicago Press, 1957), 856.
7. Richard C. Trench, *Notes on the Parables of Our Lord* (London: John W. Parker & Son, 1855), 503.
8. Bailey, *Through Peasant Eyes,* 148; and Joachim Jeremias, *Rediscovering the Parables* (New York: Charles Scribner's Sons, 1966), 113.
9. Eta Linnemann, *Parables of Jesus: Introduction and Exposition* (London: SPCK, 1966), 144; and Joachim Jeremias, *The Parables of Jesus* (London: SCM, 1954), 114.

Chapter 13: Final Parables on Rewards in the Kingdom

1. Robert Stein, *Introduction to the Parables of Jesus* (Philadelphia: Westminster, 1981), 126–27; and William Taylor, *The Parables of the Savior* (New York: A. C. Armstrong & Son, 1901), 104.
2. Warren S. Kissinger, *The Parables of Jesus: A History of Interpretation and Bibliography* (Metuchen, N.J.: Scarecrow, 1979), 23.
3. Carl L. Blomberg, *Interpreting the Parables* (Downers Grove, Ill.: InterVarsity, 1980), 222.

4. R. C. Trench, *Notes on the Parables of Our Lord* (London: John W. Parker & Son, 1855), 164.
5. Eta Linnemann, *Parables of Jesus: Introduction and Exposition* (London: SPCK, 1966), 27, 87.
6. Stanley D. Toussaint, *Behold the King* (Portland: Multnomah, 1980), 231.
7. Trench, *Notes on the Parables of Our Lord,* 177.
8. William O. E. Oesterley, *The Gospel Parables in the Light of Their Jewish Background* (New York: Macmillan, 1936), 104ff.
9. Nathan Levison, *The Parables: Their Background and Local Setting* (Edinburgh: T & T Clark, 1926), 198.
10. Montague R. James, *The Book of Tobit and The History of Susanna.* Reprinted from the Revised Version of the Apocrypha (London: The Haymarket Press, 1929), 5:15.
11. A. M. Hunter, *The Parables Then and Now* (Philadelphia: Westminster, 1971), 72. See also a recent expression of it in Blomberg, *Interpreting the Parables.*
12. Taylor, *The Parables of the Savior,* 108.
13. Joseph A. Fitzmyer, *The Gospel According to Luke* (Garden City, N.Y.: Doubleday, 1985), 1235. The "pound" or "mina" (only here in the New Testament) was valued at one hundred *drackmae* or about twenty dollars, which is one-sixtieth of the value of the "talent" of Matthew 25:15ff.
14. Flavius Josephus, "Jewish Antiquities," in *The New Complete Works of Josephus,* trans. William Whiston (Grand Rapids: Kregel, 1999), 17.11.4.
15. Bernard B. Scott, *Hear Then the Parables* (Minneapolis: Fortress, 1989), 223.
16. John D. Crossan, *In Parables: The Challenge of the Historical Jesus* (New York: Harper & Row, 1973), 99–102.
17. Joachim Jeremias, *The Parables of Jesus* (London: SCM, 1954), 48.

Chapter 14: Final Parables to Rejecters on Loss of the Kingdom

1. Flavius Josephus, *Wars,* 6.9.4, notes that 2,565,000 lambs were slain on Passover in A.D. 70 for 2,700,000 people, as also thirteen ate of one lamb at the Lord's last supper.
2. Sir Robert Anderson, *The Coming Prince,* 15th ed. (Grand Rapids: Kregel, 1963), 122–28; and Harold Hoehner, *Chronological Aspects of the Life of Christ* (Grand Rapids: Zondervan, 1977), 137.
3. Frederick W. Farrar, *The Life of Christ,* vol. 2 (London: Cassell Peter, & Galpin, n.d.), 334–35.
4. Ibid., 330f.
5. Cunningham Geikie, *The Life and Words of Christ,* vol. 2 (New York: D. Appleton, 1891), 222–28.

6. Simon J. Kistemacher, *The Parables of Jesus* (Grand Rapids: Baker, 1980), 84; and Bernard B. Scott, *Hear Then the Parables* (Minneapolis: Fortress, 1989), 80–83.
7. Joachim Jeremias, *The Parables of Jesus* (London: SCM, 1954), 52–62.
8. Robert W. Funk, Roy W. Hoover, and Jesus Seminar, *The Five Gospels* (New York: Macmillan, 1993), 510–11.
9. Warren Kissinger, *The Parables of Jesus: A History of Interpretation and Bibliography* (Metuchen, N.J.: Scarecrow, 1979), 70–71; and A. Guillaumont et al., *The Gospel According to Thomas* (New York: Harper & Row, 1959), 39, Log. 65–66.
10. That tendency to slim down the parable to its bare bones has also been fueled by the discovery of the so-called "Gospel of Thomas." That Coptic collection of Jesus' sayings includes this "Vineyard" story, but without its metaphorical language. In this form it is accepted by members of the "Jesus Seminar," who reject the Synoptic version. In spite of the Gnostic strains of this collection and its many nonsensical statements attributed to Jesus, they favor its stripped down version. It should be recalled, however, that this "Gospel" of Thomas is hardly authentic (in contrast to the four Gospels found in the New Testament). It is a group of 114 sayings of Jesus without historical structure or redemptive basis, omitting the Passion story. It is made up largely of wisdom sayings in proverbial form with an emphasis on "knowledge," which is assumed as salvation. Its final Logia (114) is strongly anti-feminist, a feature quite foreign to the Synoptics, especially Luke.
11. John P. Lange, "The Gospel According to Matthew," *Commentary on the Holy Scriptures: Critical, Doctrinal, and Homiletical,* ed. Philip Schaff (Grand Rapids: Zondervan, 1978), 8:385.
12. Anthony J. Saldarini, "Sanhedrin," in *The Anchor Bible Dictionary,* ed. David N. Freedman (New York: Doubleday, 1992), 5:976–77.
13. V. Gilbert Beers, *The Victor Handbook of Bible Knowledge* (Wheaton: Victor Books, 1981), 245; and R. K. Harrison, "Vine," in *The Inter-national Standard Bible Encyclopedia,* ed. Geoffery W. Bromiley (Grand Rapids: Eerdmans, 1988), 4:986.
14. E. M. Blaiklock, "Inheritance," in *The Zondervan Pictorial Encyclopedia of the Bible,* ed. Merrill C. Tenny (Grand Rapids: Zondervan, 1976), 3:278; and F. E. Hirsch and D. K. McKim, "Inherit," in *The Inter-national Standard Bible Encyclopedia,* ed. Geoffrey W. Bromiley (Grand Rapids: Eerdmans, 1982), 2:824.
15. Donald Guthrie, *New Testament Theology* (Downers Grove, Ill.: InterVarsity, 1981), 311.

16. Stanley D. Toussaint, *Behold the King: A Study of Matthew* (Portland: Multnomah, 1981), 250–51.
17. George W. Peters, *A Biblical Theology of Missions* (Chicago: Moody, 1982), 22–23.
18. Alan H. McNeile, *The Gospel According to St. Matthew* (Grand Rapids: Baker, 1980), 312.
19. Earl Radmacher, Ronald B. Allen, and H. Wayne House, eds., *Nelson's New Illustrated Bible Commentary* (Nashville: Nelson, 1999), 1182.
20. Alfred Plummer, *An Exegetical Commentary on the Gospel According to St. Matthew* (Grand Rapids: Baker, 1982), 301; D. A. Carson, "Matthew," *The Expositor's Bible Commentary,* ed. Frank E. Gaebelein (Grand Rapids: Zondervan, 1984), 8:455–56; and Craig L. Blomberg, *Interpreting the Parables* (Downers Grove, Ill.: InterVarsity, 1990), 237.
21. Beers, *The Victor Handbook of Bible Knowledge,* 347–48; and J. I. Packer and M. C. Tenney, eds., *Illustrated Manners and Customs of the Bible* (Nashville: Nelson, 1980), 433.
22. R. K. Bower and G. L. Knapp, "Marriage," in *The International Standard Bible Encyclopedia,* 4:263.
23. P. Trutza, "Marriage," in *The Zondervan Pictorial Encyclopedia of the Bible,* ed. Merrill C. Tenney (Grand Rapids: Zondervan, 1976), 4:97.
24. Ibid.
25. William Hendriksen, *The Gospel of Matthew* (Grand Rapids: Baker, 1973), 793.
26. Alan Millard, *Discoveries from the Time of Jesus* (Oxford: Lion Publishing, 1990), 147.
27. John F. Walvoord, *Matthew: Thy Kingdom Come* (Grand Rapids: Kregel, 1998), 165.
28. Hendriksen, *The Gospel of Matthew,* 797–98.

INDEX OF PARABLES